Ex libris: James J. O'Brien

**With best personal and professional
regards.**

10/77

Construction Delay

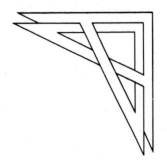

Construction Delay
Responsibilities, Risks, and Litigation

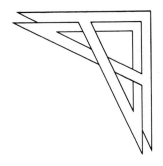

James J. O'Brien, P.E.

Cahners Books International, Inc.
221 Columbus Avenue
Boston, Massachusetts 02116

International Standard Book Number: 0-8436-0162-0

Library of Congress Card Catalogue Number: 76-19110

Printed in the United States of America

Designed by Designworks, Inc.

Second Printing

Library of Congress Cataloging in Publication Data
O'Brien, James Jerome, 1929-
    Construction delay: responsibilities, risks, and
litigation.

    Bibliography: P.
    Includes indexes.
    1. Building—Contracts and specifications—United
States. 2. Construction industry—Law and legisla-
tion—United States.   I.   Title.
KF902.027   343'.73'078   76-19110
ISBN 0-8436-0162-0

Contents

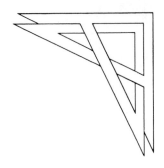

Foreword

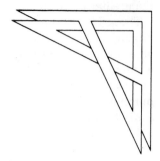

Buildings have several unique characteristics when compared with virtually all other products of our society. Washing machines, automobiles, furniture, and almost any other type of manufactured item are designed and constructed by and bear the warranty of a single business entity. Such products may be inspected by a potential purchaser in their finished and operating state. Since one can compare such products, there are few, if any, surprises after purchase. There is usually a single source of responsibility if problems do occur.

Buildings, on the other hand, are quite different. When something goes wrong, there is seldom a single firm to blame. In addition to the client or owner of a construction project, many others are involved, each with a separate and distinct interest: the money lenders, the architect, possibly several engineers, special consultants, one or more prime contractors, a host of subcontractors, and any number of reviewing governmental agencies. There is no other product that is designed by one entity, constructed by another, often financed by another, and that has its feet planted inseparably in unpredictable mother earth.

Another unique characteristic of building construction compared with other man-made products is the extended time of the process. It takes a year to design and construct even a simple house. It can take as much as three, four, or even five years to complete the process for a complex project such as a hospital or government building. In that kind of a time span, the personnel, financial condition, and attitudes of the firms involved can change; even construction and labor practices may change. And it is axiomatic that the longer the time span, the greater the impact of escalating cost.

There is, of course, still another ingredient that makes the procurement experience quite different for buildings than for other products. For many owners, the acquisition of a building is the most significant and largest single purchase in their lives. For all owners, whether the project is a once in a lifetime purchase or only one of several buildings to be acquired, the capital outlay is a very major consideration.

The size of the firms involved (architects, engineers, construction contractors) also makes building design and construction unique. Most such firms are relatively small. For the architectural/engineering firm, the design of a $5 million project may represent all or at least a large percentage of the current or annual capacity. A general contractor on the same job may only execute three or four like-size projects at any one time. If a faulty engine on an occasional Mustang must be replaced, hardly a ripple is felt in the financial condition of Ford Motor Co. By contrast, if something goes wrong on a construction project—delays, litigation, etc.,—it can result in financial disaster for the architect or the contractor.

Another factor that is having an effect on the construction process today is the current wave of consumerism. This new phenomenon is, of course, not restricted to construction. It developed first in relation to more conventionally manufactured products but the concept that every item a person purchases must be perfect does not wholly apply to facilities construction. An owner may rightfully expect each item to perform when the project is completed. However, the fitting together of all the parts under a number of responsibilities makes it difficult if not impossible for the total facility to be completed without the occurrence of some conflicts, the emergence of some unforeseen problems, or the need of a few unpredicted expenditures. When an owner undertakes a construction project, he takes on certain risks that cannot be delegated. With all of these important and complex conditions, unique to building construction, is it any wonder that acquiring a building or adding to or adapting an existing one is such a complex process?

With an owner who may be inexperienced in acquiring a facility with a host of designers, contractors, and subcontractors—each with separate responsibilities and contractural arrangements but with inextricably interwoven roles—and with the project representing a major endeavor for all parties, it is certainly not surprising that complicated claims, counterclaims, and litigation result.

When a dispute arises during construction several parties are involved, each with overlapping contractural responsibilities: each party may have much to lose, perhaps reputation, as well as dollars. It is very easy to suggest that all parties amicably settle their claims with mutual respect for each other but a great deal may be at stake for each. This is particularly true of the owner or purchaser who, if inexperienced, finds it difficult to comprehend the differences between buying a new car and acquiring a new building.

In buildings or any type of facilities construction, an understanding of the process and the roles of all those involved is of utmost importance. *Construction Delay* describes in detail the complexity of the process and the various roles of its participants. This can go a long way to mitigating the disruptive consequences of major disputes and litigation.

LOUIS deMOLL, FAIA
President, The American
Institute of Architects

Preface

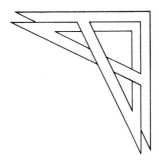

In years past, delay in the completion of construction used to be a mutually accepted condition; even the courts on occasion recognized that delay was a normal situation in the construction process.

Today, with tight budgets on the part of the owners, who usually want to expend right up to the limit of that budget, and the real cost of staying on the job longer than planned—delay is a real cost item. During the construction process, the parties attempt to shift the cost of delay to the other party. If litigation does result after failure to negotiate, the litigation is between two (or more) losers who are attempting to mitigate their loss. There are no winners in delay.

The typical project goes through several romance-marriage cycles. First, the user has to convince his budgetary authorizing body (legislature, corporate powers, bank, or similar holder of the purse strings) that the project is necessary, and should be included in the budget. Later as the pressures of unexpected changes, unforeseen delays, and expansion of the program occur—as they almost inevitably do—this relationship tends to deteriorate.

The second romance cycle starts with the selection of the design team—usually an architect in the case of a building, or an engineer for heavy construction. The selection is made with mutual high hopes, and works well for a time, usually. This relationship reaches its straining points during construction, when the contractor as an adversarial party imposes unexpected strain.

The romance-marriage cycle varies in construction with the type of contract. The sealed bid-low bid type contract utilized in public bidding is almost a shotgun marriage and starts to fall apart immediately, or at the best comes under heavy strain. The negotiated contract has a much better opportunity to survive, since it is a marriage of convenience, and has more funding available for the natural give-and-take of the construction process.

Litigation

In most construction litigation, the lawyers for both sides (in the privacy of their own conference rooms) often, in fact almost always, look askance at many of the important actions taken by their parties during construction. While sympathetic, they find it difficult to understand why the parties take substantial actions that will have unfavorable legal implications in the event of litigation.

The answer to the lawyer's puzzlement is relatively easy. Most parties to construction contracts do not enter the contract with the specific idea that it will have to go to litigation ultimately. The owner clearly does not want a contractor who is going to litigate, and the contractor works on such a narrow profit margin that he can ill-afford litigation, even if he wins, for the winner usually has to wait years for his money.

This book is divided into four major areas. Most of it discusses the actions during the construction process (or the preceding design process) that may have substantial legal implications not immediately obvious to the party taking the action. This type of education of the parties usually occurs after the fact, and much too late. The purpose of the presentation is to attempt to provide some foresight on those factors that might be damaging later. Of course, even when informed, a contractor or owner may still find that he must tread a perilous path, but at least he can do so knowledgeably.

The second section of the book is a discussion of the litigation process itself, including the process, trial procedures, arbitration proceedings, setting of damages, and the preparation of the case for trial.

The third section of the book is made up of a series of reference cases. These cases are cited in more than one instance within the text, and they are presented as a group for convenience. Most of the cases are described by extracts from the actual court records and opinions.

The final section is a case study of the John Hancock Tower in Boston. The article was written by Rita Tatum former associate editor of *Building Design and Construction.*

This book is not intended to be a do-it-yourself law book. There are two sides to every argument and the establishment of the facts and responsibilities of delay, and there are two sides to every page in a law book. The law is often interpreted quite differently in different courts for the same set of facts. Accordingly, the approaches described cannot be expected to plot a successful legal path. Much more legal training and many more appropriate volumes of references would be required. The book is really attempting to point out those clearly hazardous legal paths that would almost guarantee failure. Litigation costs money. It should be entered into most carefully and thoughtfully. The first and last piece of advice given by most lawyers is: settle.

Part I · The Situation

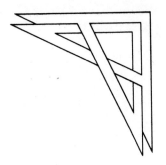

Chapter One · Delay

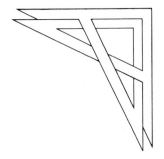

Delay is a relative term. In construction, it means the time over-run either beyond the contract date or beyond the date that the parties agreed upon for delivery of the project. In both cases, delay is usually a costly situation.

To the owner, delay can mean loss of revenue through lack of production facilities and rentable space, or a continuing dependence on present facilities. To the public owner, it means that a building or facility is not available for the use to which it will be put. The service revenues lost through delay can never be recovered. To the contractor, delay means higher overhead costs because of the longer construction period, higher material costs through inflation, and escalation costs due to labor increases. Plus, his working capital is tied up so that he cannot pursue other projects.

In a construction delay situation, there is not usually a winner and a loser, but rather two (or more) losing situations. Delay litigation, then, involves an attempt by one party to shift more of the cost to the other party.

The assignment of responsibility for delay is usually difficult, and the courts have often remarked that delay is a situation that should be anticipated in a construction endeavor. Traditionally, the courts have protected the owner more than the contractor. Until recently, no damage for delay clauses have often been enforced, with the contractor receiving only an extension in time. Time extensions avoid another owner's remedy: liquidated damages. Even with courts that are more inclined to consider recovery of damages for owner-caused delay, the burden is on the contractor to prove active interference on the part of the owner in order to receive a favorable decision.

As the cost of individual projects increases dramatically, the costs of delay seem to increase at an even greater rate. For instance, Consumer's Power Company of Michigan estimates that its 1300 megawatt nuclear power plant under construction near Midland, Michigan will cost almost 50 percent more to complete ($1.5 billion rather than the original estimate of less than $1 billion), due principally to the costs of a two-year construction delay. The delay was the result of funding problems and design changes, and the cost increase is ascribed principally to inflation. Consumer's Power had previously filed suit for $300 million or more for delay damages due to costs involved in start-up delays for another nuclear power plant. Delay costs included loss of revenues.

The joint venture for the Grand Coulee third power plant suffered losses due to delays on a $112.5 million fixed price contract. They are claiming a delay cost on the order of $30 million to $35 million.

A joint venture of contractors on the Oroville Dam in California is suing for $15 million for delays resulting in extra costs during excavation. The joint venture contractors claim that the rock did not react in the expected manner, and they incurred additional costs that should be paid by the state. The state, in turn, is countersuing. In its countersuit is a claim for almost $2 million in compensatory damages because the job was completed in forty-eight months rather than the contractual forty months.

Not only are the amounts of costs resulting from delay large numbers, but they also represent substantial percentages of the overall contract value.

Responsibility for Delay

There are four general categories of responsibility:

1. Owner (or his agents) responsible
2. Contractor (or his subcontractors) responsible
3. Neither contractual party responsible
4. Both contractual parties responsible

In the case of the owner (or his agents) causing delay, the courts may find that the language of the contract, in the form of the typical no damage for delay clause, protects the owner from damages but requires him to give a compensatory offsetting time extension to avoid liquidated damages. If the owner can be shown to be guilty of interference with the progress of the contractor or has committed a contractual breach, then the contractor can probably recover damages caused by the owner due to delay.

If the contractor (or his subcontractors) causes damage to the owner through delay, the contract does not generally offer the contractor protection against litigation to recover.

If the delay is caused by forces beyond the control of either party to the contract, then the general finding is that each party must bear the brunt of the damages suffered.

If both parties to the contract contribute to the cause of a delay or cause concurrent delays, the usual finding is that the delays offset one another. An exception to this generalization would occur in those instances where the damages can be clearly and distinctly separated, although the courts are not quick to allow such distinction.

Types of Delay

There are three basic types of delay: classic, concurrent, and serial.

Classic delay occurs when a period of idleness and/or uselessness is imposed upon the contractural work. In *Public Construction Contracts and the Law* (p. 267), Cohen cites the case of *Grand Investment Co. v. United States* (102 Ct. Cl. U.S. 40; 1944) in which the government issued a stop order by telegraph to the contractor that resulted in a work stoppage of 109 days. The contractor sued for damages due to the delay. The basis for the suit was breach of contract. The court found that the stop order was not justified and resulted in a breach of the government obligations in the contract. The court allowed, among other things, a damage due to the loss of utilization of equipment on the job site, finding: "When the government in breach of its contract, in effect, condemned a contractor's valuable and useful machines for a period of idleness and uselessness . . . it should make compensation comparable to what would be required if it took the machines for use for a temporary period." This is what many lawyers term *classic delay*.

In *Johnson v. Fenestra* (Reference Case 34*), the situation involved a classic delay when workmen were idled by the failure of the general contractor to supply materials. This delay, to have legal effect, must be substantial, involving an essential segment of the work and must remain a problem for an unreasonable time.

*Editor's Note: Reference Cases are described in more detail in Part III.

Generally, if two parties have concurrent delays, the court will not unravel the factors and will disallow the claims by both parties. Thus, in *United States* v. *Citizens and Southern National Bank* (Reference Case 58), a subcontractor was able to show delay damages on the part of the general contractor. However, the general contractor, in turn was able to demonstrate that portions of the damages were due to factors for which he was not responsible. In the absence of evidence separating the two claims, the court rejected the entire claim stating: "As the evidence does not provide any reasonable basis for allocating the additional costs among these contributing factors, we conclude that the entire claim should have been rejected."

Similarly, in *Lichter* v. *Mellon-Stuart* (Reference Case 36), the court found that the facts supported evidence of delay imposed upon a subcontractor by a general contractor. However, they also found that the work had been delayed by a number of factors including change orders, delays by other trades, and strikes. The subcontractor had based its claim for damages upon all damages due to delay, and both the trial court and the appeals court rejected the case on the basis that: "Even if one could find from the evidence that one or more of the interfering contingencies was a wrongful act on the part of the defendant, no basis appears for even an educated guess as to the increased costs . . . due to that particular breach . . . as distinguished from those causes from which defendant is contractually exempt."

Serial delay is a linkage of delays, sometimes of different causes. Thus, the effects of a delay may be amplified by a following delay. For instance, if an owner's representative delays in the review of shop drawings, and that resulting delay causes the project to drift into a strike or severe weather, then a court may find the owner liable for the total serial delay resulting from the initial incremental delay.

In *Legal Pitfalls in Architecture, Engineering, and Building Construction* (p. 146), the authors (Nathan Walker and Theodor Rohdenburg) describe such a case of serial delay. In the case of *Murphy* v. *U.S. Fidelity* (100 App. Div. 93, N.Y.; 1905), a general contractor sued a subcontractor stone company for losses due to damage through delay and delivery. Stone was to have been delivered by August 1, and on that date, the stone company defaulted. The general contractor relet to another stone company, but despite efforts to expedite the delivery, the work ran into the winter and increased costs resulted. The court found for the general contractor.

Force Majeure Causes

These forces include acts of God. The general contract usually provides a list of events such as fires, strikes, earthquakes, tornadoes, floods, and similar unforeseen circumstances that, should they occur, provide a mutual relief from demands for damages due to delay. In the case of force majeure occurrences, the owner is obliged to provide a reasonable (usually a day-for-day) time extension.

In the case of weather, only those occurrences shown to be beyond the average expected for the area based upon past records can be considered as a reason for time extension.

Many contracts carry clauses to the effect that extensions for acts of God shall apply only to those portions of the project that are specifically affected. Thus, a severe downpour after the site has been graded, drained, and the building closed in may cause no actual delay, even though it would qualify under other methods of evaluation as a force majeure act.

The Arundel Corp. v. *United States* (103 Ct. Cl. U.S. 688; 1945) was a situation in which an act of nature in the form of a hurricane reduced the amount of work to be accomplished in a contract. Before the contract was executed, the hurricane set up currents that scoured a channel and removed a large amount of material that was to be dredged. Because the amount to be dredged was reduced, the contractor filed a claim for increased overhead per unit to be removed. The court stated: "The plaintiff [contractor] assumed the risk of the amount of material to be dredged being reduced, as it was, by the hurricane, an Act-of-God, just as the government would have had to assume the risk of having to pay for an increase in the material necessary to be dredged for the same reason. . . . It is a general principle of law that neither party to a contract is responsible to the other for damages through a loss occasioned as a result of an Act-of-God."

The distinction between causes is not always clear. In *Hammermill Paper Co.* v. *Rust Engineering* (Reference Case 28), Hammermill (the owner) contended that the wall collapse involved in the case was the result of faulty and negligent construction, while Rust (the designer/engineer) pleaded that the collapse was an act of God due to excessive rains.

Unforeseen Conditions

The distinction between unforeseen conditions and force majeure delays is not always clear. In *Luria Engineering* v.

Aetna (Reference Case 37), the original roofing subcontractor was delayed due to labor difficulties. He claimed that the change in conditions required that he receive increased compensation. Luria hired a new roofer and sued the surety company (Aetna) for the increase in cost incurred by the original roofer's failure to perform. The court agreed that the original roofer had to provide for the additional cost: "Acts of a third party . . . causing a delay resulting in substantial increase in expense . . . do not excuse failure to perform if such acts were foreseeable." The court held that the possibility of labor difficulties was not unforeseeable, and therefore, should have been a contingency in the bid.

In the case of *Moore* v. *Whitty* (Reference Case 42), Moore was the contractor for installation of bath fixtures in buildings being constructed by Whitty. Whitty had originally called for union labor in the contract but agreed to drop the provisions as part of the negotiations. The Moore crews (nonunion) triggered a labor dispute, and Whitty terminated the contract. The court refused to agree with the termination because both parties had been aware of the labor situation. Because of this awareness, they were not allowed to use the problem as a reason to avoid the performance of their part of the contract.

In *Wertheimer Construction* v. *United States* (Reference Case 62), the construction company claimed a number of acts of God and unforeseen circumstances. A request for delay due to bad weather or unseasonable nature was evaluated after a comparison with weather conditions over the preceding eight-year period. The trial commissioner granted an extension of twenty-two days for each group of buildings, although the contractor had requested a longer period of delay. The trial commissioner found that the contractor's evidence on this point was vague and intangible.

The contractor had indicated that vandalism was an unforeseen problem. In so claiming, the contractor noted that he had planned on a certain amount of vandalism and had allowed for watchmen. However, the trial commissioner found that the evidence was clear and uncontradicted that there was extensive vandalism and that the contractor was delayed by the vandalism. In this case, a time extension was permitted since the contractor had "adopted reasonable and continuous protective methods, but was delayed by vandalism which was unforeseeable, beyond its control, and without fault or negligence."

One of the most common unforeseen condition situations is

that of subsurface conditions. The case of *Cauldwell-Wingate Co. v. State of New York* (Reference Case 12) is a classic in this regard. Cauldwell-Wingate was superstructure contractor for a building project. The state had assigned the foundations stage to another contractor, who anticipated that he would be able to meet the schedule. During the initial demolition, the foundation contractor discovered many old walls and masonry footings that required a different treatment. After this discovery, the state conducted a subsurface study and an appropriate redesign. Change orders extended the work of the foundation contractor for nine months. The superstructure contractor sued for the cost of the delay. The court agreed that the superstructure contractor had a right to rely on the plans and specifications, and, therefore, the delay was unforeseen.

In a similar case, *Citizen's National Bank of Meridian v. Glasscock* (Reference Case 13), the contractor had encountered unexpected foundations, which precluded the placement of new concrete piling. The specifications generally anticipated the existence of the old foundations but gave no details regarding their location or size. The contractor had interpreted the specifications as not requiring removal of foundations before placing his piling. The court found that the situation was not unforeseen and that the contractor could not recover for the delay damages incurred.

The case of *Hersey Gravel Co. v. State of Michigan* (Reference Case 31) is a combination of the two situations. The contractor found that the material encountered in the right-of-way was not the kind anticipated, and thereby caused extra work and delay. The court held that the contractor was "entitled to rely upon the contract, blueprints, plans and specifications prepared by the State, and upon the engineering practice in that connection, and he stated that it was the duty of the public authorities, when preparing proposals to provide all available information and data in unmistakable and clear-cut terms."

However, the contractor also attempted to recover on the basis of poor soil conditions in borrow pits not in the roadway. In that regard, the court held: "I can find no ground for raising any implied warranty in this contract except the one that the material from those pits was reasonably suited to use as fill material in the making of grades. In point of fact, the material was suitable for that use as such material. It was difficult to excavate with shovels, but it was excavated with shovels. . . . The petitioner is entitled to compensation for highway excavations, but not for excavations in the pits."

Causes of Delay

Clause 5 of the standard federal contract states that the contractor will not be assessed liquidated damages by reason of delays "due to unforeseen causes beyond the control and without the fault and negligence of the contractor." These causes of delays include, but are not limited to:

1. Acts of God
2. Acts of the public enemy
3. Acts of the government (sovereign or contractual)
4. Acts of another contractor in performance of a government contract
5. Fires
6. Floods
7. Epidemics
8. Quarantine restrictions
9. Strikes
10. Freight embargoes
11. Unusually severe weather
12. Delays of subcontractors or suppliers due to similar causes

Delays caused by owners can include, but are not limited to:

1. Failure to provide access, property, or right-of-way
2. Failure to fund the project
3. Owner-furnished materials not available
4. Stop order or reasons including safety
5. Introduction of major change in requirements
6. Failure to make progress payments
7. Interference by other prime contractors working for this owner

The owner is also subject to the consequences of acts by his designated representative, including the architect/engineer and/or the construction manager. These delay causes can include, but are not limited to:

1. Defects in the plans and specifications
2. Unreasonable delays in review of shop drawings or approval of material
3. Improper or delayed change orders
4. Orders to stop work
5. Direction to accomplish the work in a certain manner
6. Failure to coordinate between prime contractors
7. Inadequate information
8. Inadequate supervision
9. Failure to provide temporary heat (if contractually required)

The contractor may be delayed as the result of some of the causes above, or may cause delays for reasons including, but not limited to:

1. Slow to mobilize
2. Failure to man the project
3. Failure to provide sufficient equipment
4. Poor workmanship
5. Failure to coordinate
6. Inadequate supervision
7. Unforeseen accidents
8. Cash flow limitations
9. Bid shopping
10. Poor planning

Notice of Delay

Contracts usually include in their general conditions a requirement that the contractor shall notify the owner of delay, usually within ten days from the beginning of the delay. The following clause is taken from the general conditions form used by the state of New Jersey: "The contractor shall, within ten days from the beginning of such delay, unless the Director shall grant a further period of time prior to the date of final settlement of the contract, notify the State, in writing, of the causes of the delay."

The general conditions of the New York State Dormitory Authority contracts include a similar clause: "The contractor shall, within ten days from the beginning of such delay, notify the Owner, in writing, of the causes of the delay."

The legal ramifications of failure to give due notice are discussed in Chapter 7, "The Contractor." The giving of notice in writing is a part of normal project administration. The form need not be argumentative. Some contractors are reluctant to continually give notice of apparent delay, because of the overtones of litigation which are implied. For instance, each day of weather considered to be in the category of force majeure must be the subject of formal notification. To meet this requirement, the contractor should set up criteria for determination that weather is excessive in comparison to an established prior record from the U.S. Weather Service.

Failure to give due notice of delay as required by the contract can be overcome, but not in all cases. Therefore, prudence indicates that a documentation approach should be established.

One of the early cases supporting the requirement for notice was *Louisville and N.R. Co. v. Hollerback* (5 N.E. 28, Ind.;

1886). In this case, the defendant delayed plaintiff's work by failing to prepare adequate foundations. The plaintiff sent a notice indicating the cause for his inability to complete. The court affirmed recovery of delay damages noting: "The contractor may not acquiesce in the suspension in silence . . . but if notice be given of his readiness and willingness to prosecute the work to completion within the time agreed upon, and that its suspension will involve him in loss, we can discover no principle upon which it can be held upon the contractor."

Peter Kiewit Sons Co. v. United States (60–1 B.C.A. 2580; 1960) was heard before the Federal Board of Contract Appeals. Despite contractual requirements for an on-site source for sub-base material, this material had to be obtained elsewhere at greater cost. Kiewit sued for damages due to the extra work and delay involved. The board noted: "The government's defense is in part based upon the fact that it did not receive notice of this claim until . . . after completion of the construction work called for by the contractor, but prior to final payment. The government was, however, completely familiar with the difficulties appellant was experiencing. . . . Under these circumstances, a formal written notice of changed conditions or a formal notice that a claim would be filed was unnecessary."

However, in the two preceding cases, the owner had either interfered with the contractor or there were changed conditions that created a situation outside of the contract.

Other citations that permit recovery without notice also involve changes in the contract beyond the scope of the contract. These include: Nat Harrison Associates Inc. v. Gulf States Utilities Co. (491 F. 2d 578, 5th Cir.; 1974); Mullen Construction Inc. v. United States (72–1 B.C.A. 9227; 1972) and Eisen-Magers Construction Co. v. United States (59–1 B.C.A. 2234; 1959).

It is clear that failure to fulfill the requirement for notice to the letter and the spirit of the contract can jeopardize a contractor's proper claim to damages for delay.

Basis for Delay

In most cases, the starting date for the contract is established as the date upon which the contractor was notified that he could proceed with the work. However, some contracts have special built-in situations which stipulate that the contract will commence upon completion of another contractor's work, availability of the site, or some combination of special events. In the ultimate calculation of delay, the establishment of the true starting date is important because most contracts run a specified number of days from the "start of the contract."

In *Bloomfield School District* v. *Stites* (Reference Case 6), the contractor claimed that the amount of delay should be calculated on the basis of a delayed start date. He based this on the fact that he did not receive an executed contract from the architect until about September 23, while the date on the contract was August 8. The court disagreed, however, noting that the contract "unambiguously said 'this agreement made the 8th day of August . . . ' and there was no objection to the date or suggestion that it be changed. . . . In these circumstances, the parties having elected that their mutual rights and obligations are to be determined according to the letter of the contract, its effective date was August 8 . . . . It is of first importance that a contract shall have definitely ascertainable dates of commencement and termination. To that end, those dates should be determinable from the recitations in the contract itself; there should be no room for conjecture or speculation. . . . Obedient to that rule, the courts have generally construed contracts to run from the date they bear, and not from the date of delivery."

The date much more in contention is that of the actual completion. The courts have generally agreed that when a contract has been substantially completed, delays are ended. Substantial completion may be established by either substantial performance, or by the owner taking beneficial occupancy or use of the facility.

In *Benjamin* v. *Toledo Plate & Glass* (Reference Case 3), the owner had contracted for a replacement of large plate glass windows. After installation of the windows, acid used by another contractor to clean fire damage from the walls of the building etched the glass. The owner refused to pay the glass contractor on the basis that he had not completed the installation, which included washing of the glass. The court disagreed finding that the glass contractor had substantially completed.

In *Clark* v. *Ferro* (Reference Case 16), the work included a production facility for production of tile. The contract was to be evaluated on a performance basis. The court agreed that the contractor had not fulfilled his contract, but limited recovery for damages to the amount of the cost to put the new equipment into proper working condition.

In *Collins* v. *Baldwin* (Reference Case 17), Collins (the owner) had a contract with Baldwin (the contractor) to build a motel. This contract included a provision which would sell 25 percent interest in the completed motel to Baldwin. Collins alleged that Baldwin had failed to perform. He sought to recover damages under the contract and to preclude Baldwin from acquiring the 25 percent interest.

While the court did find damages in favor of the owner, they also found that Baldwin had substantially completed: "When a contractor and builder have in good faith endeavored to comply with the terms of a contract, literal compliance in all details is not essential to recovery, especially where the owner has taken possession of the building."

In *Nathan Construction* v. *Fenestra* (Reference Case 44), Fenestra was subcontractor for windows and curtainwall for a building in Omaha. Nathan, a general contractor, refused to pay the final progress payment asserting that the curtainwall was not in conformance with the specifications. Nathan asserted that the curtainwall permitted excessive infiltration of air, water, and dust, did not move freely with changing temperatures, and was improperly sealed. The court found that the contractor and owner were not able to prove their allegations and found in favor of Fenestra.

The court presented three reasons for agreeing with Fenestra's posture in regard to substantial completion:

1. That work on a building is such that, even if the owner rejects it, he receives the benefit of it and it is equitable to require him to pay for what he gets.
2. Literal compliance with every detail of specifications is impossible.
3. It is implied that the parties have agreed to do what is reasonable under all the circumstances with respect to performance.

In *Wertheimer Construction* v. *United States* (Reference Case 62), the contractor Wertheimer claimed that substantial completion occurred when the building was ready for inspection and asserted that the government failed to properly conduct acceptance inspections. The contractor claimed that he should be allowed a time extension in the period between substantial completion and the actual acceptance. The court disagreed, quoting the contract conditions and saying: "A fair reading . . . compels the conclusion that when the work was substantially completed, plaintiff [contractor] was obligated to notify defendant [owner] of that fact, but that defendant was not then obligated to accept the buildings." The court went on to note: "The record does not support [contractor's] contention that [owner's] inspectors were tardy in making inspections or that the inspections were unnecessary or improper, or that the [owner] failed to accept the buildings promptly after they were completed and ready for occupancy."

While the start and conclusion dates are key to the determination of delay, milestone dates may also be a factor. Thus, in *Bethlehem Steel v. City of Chicago* (Reference Case 5), Bethlehem missed a required date for the erection of superstructure steel for a super highway. However, Bethlehem, in defending its delay, held that although this interim contract milestone date had been missed, the city really suffered no damage, since it was able to open on the announced schedule. The courts did not agree, noting that Bethlehem admitted to fifty-two days of unexcused delay in the completion of the contract.

It is sufficient that the contractor did not meet the date and admitted to the unexcused delay. In the case of *Bethlehem v. City of Chicago*, Chicago may have had to expend additional monies to accelerate another contract in order to meet the end date. Even if it did not, and had good fortune in the implementation of other contracts, the city had the right to gain the use of the highway at an earlier point in time.

The concept of acceleration can be applied as a basis for damages even when delay does occur. For instance, in the Apollo program at Cape Kennedy, there were many delays, but a hard launch date to meet. In situations where excused delay (or unexcused delay by another contractor) occurred, the government would often pay to buy back time or to accelerate the remaining work. Even though the actual end dates of many contracts were exceeded, these same contracts or other contracts were accelerated to counteract the delay. Thus, the amount of delay cannot be ascertained by simple arithmetic without support of the facts behind the various delays.

Delays Due to Change Orders

Most contracts start with a very limited time frame for the accomplishment of a substantial amount of work. The majority of contracts, for a variety of reasons, exceed the initial completion estimate. Accomplishment of the basic contract work is usually difficult enough in a timely fashion. However, the owner typically reserves the right to change the contract. This right, combined with the "no damages for delay" clause operates to require the contractor to take on additional work, even when meeting the base contract schedule is difficult.

In the negotiation of each change order, there should be an evaluation of the impact upon the overall time frame and additional days should be added to the base contract.

The ability of the government (owner) to impose additional work on a contract, even when behind schedule, was affirmed in the case of *Crook Co. v. United States* (270 U.S. 4; 1925). The court stated: "The contractor . . . must satisfy the government of his having the capital, experience, and ability to do the work. Much care is taken, therefore, to keep him up to the mark. Liquidated damages are fixed for his delays. But the only references to delays on the government's side is the agreement that if caused by its acts, they will be regarded as unavoidable, though probably inserted primarily for the contractor's benefit as a ground or extension of time, is not without bearing on what the contract bound the government to do. . . . The [contractor] agreed to accept in full satisfaction for all work done . . . the contract price. . . . Nothing more is allowed for changes, as to which the government is master. . . . The [contractor's] time was extended, and it was paid the full contract price. In our opinion, it is entitled to nothing more."

In *Frazier-David Construction Co.* v. *United States* (97 Ct. Cl. U.S. 1; 1942) the contractor filed a claim for additional costs due to subsurface conditions different from those shown in the plans and specifications. A change order had been issued for the basic increase in costs and an extension of time was granted. However, the claim was for additional costs due to the delay, which the court dismissed.

There is obviously a point at which the number and value of change orders will operate to materially change the nature of the contract by either increasing it, or requiring the contractor to employ a different level of resources, funding, equipment, and supervision than he had contemplated.

Based on the authority of officials in many jurisdictions to approve change orders up to 5 percent of the contract value without going back to higher authority for approval, it is the general custom of the construction trade that change orders in this magnitude of percentage value of the contract are to be expected. (The actual number of change orders has little meaning, since small changes can be packaged into individual larger change orders.)

In *Magoba Construction Co.* v. *United States* (99 Ct. Cl. U.S. 662; 1943) the court held that the issuance of sixty-two changes during the progress of the work did not constitute a change in the basic scope of the contract. The contract was for approximately $2 million for post office reconstruction.

An even more extreme example occurred in *Great Lakes Construction Co.* v. *United States* (95 Ct. Cl. U.S. 479; 1942) where during the construction of a federal penitentiary, 109 change orders were issued. However, this understated the real situation. The basic bid was made on an incomplete set of plans and specifications. Shortly after the contract was made, a new set of plans and specifications was delivered, which included some 700 additions, revisions, and corrections. The court of claims found that this number of changes did not violate or breach the contract, and a claim for damages due to delay was disallowed.

An important case which counteracted the premise that the owner could impose virtually unlimited change upon a contract is *Ross* v. *United States* (Reference Case 52). In this case, the contractor was granted a number of time extensions for changes, but the change orders compensated him only for the cost of the changes, and not for the loss due to delay. The court found that the contractor was "entitled to recover because this was a breach of contract."

Chapter Two · Construction Law

The title of this chapter is a misnomer, since no separate body of law exists for construction projects. The law is really a massive heterogeneous mixture of laws, statutes, ordinances, and regulations prepared by the various independent and overlapping jurisdictions of legislature. In the United States' system of government, these legislated bodies of law are administered by executives. Where problems occur, the judiciary system is utilized to adjudicate the problem.

In criminal justice, when a law has been broken, there is a recognized procedure for apprehending, trying, and sentencing those who perpetrated the crime or misdemeanor. The rules of evidence are well established, and the criteria for conviction generally well structured. The system is one which deals with extremes.

Civil law is designed to handle disputes rather than crimes. In a dispute there tends to be less black and white, and much more gray area to study. While the rules of evidence are the same, the question most often occurring is: What was the agreement between the parties? Once that is established, the next question to be addressed is: How did the parties respond to their obligations?

The rules of law under which these two questions are addressed have evolved through the English common law system. Through usage, the general common sense laws laid down have become structured. The precedent case is an indispensable part of our legal system. It is complicated, however, because given the same set of facts, courts in various jurisdictions have come up with different answers. Generally speaking, therefore, precedent cases in the jurisdiction in which the project dispute is to be heard would have priority or precedence over those from other jurisdictions. Nevertheless, precedent cases with analogous facts or situations are considered by the courts in arriving at findings. Thus, construction law really is a term that applies to a loosely structured set of procedures that has evolved within the specific jurisdiction within which the contract has either been agreed upon, or is being implemented.

When the parties to a contract have not been able to settle their disputes through the machinery established in the contract, or inherent in their situation, then they may litigate. There are levels of litigation, and beyond the basic litigation—appellate courts and higher courts.

In litigation, juries determine the facts, while the jurists interpret the law. In nonjury trials or during appeal, jurists review both findings of fact and interpretations of the law.

In the following case study, a single case is discussed in depth and greater detail than the basic reference cases incorporated in this text. First, the situation is discussed in narrative fashion on the basis of a review of the records of the case, as well as discussion with one of the parties. This is followed by extracts from the legal arguments (i.e., briefs) presented by each side. The arguments from the briefs point out simultaneously the importance of precedent cases, and the difficulty in applying them to a current case.

A Contractor's Story: *Joseph F. Egan, Inc.* v. *City of New York* (17 NY 29 90; 18 A D 2d 357):

Joseph F. Egan, Inc., was plumbing contractor for New York City on the construction of the Elmhurst General Hospital and Nurses' Residence for the contract price of $2,169,000. However, the city's plans were so defective that the hospital could not have been constructed without a complete redesign. Egan was directed to hire an engineer to work with the city's architect in revamping the plans in order to provide sufficient space to permit the installation of the various mechanical lines. The direction to furnish the engineering services was made by Bernard J. Farrell, the Director of Buildings, in charge of Construction and Design, of the Department of Public Works. The changes were so extensive that their overall financial effect could not be ascertained until the conclusion of the work, and the city concededly did not have the staff available to evaluate the financial effect of such changes. Farrell specifically directed that the determinations of the engineering services and related items as contract work or extra work would be made at the conclusion of the work.

Leonard Johnson, who had been the city's resident engineer on the project, and who was now Chief of Construction, testified that Farrell was in direct charge of all construction on Department of Public Works projects. Because of the defendant's inability to handle the extensive redesign work in normal course, Farrell had actual, and the commissioner only "theoretical," authority over the progress of the work and the issuance of change orders. In fact, letters directed to the commissioner were referred to, and answered by, the director.

Pursuant to Farrell's directive, Egan continued employing the otherwise unnecessary engineer for redesign work over a period of two and one-half years, during which time Egan submitted daily reports to the city noting the continued engineering expenses resulting from the redesign. The city utilized these engineering services to issue supplementary plans, to revise change orders and plan drawings, and to make plan changes for all trades necessary to enable construction of the building.

Upon substantial completion of the work, Egan presented ninety-one claims for extra compensation that had been held in abeyance, without formal claim notice, in compliance with Farrell's direction, including the claim for engineering services. Pursuant to such procedure, defendant did, in fact, entertain all such claims and ultimately issued change orders on eighty-two of them. Of the remaining nine claims, eight were conceded at trial to be justified and were settled. The remaining claim was for the engineering services.

Johnson admitted that all contractors were required to proceed on the oral orders of the city's engineer with the performance of undisputed items of extra work, and that change orders were processed, and written confirmation given by the commissioner, only years after the work was done. Where it could not be immediately determined whether the work was extra or contract work, it was ordered to be performed subject to future determination. More than four hundred change orders, totalling more than $1.5 million, were issued on this project, after years of delay, and were, necessarily, subsequently confirmed by the commissioner.

Delay Damage: The contract provided for performance to commence on November 10, 1952, and to be completed within

840 days, or by March 9, 1955. Because of the defects in the plans, the work was delayed and disorganized so that substantial completion was not obtained until March 26, 1956, a delay of 383 days, and was further delayed an additional two and one-half years until final completion, acceptance, and payment in October 1958, a total delay of almost four years.

The major difficulty involved was the failure of the plans to allow sufficient space in hung ceilings and partitions to accommodate the mechanical installations. The problem was particularly acute on the first four stories of the fourteen-story main building, where the installation of the major mechanical equipment was concentrated. These installations could not be made because the inadequate design left insufficient space for coordinated installations by all contractors on the site. As a result, Egan commenced work in the normal manner, from the bottom up, but was required to suspend operations until concrete arches and interior redesigns permitted installations to be made on the upper floors. The continuing redesign delayed the pouring of the lower four floor slabs one and one-half years beyond schedule. The mechanical contractors, therefore, had to begin their installations in partitions on the upper floors and work directly on top of the general contractor. This prevented the normal, economical, and continuous procedure under which plaintiff's work would begin with the main runs in the basement, branch from them into vertical risers running through the pipe spaces and partitions, with the horizontal runs taken off the risers on each floor as they progressed, passing through the corridors where further branches would run to the room fixtures.

Because of the redesign work, Egan had to begin with the vertical risers on the first floor and run them up. Egan could not take the horizontal runs off these risers until the redesign of the corridor hung ceilings, where multiple mechanical installations were required, was completed. Therefore, beginning on the higher floors, it was necessary to put in short branches in each room running from the fixture outlet to the corridor. The delay on the corridor installations made it necessary to individually test thousands of these short water, compressed air, oxygen, vacuum, drainage, and duriron lines, rather than to utilize the normal procedure of making a total of some thirty or forty pressure tests on large segments of the entire systems. Further delay resulted from the necessity to close up the corridor ends of these short branch lines in order to obtain sufficient pressure for the tests, and to make an otherwise unnecessary special coupling between the short branch lines and the corridor lines, when the latter were finally installed. This was all done at tremendous labor costs not otherwise necessary. When the redesign of the lower areas was finally completed, one and one-half years later, Egan had to work backwards to open up the previously installed and plugged horizontal runs in order to connect them with the main lines which they could now install in the lower areas. Egan was further delayed two years by extensive architectural redesign of the maternity divisions of three wings; by changes in toilet locations from the fourth through the tenth floors; and by changes in the incinerator and equipment installations, particularly, extensive kitchen equipment changes.

As a result of the four hundred change orders issued to the various trades and the direction to bypass areas in which conflicts existed or changes were being planned, the work could not progress in each wing simultaneously, floor by floor, in an economical, continuous operation. Egan had to perform the work in a segregated and piecemeal manner requiring many work gangs in many places at a given time and five foremen rather than the two normally necessary. Furthermore, by being forced to work directly on top of the general contractor, Egan was affected by the confused and disjointed performances of precedent trades resulting from the uncoordinated issuance of their change orders and from their continuous confrontation of field conflicts.

The city attributed no fault to Egan for these delays. The certificate of the city engineer annexed to all payment requisitions, and approved by the commissioner, in listing causes of the delays, attributed no responsibility to the defendant. The city conceded it held the plans eight months after their receipt from the architect, but that its architectural bureau was too busy to properly check them before the bid, as required.

Egan testified that the city was responsible for 348 of the 383 days delay until substantial completion. This included 88 days of conceded delays for foundation changes, 210 days of mechanical redesign delays on both buildings, and some 50 days delay due to strikes occurring after the original termination date that otherwise would not have affected the progress of the work. These delays, the irregular and uneconomical work schedules, and the additional testing procedures resulted in the substantial loss of labor productivity and increased the labor cost far above that reasonably anticipated for the job on the basis of Egan's extensive prior experience in hospital and public construction work.

As a result of these delays and resulting disorganized performances, Egan sustained huge costs and damages. The city stipulated, without conceding liability therefore, that Egan expended an additional $103,224 for wage increases, additional supervision, field expenses, and additional insurance payments as a result of the delays. In addition, the chaotic job conditions so decreased Egan's labor productivity on the job, that his labor cost ran $676,626 or $260,807 more than it should have under normal and anticipated conditions. Deducting the conceded sums of $39,827 for supervisory costs and $26,102 for wage increases and the stipulated sum of $23,952 for engineering services, Egan's loss of productivity expense resulting from the delay was $170,927. In addition, Egan also carried the substantial financial burden of the extra work which the city failed to process or pay for until after Egan had substantially completed its contract.

On award of the contract, Egan had been approved by the city as financially qualified to perform the work. This was the only contract Egan performed from April 1953 to shortly before substantial completion on March 26, 1956. Because of the tremendous losses and outlays for unprocessed extras, Egan, at the time of substantial completion, had only $303 in the bank, plus a receivable of some $5,000 due from the defendant on another contract. Egan owed $239,079 to creditors and $75,000 on a bank loan, due May 1, 1956, taken to finance increased labor costs on this job. Any further delay of payment would cause the creditors to report the delinquency to a central credit association, and Egan would have been placed on a cash basis by the suppliers. This would have caused plaintiff's financial ruin.

Egan's work was approved as substantially complete on March 26, 1956. Egan was then entitled to a substantial completion payment of $179,434 that the city was particularly obligated to pay in view of the long delay for which it was responsible. There is no question that Egan, at that time, had a valid claim for damages for delays and disorganized performance resulting from the defective plans. However, as a prerequisite to its substantial completion payment, Egan had to obtain an extention of time. Since the delays were concededly not Egan's fault, the extension was a matter of right.

On applying for such time extention, John E. Egan, general manager, was advised that the commissioner would insist on a waiver of Egan's valid delay claim as a condition to granting it. He saw the commissioner and advised him that the company was in dire need of funds because of its tremendous obligations resulting from the delay losses on this contract. The commissioner told Egan he would not act on the granting of such extention of time unless the delay claim was waived, giving Egan the alternative of waiving its delay claim or not getting its substantial completion payment. The commissioner revealed to Egan that he was exerting the same pressure on Jesse E. Kahn, Inc., the plumbing contractor on another hospital project, whose application for extension of contract time had been held up for one and one-half years because of an asserted claim for delay damages. (No proof to disprove the commissioner's refusal to process Jesse Kahn's application was presented by the city.) Faced with financial ruin unless he complied, Egan executed a waiver of his just claim for delays and disorganized performance. Thereupon the commissioner granted the extension, but expressly reserved the city's right to impose liquidated damages for the entire delay on Egan although the commissioner, in approving Egan's prior requisitions, had conceded such delays were not Egan's fault.

Even after receipt of the substantial payment, there was still an unpaid contract balance due Egan, plus claims for extra work not yet passed upon by the comissioner, of a total sum ultimately found to be $206,612. Egan was afraid that the commissioner might take action against the large pending claims for extras. With the possibility of arbitrarily imposed liquidated damages, and other available ways of creating difficulties to the completion and acceptance of the project, and just before receiving a large payment of $98,831 against the then $104,552 contract balance, Egan, in disregard of, and contrary to the coerced waiver, served written notice of claim for damages for delays and disorganized performance.

The fact that this was done two and one-half years after the execution of the waiver was not Egan's fault. Egan felt subject to the duress until the last payment. The continuing delay until such payment was a result of the defects in the plans. Moreover, the extent of the delay and the resulting damage could be ascertained only upon completion of the project. It was only then that Egan's claim accrued, and Egan acted immediately. The filing of the notice of claim was the first and prerequisite step to the commencement of an action to recover the delay damages, which was instituted some months later.

After the notice of claim was filed, the comptroller held an examination. Upon being asked whether Egan had waived the claim, Egan's counsel stated that a waiver had been executed, but gave an explanation that the waiver was made "in order to obtain a large overdue payment." There can be only one reasonable inference from the statement that unless the waiver was executed, the payment would not be made. At that hearing the comptroller demanded no further details as to why Egan had signed a waiver in order to get the payment.

The Trial

In regard to the engineering change of scope, the trial court charged the jury that it could find the actions of the director of construction, in ordering the engineering services by Egan, and the action of the Commissioner, in utilizing such service, constituting a waiver of the requirements of Article 27 of the contract as regarding requests for ruling of the commissioner and protests. The jury found for Egan and awarded $23,952.

In regard to the damages due to the delay, the trial court charged the jury that it could (1) based upon its finding of the defendant's proportionate responsibility for the delays, find for Egan up to the sum of $120,000; (2) determine whether the Comissioner had used economic duress to compel Egan to execute the waiver of the delay claim; and (3) determine whether Egan had acted as promptly as circumstances would permit to repudiate the transaction within a reasonable time after the duress was removed. The jury found for Egan in the amount of $120,000. The total award, including interest, was $160,090.

At this point, it would appear that equity had prevailed, and the long-suffering contractor had been vindicated. However, the appellate division (first department) reviewed the case and reversed the judgment of the jury on the grounds that a contract provision could not be waived by the city's field representative on the job. Further, they found that Egan had waived his right to a delay claim.

As described in Reference Case 21, the courts finally approved payment of the extra scope of work for the imposed change of scope requiring the hiring of a coordinating engineer by Egan. Our principal interest here is in the delay claim. In arguing, the counsel for plaintiff had to argue on several bases, on the premise that their interpretation of the law could be turned aside. Similarly, the counsel for the City of New York defended the appeal on a number of bases.

The following presents the initial arguments in regard to the delay damage claim by plaintiff counsel Max E. Greenberg et al.:

Point A:

The refusal of the Commissioner to grant an extension of time prerequisite to the payment of the large substantial completion payment, unless plaintiff's valid claim for delay was waived, made with full knowledge that plaintiff would have been financially ruined if the payment was not made, constituted duress.

The jury found that the Commissioner had obtained the waiver from the plaintiff by duress. Since that finding was not reversed in the court below, which only expressed grave doubts as to whether the facts constituted duress, it is submitted that duress must be assumed, limiting this appeal to the question of whether the waiver was ratified.

In any event, the testimony supported the jury's finding that the waiver was made under duress.

Although the court below stated that there was no adequate showing that the City was responsible for plaintiff's financial condition, it is submitted that there is no other conclusion from the conceded facts but that plaintiff's financial plight resulted directly from the huge losses sustained by it as a result of the defective plans.

Plaintiff had originally been approved by defendant as financially capable of performing the contract. From the start, this was its only contract until shortly before substantial completion. There is no dispute that large sums were invested in extra work, ultimately allowed in the sum of $92,025, the processing of which was delayed for years by defendant. Defendant conceded plaintiff sustained $103,224 damages by reason of the delays, apart from its further losses of some $107,927 from unproductive labor resulting from disorganized performance. Plaintiff had to borrow $75,000 from its bank to cover its excessive labor costs.

However, even assuming plaintiff's financial condition did not result from defendant's fault, we still have a situation, where plaintiff, in dire need of funds to avoid financial ruin, is entitled to an extension of time by reason of delays due to the default of the defendant, which knowingly took advantage of plaintiff's financial straits by refusing the extension plaintiff was legally entitled to receive, unless it waived its valid claims.

The act of the Commissioner, in threatening not to process the extension, knowing that such refusal was improper and for the purpose of coercing the waiver of plaintiff's valid claim in order to obtain a payment which should have been made a year before, constituted duress.

The basis of economic duress is the taking advantage of the known circumstances of the coerced party by an unjustified threat to do something there is no justifiable right to do, or to improperly withhold rights of the threatened party, with a purpose of coercion where there is no adequate alternative available to the coerced party. . . .

. . . . The government's refusal to grant a time extension to which a contractor is legally entitled, or to improperly threaten to assess liquidated damages in order to coerce a release of a valid right of a contractor constitutes economic duress. . . . The Court charged the jury that if the Commissioner unjustifiably insisted on the waiver of plaintiff's delay claim as a condition to the granting of an extension of time, it must be deemed an improper demand.

Implicit in its verdict is the jury's finding that the Commissioner insisted upon the waiver as a condition to the granting of the time extension, without justification, and for the purpose of coercing the waiver of plaintiff's valid claim. The Appellate Court below incorrectly stated that "It was the plaintiff who injected the condition into the bargain, namely, that both sides waive any rights to due delay," and that the Commissioner would have taken this position whether or not plaintiff was in financial difficulties. The plaintiff merely asked that it be given the extension of contract time it was entitled to without being forced to waive its delay claim. The Commissioner took unfair advantage of plaintiff's unfortunate financial condition by refusing the extension, made necessary through defendant's fault, although plaintiff had a legal right to receive it. Almost any contractor would be put under tremendous pressure by this unjustifiable device. Under the circumstances of the long delay and the huge expenditures under the unprocessed change orders, in themselves long delayed, the Commissioner was abusing his discretion in refusing to pay the substantial completion payment unless plaintiff waived its proper delay claim. The plaintiff did not seek a "bargain", nor did it request that defendant, in turn, waive any rights it might have against plaintiff by reason of the delay. Defendant obviously had no right to delay damages. The contention that plaintiff offered to waive its right to delay damage in consideration of defendant waiving a similar claim against plaintiff is simply unrealistic. It means plaintiff would be waiving a valid right in consideration of defendant waiving a right which both sides knew defendant did not have. As in any case of duress, the Commissioner had the ability, but not the right to carry out a threatened improper act or to withhold something he had no right to withhold in order to obtain what he wanted.

Furthermore, and this the Court below apparently completely overlooked, the defendant, in granting the extension gave nothing in return, as it specifically reserved the right to impose liquidated damages against the plaintiff for the entire delay, if it had any such right.

The threatened refusal to extend plaintiff's contract time and thus deny it payment long overdue, because of delays caused by the defendant, was an improper attempt to impose the result of the City's own default upon the plaintiffs.

The defendant was not entitled to impose conditions upon the granting of an extension of time necessary through no fault of plaintiff, but by reason of defendant's own breach of contract. Town and Country Engineering Corp. v. State, 46 N.Y.S. 2d 792, 822; Good Roads Engineering & Contracting Co. v. State, 176 Misc. 1012, 29 N.Y.S. 2d 848; Oswald v. El Centro, 211 Cal. 45, 292 P. 1073, 71 A.L.R. 899.

Obviously there was no reason for plaintiff to waive its claim for the large damages suffered by it through defendant's fault except for the pressure exerted on it by the Commissioner. Where a transaction results from an improper demand made under circumstances of coercion and without consideration, it has been held [that]: "it would be a disgrace to the Court that such a transaction be permitted to stand." Van Dyke v. Wood, 60 App. Div. 208, N.Y.S. 324, 331.

In 17 N.Y. Juris., Duress & Undue Influence, pp. 210–218, it is stated that duress applies where one yields to an extortionate claim as an alternative to a serious loss or damage to its property, or where one yields to an exaction in order to obtain a release of property improperly withheld, there being no apparent alternative of practical adequacy. It is further stated:

> Cases from other jurisdictions indicate that requiring as a condition of the delivery of property to one entitled to the immediate possession thereof, the giving of a release from liability in reference to the property, constitutes duress, especially where the parties do not stand on an equal footing. (Sec. 10, pp. 216–217)

Since the Courts are ever mindful of the disparities of the parties in duress cases, they will, in a proper case, find economic duress exerted against contractors or individuals by government authorities.

The exact fact pattern as we have here was determined to be duress by the Board of Contract Appeals of the federal government in the matter of Paccon, Inc. [v. United States].

There, work suspensions for contract changes ordered by the Government seriously delayed the Contractor. The contracting officer, with knowledge that the contractor had limited financial resources, threatened to withhold other payments under the contract unless the contractor signed a modification granting a time extension containing a waiver of claim for delay damages. The Board, reversing the determination below, held a refusal to make payments otherwise due conditioned upon plaintiff's waiving its claim in the extension of time was a wrongful and unlawful act. The Board said:

> As to modification #79 the contractor was legally entitled to an extension of time, but the Government was not legally entitled to a waiver clause, and for the contracting officer to refuse to grant a time extension unless the contractor would agree to the waiver clause, and to threaten to assess liquidated damages, which the contractor did not owe, was a wrongful act. We find that the contractor was pressured and coerced against its will into signing the three contract modifications only because it believed with good reason that the contracting officer would carry out his threats if it did not sign, and that its only alternative to signing was financial ruin. We find that the acts wrongfully threatened by the contracting officer for the purpose of coercing the contractor into signing the contract modifications with waiver clauses would have caused irreparable damage to the contractor, to wit, financial ruin. The economic duress is aggravated by the fact that the contracting officer, was not only fully aware that the threatened action would bankrupt the contractor, but the contractor's financial straits were caused by the Government itself in suspending, delaying and disrupting the contractor's work and ordering changes in work without establishing prices under which the contractor could be paid. (pp. 18, 354)

In American Dist. Telegraph Co. v. City of New York, 213 App. Div. 578, 211 N.Y.S. 262, the Court held that where plaintiff, on threat of the City to put it out of business, entered into a new franchise agreement, without protest, whereby it was to place its lines underground, although it had been chartered to use overhead cables, recovery for its costs would be allowed since the transaction was coerced and the City could not uphold the fruits of fraudulent oppression. The Court stated:

> The franchise agreement was not a voluntary act. It was made in order to preserve rights which plaintiff feared would be destroyed, if it did not acquiesce in the demands made by the representatives of the City and entered into agreement. There is

*duress sufficient to require the judgement it has obtained. In
most cases which appear to the contrary, facts appeared which
warranted the view that the payment of the contract had been
voluntarily made to obtain some benefit sought. The plaintiff by
this contract relinquished valuable rights which were
surrendered in the belief that if the contract were not entered
into, its business would be destroyed. The contract was not to
the plaintiff's benefit, for without it, plaintiff was in a better
position. (p. 269)*

The Courts have long held that threats by governmental
bodies to make improper exactions against contractors
nullified the transactions coerced thereby. . . .

The United States Supreme Court has held that where public
officials improperly withheld a right to which the plaintiff was
entitled and which was essential to the conduct of his business,
a contract entered into with those public officials to secure that
right was voidable under the doctrine of business compulsion.
Oceanic Steam Navigation v. Stranahan, 214 U.S. 320, 53 L.Ed.
1013, 29 S.Ct. 671.

Similarly, releases or modification agreements entered into
because of an unjustifiable threat by a public agency to
repudiate its contract, leaving the plaintiff to an inadequate
remedy, have been voided for duress. Precedent cases do not
require the coercing party be solely responsible for the
compelling financial necessity causing the plaintiff to accede
to the wrongful threat. The crux of duress is that the offending
party threatens a wrongful act which would cause irreparable
damage without remedy.

In Tri-State Roofing Co. of Uniontown v. Simon (142 A.2d
333, 187 Pa. Super. 17), a subcontractor claimed a contract
balance against the general contractor, who counter-claimed
for delay damages which he had previously released, claiming
the release had been coerced by the subcontractor's threat not
to perform its subcontract. The Court held that no lack of
adequate remedy had been shown, but that had the general
contractor been able to show that no other subcontractor would
have completed the work, the threatened refusal to abide by its
contract obligations would be duress if it resulted in a threat of
financial loss so serious as to afford no alternative but to
comply with the improper demand.

The case of Fitzgerald v. Fitzgerald & Mallory Construction Co. (44 Neb. 463, 62 N.W. 899, 909), is similar
to ours in that there, too, the owner took advantage of the
financial pressures caused by a large outstanding and
overdue contract balance to force the contractor to agree to

a reduction in the unit price per mile for railroad track. Despite the owner's specious claim of consideration based on poor workmanship, the Court held that the modification was procured under "practical compulsion," since plaintiff otherwise would have gone out of business. The Court said:

> A payment of concession exacted will be held compulsory when made or allowed through necessity in order to obtain possession of property illegally withheld where the detention is fraught with great immediate hardship or irreparable injury.

Similarly, see Thomas v. Brown, 116 Va. 233, 81 S.E. 56, where the owner improperly withheld monies due on the contract to pressure the contractor to agree to conditions the owner had no right to insist upon.

In Parkside Clothes, Inc. [v. United States], 4 CCF 51, 387, the Armed Services Board of Contract Appeals held [that] a contractor's acceptance of an excessive reduction of contract price for failure to meet specifications was made under duress because the contractor's financial condition forced it to accept the Government's demand. The Board held that although the contracting officer was not responsible for the contractor's difficulties, the effect of his excessive demands upon the contractor, with an awareness that those circumstances, subjecting it to pressures it could not withstand under the circumstances, constituted economic duress. See, also, Aronoff v. Levine; Sheinberg v. Sheinberg, 249 N.Y. 277, 164 N.E. 98; Kalbfleisch v. Anderson, 201 App. Div. 158, 194 N.Y.S. 692; Ring v. Ring, 127 App. Div. 411, 111 N.Y.S. 713.

The Trial Court . . . charged that if the jury found the plaintiff's financial condition was precarious, and the Commissioner, knowing it would mean financial ruin for plaintiff, and seeking to take advantage of that fact, threatened not to grant an extension of time to plaintiff unless it waived its intended delay claim, thereby depriving plaintiff of its freedom of will, it could find the waiver voidable for duress. The jury so found. And, as stated, the court below did not reverse that finding.

Point B:

The jury's finding that plaintiff did not ratify the waiver was justified and is not reversible as a matter of law.

On October 3, 1958, upon completion and acceptance of the project but before final payment, some 2½ years after plaintiff executed the waiver of its delay claim as a condition to receiving its substantial completion payment, and some 3½ years before trial, plaintiff, in complete disaffirmance of said waiver and as a prerequisite to this action, filed its formal notice of claim to recover its damages resulting from defendant's delays. Consequently, issues of fact existed as to whether the notice of claim constituted a disaffirmance of the waiver, and whether such disaffirmance was timely made.

The jury, charged by the Trial Court, without exception taken by defendant, that it could determine whether plaintiff had disaffirmed the waiver with reasonable promptness after its vulnerability to the duress was terminated, found the plaintiff had disaffirmed and had not ratified the waiver.

Plaintiff showed that for the 2½ years after the waiver, while it continued performance on extra work and contract completion items, it remained in fear of anticipated acts of reprisal on the part of the Commissioner with respect to his approval and valuation of extensive extra work items, his ability to impose liquidated damages for the total job delay, and to further delay or prevent payment of the much needed contract balances on completion of the project. Since $206,000 was finally approved for payment during this period after the waiver, of which $98,831 was paid on October 3, 1958 immediately prior to the filing of the notice of claim, there was, in view of plaintiff's continued financial plight, sufficient basis for finding that plaintiff remained subject to the duress until acceptance of its work and the filing of its claim. Moreover, the logical time for plaintiff to have asserted its claim was when it finally accrued, which occurred only upon entire completion of the work.

Under the circumstances, the Trial Court having presented the issue of ratification to the jury as a question of fact, without exception taken by the defendant, and the jury having found there was no ratification, it is submitted that the court below could not reverse the finding as a matter of law. . . .

. . . It is submitted that the mere passage of 2½ years before the filing of the notice of claim, during which period plaintiff continued under the influence of duress, and its entire claim had not accrued, is not sufficient basis to find ratification as a matter of law. Courts have refused to uphold the fruits of coercion because of long silence of even greater periods where there is no action unequivocally showing an intention to condone the wrong and a purpose to abide by its consequences, so long as the rights of innocent parties have not intervened. . . .

The above is only an extract from the brief presented by counsel for the plaintiff, and speaks only to the question of duress. Many citations and extensions of the argument have been deleted, but the basic argument is evident. On the basis of legal precedent and realities of the construction industry, as well as the fact that this contractor was working only for one client—the New York City Department of Public Works—over a period of many years, even though on low bid basis, it would appear that a convincing argument for duress had been made.

Despite this convincing argument, the city countered with an argument of its own. An extract from that argument follows:

Re: Points A and B

The court below stated that there was very great doubt whether the Commissioner's action in making plaintiff's waiver of a valid delay claim, arising out of the defective plans, a condition of granting plaintiff an extension of time for such delays, for which plaintiff concededly was not responsible, constituted duress, even though the Commissioner knew said extension was a prerequisite to a large substantial completion payment then due plaintiff, without which plaintiff would have been forced out of business because of the large losses it sustained as a result of the defective design. The court below held there was no adequate showing that defendant was responsible for plaintiff's financial condition at the time of the alleged duress. The court below further stated there was a bargain whereby both sides waived any right due to delay, although defendant, despite its knowledge that plaintiff was not responsible for the delay, expressly retained its right to improperly impose liquidated damages on plaintiff for the delay.

The court below held, as a matter of law, that the plaintiff did not disaffirm the waiver promptly nor assert the claim until trial, and that the filing of the notice of claim for the delay damages with the Comptroller at the conclusion of the work, when it accrued, as a contractual prerequisite to suit thereon, did not constitute disaffirmance of the waiver of that claim.

The validity of an extension of time which was granted to a contractor upon his waiver of delay claims was passed upon in Sundstrom v. State of New York, 159 App. Div. 241, 247–249 (3rd Dept.; 1913), *and idem,* 213 N.Y. 68, 75; 1914.

The application for the extension of time, Defendant's Exhibit B, sets forth seven alleged causes of delays as causing a total delay of 383 days. No specific number of days is attributed to each cause although Egan attempted to do so orally.

Egan had reserved 46 claims for extras. The Board of Extension for Contract Time permitted him to reserve these claims for extras subject to the contract provisions.

However, insofar as an extension of time for delay was concerned, Article 13 governed. The contractor was entitled to an extension of time for delays due solely to certain causes as determined by the Commissioner or the Board for Extension of Contract Time. Granting an extension of time for causes of delay other than those enumerated is entirely within the discretion of the Commissioner or the Board, whose determination is binding and conclusive upon the contractor. In granting the extension the Board decided the contractor was entitled to it for the reasons set forth in the application provided no delay claims therefor were made against the City. The Board could have refused to recognize any one or all of the reasons for delay given by the contractor and refused to grant a full 383-day extension. Liquidated damages for delay might have been assessed under Article 16.

It must be observed that under Article 43 the Commissioner, when, in his opinion, the work had been substantially but not entirely completed, could, in his discretion, issue a certificate of substantial completion and a voucher calling for payment of any part or all of the balance due under the contract.

Egan was seeking a payment which he wanted expedited. The granting of the extension was implemented by Defendant's Exhibit E, Change Order No. 2-30, which specifically stated: "The City grants this extension so as to expedite a payment to the Contractor." There being a question as to whether the alleged causes of delay set forth by Egan entitled him to an extension of 383 days, and as to whether he was entitled to damages for any such delays, the matter was resolved by the City granting the extension, and Egan giving the delay claim waiver and warranty and representation that only $51,006.54 in claims remained.

Since Egan's own claim at the trial, as analyzed on the schedule, enumerated 377 days, of which 35 were not attributable to the City and 55 more not allowed in evidence, it becomes obvious that the granting of an extension of time was not a cut and dried matter.

Plaintiff is predicating its contention on the invalidity of the waiver and release of delay claims set forth in its extension of time application, and the invalidity of its warranty and representation that it had no other claims arising out of the contract as of April 2, 1956, nor would it assert any other claims against the City in connection with the contract, on the

ground of alleged economic duress exercised by Commissioner
Zurmuhlen upon the plaintiff.

We submit that in the absence of proof that Egan's claimed
financial embarrassment was created by the City through the
use of coercive means, the plaintiff cannot claim economic
duress in avoidance of the waiver and release and the warranty
and representation.

As stated in Arlington Towers Land Corp. v. McShain, Inc.,
150 F. Supp. 904, 914 (Dist. Ct. D.C.;1957):

> . . . but most jurisdictions place emphasis on the fact that the
> factual circumstances reacting to the plaintiff's economic
> disadvantage must have been created by the respondents'
> action.

Plaintiff's theory is that the City delayed the performance of
the contract to such a degree that the plaintiff became
financially embarrassed as a result thereof. However, the
evidence that the financial embarassment resulted directly and
solely from such delay is vague, indefinite, sketchy and
without adequate support to give it definite probative value.
Moreover, there is no evidence that the alleged delays on the
part of the City involved any element of coercion, or that Egan
was in fact coerced. Nor, as stated by the Appellate Division,
was there an adequate showing that the City was responsible
for plaintiff's financial condition.

Although requested to, Egan never produced the corporate
books that would show plaintiff's financial condition and the
various changes therein from the time it was awarded the
contract to the time it made up its application for an extension
of time. Egan's testimony, although allegedly based on his
knowledge of the plaintiff's activities, was not buttressed in
any documentary manner, except for some letters and bills.
These were certainly not evidence that the City had caused
Egan's financial embarrassment, if such there was, nor coerced
him into it.

It must be remembered that the alleged duress rests solely on
this alleged financial embarrassment, hence the necessity of
proof relevant thereto. The only testimony relative to
Zurmuhlen's knowledge of plaintiff's financial situation is that
Egan advised him that plaintiff was put in the situation
because of the long delay, increase in wages, additional wages
and poor plans. However, Zurmuhlen was not interested in his
excuses and stated: "Either you waive the claim or you don't
get the money."

In its charge the Trial Court did not instruct the jury that in order to sustain the plaintiff's claim of duress it must find that plaintiff's financial condition when it signed the waiver and release of delay claims, and the warranty and representation of no other claims than those set forth in the bill of particulars, was the result of coercion by the City.

In the application of the rules set forth in [paragraph] 493 of the Restatement of Contracts relating to how duress may be exercised: "Whether the alleged facts are sufficient to constitute duress is a question of law, whether alleged facts pleaded as constituting duress, existed, if the existence of these facts is denied, is a question for the jury."

As stated in Meyer v. Guardian Trust Co., 296 F. 789, 792 (C.C.A. 8th; 1924): "What constitutes duress is a matter of law. Whether such duress exists as to a particular transaction is a matter of fact."

It is submitted that the Trial Court should have dismissed the third cause of action on the ground that the evidence submitted by Egan as to the alleged duress did not constitute duress as a matter of law.

In Finn v. Miller, 47 N.W. 2d 660, 662, 330 Mich. 396 (Sup. Ct. Michigan; 1951), a building contractor, after completing a contract, had a dispute with the defendant as to the amount due. The contractor claimed a $91,000 cost figure, instead of an estimated $39,000, all due to defendant's acts in changing plans and ordering extras. Moreover, such acts of defendant were the cause of plaintiff's later financial embarrassment. While the dispute was going on and before payment of the balance due, the contractor being in financial difficulties, accepted a check from defendant in full payment, and executed a release. Thereafter the contractor brought an action to have the release declared void and for the additional amount he claimed due him.

The contractor asserted the release was executed under duress occasioned by his financial difficulties which were caused by the defendant. The court stated: "There is no showing that plaintiff's financial distress was caused by any unlawful act on the defendant's part" and dismissed the complaint, reversing the court below which had given plaintiff judgement.

The application for an extension was made in writing, dated April 2, 1956, the substantial completion inspection having been made on March 26, 1956. No check would have been issued on substantial completion without an extension, although a partial payment would be issued even if the contract date was passed. Egan had submitted such an

application for an extension of time signed by his father Joseph
F. Egan. . . . It will be noted that Defendant's Exhibit B executed
by Joseph F. Egan, as president of the plaintiff, whose
acknowledgement was taken by the witness John F. Egan,
stated:

> We hereby represent and warrant, in consideration of the
> Board for the Extention [sic] of Contract Time considering our
> application for an extention [sic] of time, that we have no other
> claims arising out of the contract as of this date, other than those
> stated in this sworn statement, and we further represent, and
> warrant we will not assert any other claims against the City of
> New York, in connection with this contract.

Egan had received both forms from Friedberg, a clerk in the
Department of Public Works, who handled the issuance of all
change orders and extensions of time in the Department of
Public Works at the time. As an extension of time eventually
became a change order, it was under his jurisdiction.

Counsel for defendant drew Egan's attention to Article 13 of
the contract relative to extensions of time, which states that
extensions of time in excess of sixty days may be granted only
by a board consisting of the Commissioner, the Corporation
Counsel and the Comptroller, or their duly authorized
representatives. Egan's application for an extension of 383
days was passed upon by such board. The decision of this
board was received by Egan as Change Order No. 2-30, which
change order was admitted into evidence as Defendant's
Exhibit E.

In Defendant's Exhibit E, the change order granting the
extension of time, it is specifically stated:

> Approved by the Board of Extension of Contract Time on
> April 17, 1956 with the understanding that any claims
> heretofore waived by the Contractor shall not be revived by
> reason of this extension.
>
> The City grants this extension so as to expedite a payment to
> the Contractor and does not waive or release any claim it may
> have against the Contractor whether it be for liquidated
> damages or for any reason whatsoever.

Thereafter, Egan made out the application for an extension
of contract time, waiving the delay claim. The substantial
payment requisition was for $179,000. Egan claimed the
plaintiff could not have continued in business if it had not
received such payment. Egan received the $179,000
approximately one month after making the application and
was able to pay off part of the plaintiff's debts. It will be noted
the change order extending the time of completion after

approval by the Board for Extension of Contract Time on April 17, 1956 was dated April 22, 1956.

Egan testified that the waiver and release were executed under duress.

The following are extracts from the Egan counsel's rebuttal brief on Points A and B:

Respondent fails to refute appellant's basic contention that Egan repudiated its waiver by filing its notice of claim for such delay damages on October 3, 1958, simultaneously with its acceptance of the large outstanding contract sum of $98,831. It was not necessary that appellant specify that the waiver was being repudiated because it had been exacted under duress.

It is undisputed that one who is defrauded into executing an instrument may repudiate that instrument simply by refusing to abide by, or by acting contrary to, its promise therein, without stating the reason for the repudiation. Similarly, one who executed an instrument under duress may repudiate it by acting contrary thereto, without giving his reasons therefor. This is so because the ratification of an act coerced by duress may only be based upon acts unequivocally showing an intention to condone the wrong and abide by its consequences.

The very cases cited by respondent substantiate that repudiation on grounds of duress is similar to repudiation on the grounds of fraud, which requires no specification of the reason for disaffirmance. As stated in Colon & Co. v. East 189th St. Building & Construction Co., 141 App. Div. 441, 442 (Resp. Br., p. 61), these cases derive from Oregon Pacific R. R. Co. v. Forrest, 128 N.Y. 84. It is there stated that there is a "duty to act promptly in repudiating the agreement which it had been induced to enter into by duress. . . . One entitled to repudiate a contract on the ground of duress should, like one who attempts to repudiate a contract on the ground of fraud, act promptly. . . ." Gould v. Cayuga County National Bank, 86 id. (N.Y.) 82; Baird v. Mayor, etc., 96 id. 567.

Since both the Gould and Baird cases on which the Oregon decision is based involved repudiation on the ground of fraud, the New York doctrine of repudiation of an act coerced by duress cannot be deemed to require a specification of the duress. The filing of the notice of claim showed that Egan had no intention of condoning the wrong, as found by the jury, and, was adequate and timely disaffirmance of its prior waiver of claim. . . .

. . . . Respondent's contention that Egan did not prove duress as a matter of law is not substantiated by its arguments nor the cases it cites. The jury found duress existed; the Appellate Division did not reverse this finding.

Respondent's brief completely misconstrues the coercive aspect of duress. Business compulsion does not require one to cause another's financial embarrassment by coercion, as respondent argues; it exists where one party takes advantage of the other party's known financial distress by unjustifiably and coercively withholding something rightfully and necessarily due that party, in order to force a promise to which the coerced party would not otherwise agree. . . .

. . . . Our case does not involve a claim that work was performed under duress. The Commissioner coercively prevented Egan from asserting a claim it had a right to file by threatening not to grant the extension of contract time to which Egan was concededly entitled, thereby preventing payment of the huge, agreed, substantial completion payment which he knew Egan required in order to stay in business, and subjecting Egan to an unjustifiable assessment of liquidated damages against the agreed contract price.

Our case is, therefore, the precise factual situation as that in Paccon, Inc. [v. United States], ASBCA 7890; 1963, BCA 3659, which respondent failed to distinguish. As in the Paccon case, Egan not only showed that the Commissioner took advantage of its known condition of financial distress, but also that such financial condition was the direct result of the concededly great increase in its labor cost resulting from the delays, and the large sums unpaid for contract balances, delayed change orders and extra work items. Respondent's stress on the fact that Egan did not produce its books would have been better taken up on cross-examination rather than appeal. As the Trial Court charged, and the Corporation Counsel concurred by its recommended charge, the absence of the books went only to the weight of the evidence. Actually, Egan's records were in court, enabling the parties, including the City's auditor, to work out the value of the conceded damages. Moreover, the Corporation Counsel expressly waived his right to have Mr. Egan testify from his books.

Respondent is finally reduced to try to find consideration for the Commissioner's refusal to pay the conceded contract balance in his right to assess liquidated damages because of Egan's alleged delay in completion. There is absolutely no basis in the record for such a finding, the City conceded Egan was not responsible for delays.

Respondent's argument that Egan failed to comply with

technical notice and claim provisions of the contract with respect to the delay claim, is a factual issue beyond the scope of this appeal. The jury's finding that plaintiff complied with all relevant notices was permissible under the unexcepted to charge of the Trial Court, and was not reversed by the Appellate Division.

In any event, the City's Resident Engineer certified in writing, on requisitions approved by the Commissioner, that he had received written notification in compliance with Articles 11 and 13 of the contract.

Articles 27 and 28 are, by their very terms and captions, applicable to disputed extra work items only, and not to delay claims, which accrue only at the end of the contract. Article 42 specifically refers to the presentment of claim on final requisition in addition to those presented under Articles 27 and 28. On the other hand, although Article 42 might require inclusion of a delay claim in the final payment requisition, failure to comply therewith serves to bar a claim only upon the contractor's receipt of final payment (Art. 44 (a)). Concededly, final payment was not made herein. Egan accepted the last payment of $98,831 under a stipulation whereby the City paid it as a partial settlement and not as final payment, thereby recognizing that the payment was no bar to the maintenance of Egan's entire claim, inclusive of that for delay damages, as set forth in its notice of claim. . . .

Egan after complying with Articles 11 and 13 of the contract, was forced to abandon its claim under duress. As found by the jury on the unexcepted to charge of the Trial Court, Egan remained under duress in requisitioning the payment of $98,831, since it was mindful of the Commissioner's power to improperly impose liquidated damages if a delay claim was asserted contrary to its waiver of claim (2482). The jury found Egan remained under duress at least until the time it received the $98,831 payment, simultaneously with which it filed its notice of claim for delay damages in repudiation of its waiver.

Both sides filed briefs regarding the actual delay damages. These arguments are included in Reference Case 21, since they are illustrative of important factors in the development of specific presentation of delay for damages. However, the facts as argued in the damage portion of the briefs were never really considered in the final decision. This decision was decided on the judicial interpretation of the law, which was deemed to preclude a recovery for the delay on the basis that the Court did not find the Egan firm to have been coerced within the

definition of the law. This, in turn, made the waiver signed by
Egan valid, and precluded a recovery for damages.

Summary

The law is an uncertain thing—one that experienced lawyers
can sincerely debate. Obviously, the experienced designer,
owner, and constructor is well advised to acquire appropriate
legal consultation before entering into contractual relationships. During the implementation of these relationships, appropriate legal advice should be sought on a continuing basis.

In the broader picture, the laws of the land as they apply to
construction are undergoing evolution. The situation described
in the case of *Egan* v. *City of New York* would probably be
handled differently today—but not necessarily.

The difference behind the evolution in the law is represented
by a difference in the understanding of the roles of the parties
to the construction project, and a better perception of many of
the inequities involved in standard contractual situations. One
of the proponents of improved contractual relationships has
been Max E. Greenberg, known in the industry as the Dean of
Construction Contract Law. In *Civil Engineering* (May 1975, pp.
56–9) the editor includes comments by a more recent
Commissioner of Public Works in New York City (now assistant
Postmaster General of the U.S. Postal Service for facilities),
Alfred C. Maevis. Maevis, a hard-driving, well-organized
engineer, accomplished many major projects during his tenure.
On a number of occasions lawyer Greenberg won cases by
presenting well-prepared cases that pointed out defects
in contracts and administrative procedure. Insisting
on improvements in the city procedures, Maevis instituted
changes which achieved better quality work and earlier
completions. Maevis pointed to Greenberg's work for Standing
Subcommittee #4 on Contract Practices of the U.S. National
Committee on Tunneling Technology as "a major contribution
to better contract procedure."

Commissioner Maevis' emphasis on the positive attributes of
a professional who often undertakes an adversarial role is an
encouraging milestone in the evolution of recognition by
owners that the basic inequities in the traditional construction
contracting arrangement not only inflict harm upon the many
contractors whose projects get into trouble, but also upon
owners, in general, through higher bid prices.

Chapter Three · Construction Contract

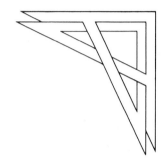

The contract for construction is the basis for all legal interpretations, judgments, and resolutions of the impact of construction delay. Yet, in the preconstruction phase, it is the area perhaps least understood by the principal parties. Contractors, owners, architects, and engineers, all refer to the contract portion of the specifications as the boiler plate.

The owner, usually through the architect/engineer, prepares the construction contract. The term "contract documents" includes not only the actual contract form, but the various additional forms used to describe the contract requirements, as well as provide the response forms which the contractor executes as part of his bid. Construction documents generally include the following:

- Advertisement for bids
- Information for bidders
- Bid form
- Notice of award
- Notice to proceed
- Special conditions
- Performance bond
- Payment bond
- Contract form
- General conditions
- Supplementary general conditions
- Plans
- Specifications

In *Public Construction Contracts and the Law* (pp. 147–152), Cohen discusses the proper manner in which a construction contract (or any contract) should be entered into. From the court decision on *Salt Lake City* v. *Smith* (104 F. 457; 1900), he quotes the following relevant definitive description of what should occur when a written contract is prepared:

The purpose of a written contract is to evidence the terms on which the minds of the parties to it met when they made it, and the ascertainment of those terms, and the sense in which the parties to the agreement used them when they agreed to them, is the great desideratum and the true end of all contractual interpretation. The express terms of an agreement may not be abrogated, nullified, or modified by parol testimony; but, when their construction or extent is in question the meaning of the terms upon which the minds of the parties met when they settled them and their intention in using them must be ascertained, and when ascertained they must prevail in the interpretation of the agreement, however broad or narrow the words in which they are expressed. In the discovery of this meaning, the intention, the situation of the parties, the facts and circumstances which surrounded and necessarily influenced them when they made their contract, the resonableness of the respective claims under it, and above all, the subject matter of the agreement and the purpose of its execution, are always conducive to and often as essential and controlling in the true interpretation of the contract as the mere words of its various stipulations.

These are rules for the construction of contracts which commend themselves to the reason and are established by repeated decisions of the courts."

Lawyers continually warn clients to carefully read any document that they sign, because they recognize that in the law a signed contract is accepted as a valid agreement between parties. From a litigation viewpoint, there is no other practical approach to take. This was the reason for the rejection of the Bethlehem Steel position in Reference Case 5, wherein the court stated: "In other words, Bethlehem now seeks to rewrite the contract and to relieve itself from the stipulated delivery dates. . . . This the plaintiff cannot do."

Similarly in *Wise v. United States* (239 U.S. 361; 1919), Wise held that the liquidated damages clause was not enforceable. The court disagreed saying: "There is no sound reason why persons competent and free to contract may not agree upon this subject as fully as upon any other, or why their agreement, when fairly and understandably entered into with a view to just compensation for the anticipated loss should not be enforced."

Max E. Greenberg starts his comments in *Civil Engineering* (May 1975, pp. 569) with the statement: "A contract is a dangerous instrument. It should always be approached with trepidation and caution. . . . Theoretically, the aim of a written contract is to achieve certainty of obligation of each party, the avoidance of ambiguities, and such definiteness of understanding as to preclude ultimate controversy. In practice, construction contracts are generally framed not to definitely fix obligations, but to avoid obligations."

Under common law, the intent of contracts (and their enforcement) is that the parties thereto shall have had a meeting of the minds. However, in the case of most prime construction contracts, this is really a case of take it or leave it.

In public work, the contractor bids on a set of documents which will become the contract. As a prerequisite to being considered, he submits an agreement to accept the contract as stated. If he conditions his potential acceptance, his bid is considered nonresponsive and his bid will be rejected. More than that, it must be rejected. Similarly, in most of the negotiated contracts, the owner (usually on the advice of his architect/engineer and his legal counsel) states the basic legal language which must be included in the contract. The contractor may be able to negotiate, but in most cases, he either will not, does not, or cannot. Often, the contractual language in the general conditions is mandated by the agency or organization, having been developed through prior experience. The courts take the position that the contractor was not forced to accept the contract, and therefore there was a meeting of the minds.

An owner may downplay the legalese portion of the contract noting that the owner can always relax or interpret the specifications. Since a contractor cannot change the boiler plate section, he accepts it for whatever value it has, trusting that he will never be exposed to litigation in regard to his performance. He carefully reviews the special conditions sections for specific information regarding the contract, leaving the legal portion to his legal staff. Even when warned that there are certain hazards in accepting certain phraseology, he has the choice of either accepting it or not bidding. Further, a contractor suffers from chronic optimism and expects that he can either meet the contract or beat it on legal terms if necessary. The contractor preparing a bid is in the romance stage, and hopes for a marriage. He is not interested in studying the litigation rules involved in an ultimate divorce.

Contract Components

The contract documents include many different components, each with its own purpose. In the interpretation of the documents, definite requirements will govern over general requirements. When provisions, such as agenda, are drafted at a later date, they will have precedence over provisions drafted earlier. Contract provisions govern over the specifications, while the specifications govern over plans.

Where the components of the contract document are in conflict, there is either a gap in information (the basis for a claim for extra work) or an overlap. Where information overlaps, ambiguity often results. The law holds generally that, given two interpretations, the courts will find against the drafter of the ambiguous information. In chapter 4, "Plans and Specifications," the problem of ambiguity is discussed more completely.

In the general conditions, it is usual to find exculpatory clauses. These clauses seek to avoid responsibility for unanticipated situations, with a view towards shifting all risk to the contractor. Exculpatory clauses are usually unenforceable, but if the contractor has taken them seriously in his bid, he may have included a substantial contingency to cover the risk of either litigation or actual damage in the field. This area is also discussed in chapter 4. The general conditions portion of the contract often includes specific clauses relating to: changes in the work; delays; notice of delay or potential delay; extensions of time; basis of final payment; and other legalistic clauses with strong potential delay litigation implications. One of the most important of these is known as the "no delay damage" clause which states that the contractor will be compensated only in the form of time for delay. Reference Case 21 (*Egan v. City of New York*) contains, in the legal brief by the city, discussion of the implications of many of these types of phrases.

The disputes clause can directly impact the progress of the job. This clause (or clauses) is made up of language that states that the owner, or his designated representative, will have the authority to settle all disputes. It is usual practice to name the designer or the construction manager as the one who is to settle disputes. As discussed in chapter 5, "The Architect and Engineer in the Field," if this dispute settling role is assigned to a professional, he may have a quasijudicial status.

No Damages for Delay Clause

This usual clause in construction contracts states that in the event of delay, the contractor will be compensated only by an extension of the contract end date. Such extension automatically extends the period of time before imposition of liquidated damages. In some cases, the clause refers to unforeseen delays rather than the broader term of delay.

In *Kaplen & Son Ltd.* v. *Housing Authority* (126 at 2d 13, N.J.; 1956), the plaintiff was the contractor for the building of public housing. Before construction could start, occupants of existing buildings had to be moved. A delay occurred, and the contractor sought to recover delay damages resulting from five months delay. The contract included a "no damages for delay clause." The clause included language to the effect that such problems would include: "hindrances or delays from any cause in the progress of the work, whether such hindrances or delays be avoidable or unavoidable, and the contractor agrees that he will make no claim for compensation, damages, or litigation of liquidated damages for any such delays, and will accept in full satisfaction for such delays said extension of time." The court ruled against the contractor's claim because the clause was found to be binding. The court went further finding that such a clause was "conceived in the public interest in protecting public agencies . . . against vexatious litigation based on claims, real or fancied, that the agency has been responsible for unreasonable delays."

In *Psaty & Fuhrman* v. *Housing Authority* (68 at 2d 32, R.I.; 1949), the contract included a no damages for delay clause and applied "whether such delays be avoidable or unavoidable." The contractor made a claim on the basis that the clause excused reasonable delay only. The court held that the clause was valid and binding unless malicious intent, fraud, or bad faith could be proven.

However, in *Cauldwell-Wingate Company* v. *State of New York* (Reference Case 12), there was a no damage for delay clause. Nevertheless, the court held that the clause did not apply to the delays incurred because of direct interference and misrepresentations of the state.

Similarly, in *DeRiso Brothers* v. *State* (161 Misc. 934, N.Y.; 1937), the no damages for delay clause was not a defense to a claim for delay caused by failure of the governmental owner to provide temporary heat for interior finishing work, as specifically guaranteed in the contract. The court saw this omission as active interference, and a condition that could not be foreseen by the contractor.

In a recent case, an owner and his architect used the premise that the acts of the owner's architect were an unforeseeable cause of delay. Accordingly, a precedent set by *Henry Shenk* v. *Erie Company* (319 Pa. 100; 1935) would apply. In Shenk, the contract included a no damage for delay clause and related this to delays due to unforeseeable causes of delay. In the instant case, the contractor's counsel successfully argued that "acts of one's agents are patently not beyond one's control. . . ." Further, he cited *George A. Fuller Company v. United States* (69 F. Supp. 409, Ct. Cl.; 1947) in which the court said:

Nor has it ever been thought that the provisions . . . providing for an extension of time for completion of the work on account of delays due to unforeseen causes, including those caused by the government would serve to relieve defendant of liability for damages for such delays. . . . This provision for an extension of time related to the assessment of liquidated damages against the contractor and had no reference to the recovery of damages by the contractor for delays caused by the government.

Counsel also cited *J. D. Hedin Construction Co. v. United States* (347 F. 2d 235, Ct. Cl.; 1965) and *Hall Construction Co. v. United States* (379 F. 2d. 559, Ct. Cl.; 1966).

In a recent arbitration between a contractor and subcontractor, the subcontractor cited *Gasparini Excavating Co. v. Pennsylvania Turnpike Commission* (Reference Case 26) claiming that the general contractor had not made the promised work site available. While the facts did not support the subcontractor's claim, the attorney for the general contractor also challenged the applicability of the law in Gasparini, because he held that the subcontractor had not demonstrated a material interference.

Another case cited by the subcontractor was *Sheehan v. Pittsburgh* (Reference Case 53). The court refused to apply the no damage for delay clause on the grounds that the delay in the minds of the parties at the time of contract was not of a nature which could subject the contractor to a large loss. The parties were referring to "loss of damage arising out of the nature of the work", while the true cause for loss was the failure by the city to procure right of way. Further, the fact that the city had not condemned the required right of way was a fact unknown to the city, and therefore, unforeseen.

The courts, in finding that a no damage for delay clause should not be enforced, look to both the unforeseeability of the cause, and the nature of the interference on the part of the owner.

In Shenk, the court defined "foreseeability" as follows:

Where a party under a delay and time extension provision on entering a contract foresees or should foresee that the work might be delayed by the failure of the owner or another con-

tractor to perform the remedy therefor . . . [is an] extension of time on the part of those who perform the work, and the presumption arises that this was intended to measure the rights of the contractor thereunder.

Chapter 6, "The Owner," includes a number of specific case references where the court held that the owner had actively interfered with the contractor, and therefore was liable for delay damages.

Interpretation of Contract

It is an accepted legal principle that the specifications should be viewed in the whole with meaning given to every part, if it is possible to do so. Thus, it is reasonable, helpful, and certainly permissible to view other paragraphs when attempting to interpret a single section or paragraph.

In *Drainage District #1* v. *Rude* (21 F. 2d 257, Neb.; 1927), the court stated:

Courts of law must enforce written contracts according to the language used by the contracting parties, giving, however, to such language a rational interpretation and one which will, so far as possible, effectuate their mutual intention, and not defeat the object and purpose sought to be accomplished. The intention of the parties as expressed by, and not divorced from their language, is what a court must seek to discover in construing a contract. It is elementary, of course, that, where language is plain and its meaning clear, there is no room for construction. In cases of doubt, however, as to the meaning of the language of contracts, preliminary negotiations, subject matter, and surrounding circumstances should be considered, not to vary the terms or change the language of the contract, but to enable the court to determine in what sense words of doubtful meaning were used.

This leads to the use of evidence regarding preliminary meetings between the parties before the execution of the written contract. While the court holds that the written contract represents the best evidence of the parties at the time of the execution of the contract, where there is doubt as to the intent of the language parol evidence may be presented. In *Hawkins* v. *United States* (96 U.S. 607; 1877), the court ruled that this type of evidence is: "in general inadmissible to vary its (i.e., contract) terms or to affect its construction, the rule being that all such verbal agreements are to be considered as merged in the written instrument." However, the courts will hear such evidence as an indication, but not controversion, of the intent of the contract.

This was further expressed in *Harnett Co. Inc. v. Throughway Authority* (3 Misc. 2d 257 N.Y.; 1956) where the court stated:

If the court finds as a matter of law that the contract is ambiguous, evidence of the intention and acts of the parties plays no part in the decision of the case. Plain and unambiguous words and undisputed facts leave no question of construction except for the courts. The conduct of the parties may fix a meaning to words of doubtful import. It may not change the terms of the contract.

The language above applies principally to acts of the parties during the execution of the contract, but can also be interpreted to apply to their acts (written as well as verbal) prior to the execution of the contract. Evidence of this type was admitted in *Clark v. Ferro Corp.* (Reference Case 15) to aid the court in interpreting the extent and meaning of the performance specification criteria.

Misinterpretation of a contract by one of the parties is not sufficient cause to permit that party to change the terms of the agreement. Thus, in *Bethlehem Steel v. Turner Construction Co.* (2 N.Y. 2d 456; 141 N.E. 2d 590, N.Y. 1957), Bethelem Steel attempted to impose a regular price change upon the structural steel for an office building. The price rise had occurred after signing of a contract for this specific project. Turner refused to pay the increase, contending that it was beyond the agreed upon price in the contract. The court agreed with Turner saying:

Mere assertion by one that contract language means something to him, where it is otherwise clear, unequivocal, and understandable when read in connection with a whole contract, is not in and of itself enough to raise a triable issue of fact. It has long been the rule that when a contract is clear in and of itself, circumstances extrinsic to the document may not be considered.

On occasion, a party to a contract depends upon the custom of the trade to support his interpretation of the contract. Thus, in *Cornell v. United States* (Reference Case 18), a contractor successfully held that the practice of the area was such that blanket-type insulation would be considered an acceptable equal to a rigid-type of insulation for air ducts required in the specification. Evidence showed that the same district office of the Corps of Engineers had previously accepted this as an alternative on twelve prior contracts by the same contractor.

In this case, the specification called for rigid-type insulation or equal. Had the specification stated that blanket-type insulation would not be considered an equal, then the case would have been decided in favor of the government. A custom of the trade, whether area or universal, cannot overrule a specific mandate of the contract.

In *Hardware Specialties Inc.* v. *Mishara Construction Co. Inc.* (311 N.E. 2d 564) a small but important detail was omitted in the specification. Mishara Construction was the general contractor and carpentry subcontractor for a housing project. Mishara subcontracted the supply of finished hardware to Hardware Specialties Inc. This subcontract called for the subcontractor to "furnish all labor and materials required for the completion of the work specified," stating the "scope of work includes furnishing, delivery, packaging and marking of all finish hardware required for completion of the building requirements."

The specifications involved carefully described quantity and quality of the hardware required. However, in using the owner's specification to describe the subcontract, Mishara felt that Hardware Specialties was to provide field installation as well as the hardware itself. Hardware Specialties disagreed, and installed the hardware under protest. Then, Hardware Specialties sought to recover the additional cost of installing the hardware in the field. When Mishara refused, the parties entered arbitration subject to review. The arbitrator found in favor of Hardware Specialties concluding: "It was the custom under the current trade practices for the subcontractor supplying finish hardware not to install it." On review, the superior court agreed with the arbitrator, ruling: "The argument that a contract may not be varied by evidence of pertinent custom and usage misconceives the role played by such evidence. Valid usages known to contracting parties respecting the subject matter of an agreement, are by implication incorporated therein, unless expressly or impliedly excluded by its terms, are admissible to aid in its interpretation."

Words or phrases which have special meaning or usage according to the custom of the trade will be interpreted to have that meaning, unless otherwise defined within the specification. Further, in preparation of a contract, a designer would be well advised to use proper terminology within the recognized customs of the trade. Failure to do so would, at best, cause confusion; at worst, unusual construction of verbiage and terminology could well be misrepresentation.

Performance

In evaluating the performance of the parties, substantial weight is given by the courts to the practical interpretation of the specification requirements by the parties, themselves, during performance of the work.

In *Bloomfield School District v. Stites* (Reference Case 6), the question of literal execution of the contract was an important one. The contract, dated August 8, 1955, provided that the building was to be substantially completed in 395 calendar days. The contract was mailed to the contractor by the architect on August 17, was signed by the contractor, and then delivered by him to the school superintendent for execution by the board. The superintendent mailed the executed contracts to the architect, who in turn on September 21 mailed an executed copy to the contractor, who received it on or about September 22.

The contractor tried to hold that the beginning of the contract was the date of the receipt of the executed contract. However, the court noted:

When signed by the parties, this contract unambiguously said "this agreement made the 8th day of August in the year 1955" and there was no objection to the date or suggestion that it be changed. Furthermore . . . it was provided that the work to be performed under the contract "shall be commenced immediately . . . and shall be substantially completed in 395 calendar days." In these circumstances, the parties having elected that their mutual rights and obligations are to be determined according to the letter of the contract, its effective date was August 8, 1955. . . . The courts have generally construed contracts to run from the date they bear and not from the date of delivery.

In *Race Company v. Oxford Hall Contracting Corp.* (Reference Case 46), Oxford signed a contract for the installation of a central heating and cooling plant. The contract noted that it was not to become effective until the plans and specifications were signed by the contracting parties. It also contained an arbitration clause. Race completed the job except for certain work not completed at Oxford's request. Race commenced an action for damages, which Oxford attempted to refute, moving to compel arbitration. Race opposed arbitration on the grounds that the plans and specifications had never been signed. All parties conceded that Race had completed the work in accordance with the plans and specifications. The court found that "under these circumstances, both parties by their conduct adopted the plans and specifications, the failure to sign them is inconsequential."

In *E. C. Ernst Inc.* v. *General Motors Corporation* (482 F. 1047; 1973), contractor Ernst notified the owner by letter that they (the contractor) could not be held liable for late start dates beyond their control without either additional compensation or extension of time. The lower court rejected the Ernst suit because they had not followed the notification procedure as described in the contract, which required that all notification of claims had to include a statement of the exact amount of damages. The court of appeals concluded that the purpose of the notice provision was to "alert the other parties that the claimant has a grievance against it," and recognized that there was evidence that the owner had been so alerted. Further, at the time of initial notice, Ernst was in no position to provide an exact cost of damages. In finding for Ernst, the court said: "Our decision should in no way be construed as relieving the parties to a contract of strict compliance with notice provisions and the like. To the contrary, it results from our conclusion that under the particular facts of this case, appellant complied with the notice provision . . . to the extent reasonable."

In *Roanoke Hospital* v. *Doyle and Russell* (Reference Case 47), one of the original points of evidence was an allegation by Roanoke Hospital that defendant contractor had not given proper notice of delay in writing, as required by the contract. One of the areas to be evaluated by the jury was whether the evidence presented indicated that the owner had waived the right to demand such notice through his own action. The findings indicated that both parties through their actions had failed to make proper formal notice. However, since the project involved was a major addition immediately adjacent to the existing hospital, and there were numerous meetings and informal communications, the evidence did indicate an exchange of information regarding progress of the project.

Scope of the Contract

Under the principle of quantum meruit, the owner must pay for what he gets or receives benefit from. In *Nathan Construction* v.

Fenestra Inc. (Reference Case 44), the owner attempted to avoid final payment on the basis that the curtainwall installed permitted excessive infiltration of air, water, and dust and other miscellaneous problems. The evidence sustained that Fenestra had demonstrated substantial performance of its obligations, and was therefore due payment for its work. One of the bases of payment was quantum meruit.

However, in *Citizen's National Bank of Meridian* v. *Glasscock* (Reference Case 13), the contractor sued Citizen's National Bank for work beyond the scope of the contract. This work had been ordered by the owner's engineer. The trial court awarded the contractor $8,902 on a quantum meruit basis. However, the reviewing authority reversed the decision, since the contract clearly set forth that "no extra work or change shall be made unless in pursuance of a written order from the owner." On this basis, the reviewing authority held that the owner had to pay for extra work only if it was authorized in writing prior to its execution. This court interpreted that the contract between the parties spoke directly to this point, leaving no leeway for an award on a quantum meruit basis.

The requirement for a written change order does not necessarily preclude a finding for quantum meruit. In some jurisdictions, including federal and New Jersey, there can be a waiver for a requirement for a written change order. In New York, similarly, there can be a waiver, but not if the contract expressly provides the agreement cannot be changed orally. (See Walker and Rohdenburg, *Legal Pitfalls*, p. 91.)

In *Lord Construction Co.* v. *United States* (28 F. 2d 340; 2d Cir.; 1928) the court stated:

The right of the plaintiff to recover for extras not covered by the contract and for which the plaintiff produced no written orders signed by the engineer . . . [wherein] the contract provided that the plaintiff should not be entitled to receive payment for any extra work as extra work unless such bill for extras be accompanied by an order in writing from the engineer, . . . the court admitted proof which tended to show that at regular meetings . . . the engineer and the plaintiff fully discussed and considered such extra items and work, and the plaintiff was then directed to proceed with them. . . . That a contract requirement such as here provided may be subsequently waived by the parties is established by the authorities.

In *Reetz* v. *Stackler* (Reference Case 48), the contractor was required to meet an exculpatory-type clause to the effect that he

would meet all building code requirements because of his signing of a rider to the contract that in effect operated as a change
order.

In *Foundation Co. v. State of New York* (Reference Case 25),
the state attempted to require the contractor to perform pumping operations on a unit cost basis as contemplated in the contract. However, the contractor had anticipated that he could
pump from one location when developing this unit price. The
situation at the site required seven pumping operations, substantially increasing the cost. The court agreed that the price
included in the contract as part of the bid was inapplicable, and
that the contractor could recover on a quantum meruit basis for
the reasonable value of the work performed.

Similarly, in *Depot Construction Co. v. State of New York*
(Reference Case 20), Depot was required to perform work in a
manner which had not been contemplated by the contractor.
The state attempted to hold the contractor to unit prices per the
contract. The court of claims held that these unit prices no
longer applied. One reason for this holding was that the state
had caused the conditions which required that additional work
be accomplished. Since it was outside any reasonable contemplation at the time of the contract, the court held that the contractor was entitled to compensation on a quantum meruit
basis.

The court made the important distinction that where there is
a qualitative change in the nature of the work described by a
unit price in the contract, the contractor is thereby not bound to
the unit prices in the contract.

Matters beyond Contract

Some contracts attempt to project areas of agreement and responsibility beyond present levels of knowledge, or even
reasonable anticipation. In *Beacon Construction Co. v. Prepakt
Concrete Co.* (375 S. 2d 977; 1st Cir.; 1967), Beacon had retained Prepakt to do piling work for a postal facility on which
Beacon was the general contractor. The contract included a
statement that Beacon intended to assign the entire project to
another contractor, and when such assignment was made, the
terms and conditions in that contract would become the contract between Prepakt and the assignee. The contract did not
include an arbitration clause. The prime contract and subcontracts were assigned to Ameco. The contract between Ameco
and Beacon did contain an arbitration clause.

Prepakt sued Beacon and Ameco over a disputed area.

Beacon insisted that the dispute should be arbitrated, contending that Prepakt's agreement in advance to any terms and conditions in the contract between Beacon and Ameco, in effect, added an arbitration agreement to the initial contract.

The trial court found for Beacon, but the circuit court of appeals reversed the verdict, holding that Beacon did not have the right to substantially change the subcontract. The court said: "We cannot say that a provision requiring arbitration with an unknown party, as a precondition to suit, is so inconsequential a change in obligation as to be ignored."

In *Randolph Construction Co.* v. *Kings East Corp.* (Supreme Court Conn; July 1973) the court held void and unenforceable the contract between a construction company (King's East) and a masonry subcontractor (Randolph Construction). The two companies met on August 5, 1970, to talk about a masonry project to be performed. They discussed plans and job specifications and made some anticipated changes in crayon marks on the drawings. At the meeting, the parties signed a contract which provided that Randolph would perform the masonry work in accordance with the plans, specifications, drawings, details, and information then available. Randolph started work but withdrew because of nonpayment. They brought action to be compensated for labor and materials rendered. Kings counterclaimed damages alleging breach of contract.

The trial court ruled in favor of Randolph and Kings appealed contending that final plans that were issued in late September did not include a substantial change from the plans dated August 5, 1970, and were thereby binding on Randolph. The court, however, found that the second set of plans included a substantial change, and thereby, there was no meeting of the minds. (However, the court did confirm that a contract that incorporated nonexistent documents could be valid if the documents were brought into existence before either party attempted to enforce performance, thus sharing a "mutuality of assent.")

Change Orders

In the general conditions of a contract, the owner generally reserves the right to make changes. Much of the law in United States claims cases flows from the Supreme Court review of *United States* v. *Rice* (Reference Case 59). This case involved an interpretation of paragraphs three and four of the standard construction contract form used by the U.S. Government. In paragraph three, "Changes", the government reserved the right "at any time, by a written order, and without notice to the sureties, [to] make changes in the drawings and/or specifications of this contract and within the general scope thereof."

The clause provides that "an equitable adjustment shall be made" for any increase or decrease in the amount due.

In paragraph four, "Change Conditions," a similar prerogative to make changes was reserved in the event of "conditions at the site materially different from those shown on the drawings or indicated in the specifications."

The Supreme Court was asked to decide whether damages for delay could be recovered under either paragraph. A unanimous court found that damages for delay could not be recovered, principally on the basis that the paragraphs called for an alteration in "the amount due." The court held that had an alteration in time been contemplated, then that dimension would specifically have been mentioned.

While enforcing the so-called Rice Doctrine, courts have generally recognized that an independent action could be entered by the contractor for breach of contract.

This was not initially true. In *Great Lakes Construction Co. v. United States* (95 Ct. Cl. U.S. 479; 1942) some 109 changes were made to the contract. The contractor was required to prepare a bid despite certain omissions in the plans and specifications. A corrected set of plans and specifications was delivered, shortly after signing of the contract which indicated some 700 additions and corrections. The parties disputed the amount of value of the changes, but work continued. The contractor's claim for damages due to delay was rejected by the court on the basis of paragraph three of the standard government contract. Further, a claim for delay due to breach of contract was not allowed by the court.

In *George A. Fuller Co. v. United States* (69 F. Supp. 409, Ct. Cl.; 1947) the court found as follows:

[The contractor] would have no right to complain if the [owner's] exercise of its reserved right to make changes set its work schedule awry. . . . At least this would be so if [the owner] has acted with due alacrity. . . .

[The contractor] had contracted to do the work in accordance with the specifications [the owner] had prepared, and [the owner] was, therefore, under a duty not to render the project more expensive than it would have been if the contractor could have complied with the plans. . . . If faulty specifications prevent or delay completion of the contract, the contractor is enti-

*tled to recover damages for the [owner's] breach of its implied
warranty.*

*This exculpatory rule [of Rice] is not applicable to a situ-
ation in which unreasonable delays were the result of the
defendant's failure to promulgate properly drawn specifications.*

Similarly, in *Luria Bros.* v. *United States* (Reference Case 38),
the court held: "Where the change is necessitated by defective
plans and specifications [the owner] must pay the entire resulting damage without any deduction for time to make changes, as
would be the case if the redesign were necessitated by a
changed condition or the like."

In *Continental Illinois Bank & Trust Co.* v. *United States* (101
F. Supp. 755; 1952) the government decided to redesign a
building and halted work. Work was delayed 175 days. An
evaluation of a reasonable time for design was estimated at 40
calendar days. The court awarded the contractor damages for
delay for 135 days saying: "We think that the government's
taking of 175 days for the redesign of the boiler house was
inconsiderate of the harm which was being caused the contractor, and was a breach of contract. The right reserved in the
contract to make changes in the work does not mean that the
government can take as much time as it pleases to consider
such changes regardless of the consequences to the other
party."

Summary

Wherever litigation occurs, the contract between the parties is
the basis upon which the judicial branch must base its evaluation of the facts in light of the applicable law. Construction law
is complicated by the multiple party situation, wherein certain
parties to the construction activity are not under contractual
relationship one-to-another. The parties to the contract may
affect its meaning through their performance, failure to perform, or waiver of rights. When a contract is changed by change
order, the original contract no longer exists. As of the date of
the agreed-upon change, the contract is now effective in its
modified form. Litigation before the effective date would be
subject to the unmodified contract.

Chapter Four · Plans and Specifications

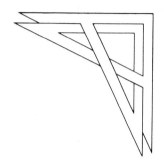

Plans and specifications are the tools prepared by the designer that the constructor uses to build the building. The terms have very definite, well-recognized connotations to both the design and construction professional. The attorney recognizes plans and specifications as a part (by reference) of the legal contract between the parties.

Traditionally, the first section of the specification is known as general conditions, and may include supplementary conditions, special conditions, special requirements, and similar sections. This first section, which includes the phrases known to the design and construction professionals as boiler plate, is discussed in chapter 3. This chapter is concerned with the technical portion of the specifications, usually starting at section or Division 2, and the plans.

The nature of the plans and specifications varies with the type of contract contemplated. The range includes, but is not limited to:

In house design: with plans and specifications; generally outline form

Design-build: more detailed than in-house design, but still very performance-oriented

Cost plus Fixed fee: more in depth detail, but not as much concern on scope or limitations

Competitive bid: must completely define the scope of the work to preclude extras or additional work costs

Generally speaking, the plans are graphic and provide a quantitative description of the work. The specifications are qualitative and specify the level of quality required. Good practice indicates that the plans and specifications should not overlap. Overlapping, that is mentioning something both in the plans and specifications, can cause confusion, particularly when the overlapping statements are in conflict.

Most of today's specifications are organized into sixteen technical divisions as described by the Construction Specification Institute (CSI). Part one is the legal section known as general conditions. The remaining fifteen divisions are:

Division 2   Site Work
Division 3   Concrete
Division 4   Masonry
Division 5   Metals
Division 6   Carpentry
Division 7   Moisture Protection
Division 8   Doors, windows, and glass
Division 9   Finishes
Division 10   Specialties
Division 11   Equipment
Division 12   Furnishings
Division 13   Special Construction
Division 14   Conveying Systems
Division 15   Mechanical
Division 16   Electrical

Delay

Plans and specifications of a poor quality can cause delay. The design professional should be striving to make the plans and specifications as clear as possible to preclude coordination problems, errors, or omissions in the field. This is their professional task—and most try diligently to meet it.

The reason for the existence of plans and/or specifications of poor quality vary considerably. Probably the principal cause is a variation in the talent of the various firms. Within that limitation, there are also considerable variables in the types of projects. Renovation work is more difficult to express clearly, because of unknown factors and the unreliability of as-built drawings, while new work should be capable of clear and crisp definition, at least from the foundations upward. In chapter One, "Delay," there is a discussion on discovery of the unexpected underground.

In some cases, the design professional who is striving for uniqueness creates certain problems because of a lack of experience in the methods or materials that he is utilizing. In other cases, either budgetary limitations or pure incompetency create problems. At one pre-bid meeting for a state agency in Pennsylvania, a prospective bidder (one of forty in the room) raised a question about one segment of the bid drawings. The prospective bidder said that he was unable to read part of the drawing because of its very small scale and complexity of mechanical systems. The unbelievable response from the state official presiding was, "You know what belongs there—so allow enough time and money for it." In this situation, poor judgment on the part of the designer had resulted in a decision to use a very small scale for the format, plus a second decision to crowd several kinds of systems on to the same drawing, creating a very complex presentation. The area questioned by the propective bidder had been partially eradicated.

In the case of *Egan v. New York* (Reference Case 21), the plumbing contractor for a New York City hospital bid on a set of defective plans. The plans were so defective, in fact, that the city directed the contractor to hire an engineer to redo the mechanical plans during construction. The basic problem was caused by a very basic mistake. The designer had left an inadequate space between floor and ceiling for all of the material that had to be placed above the ceiling line. (A similar mistake was made by another New York City designer in a major ($130 million) new hospital, wherein the architectural designer allowed chases. However, he failed to allocate the space in the chases between his mechanical and plumbing engineering designers with the result that *each* filled the total space. The result was 200 percent utilization of all openings, requiring a complete redesign after award of bids.)

Egan had to work in a piecemeal manner requiring several gangs rather than working sequentially through the building. There was substantial delay resulting from this, and the city did not really argue that it did not occur. Nevertheless, the city refused to consider a claim by Egan for the cost of delays. On the facts, Egan should have been compensated for his additional costs due to the delay, a direct result of the poor plans and specifications. Egan was an extreme case in that the owner not only provided a bad set of plans and specifications but he required that the contractor repair them.

In *Luria v. United States* (Reference Case 38), the court agreed that the original specifications were defective. The principal effect was a misunderstanding of the bearing value of the soil below the foundation of the structure. This resulted in an extensive change in the structural design. In addition to being responsible for the poor design, the court recognized that the owner should have performed expeditiously in revising the design once the errors had been noted. This was not done by the government. The government claimed that they had a reasonable time to make changes to the design. The court thought otherwise finding that : "Ordinarily, defendant is entitled to make necessary changes, and where change is necessitated by defective plans and specifications, defendant must pay the entire resulting damage without any reduction for time to make changes." (In this case, the government had sought to reduce the time of delay caused by the bad plans and specifications by the amount of time required to fix the plans and specifications.)

Warranty of Design

In *Luria* v. *United States*, the court stated that the owner implies a warranty of design that, in effect, says: "If the specifications are complied with, satisfactory performance will result." In *Public Construction Contracts and the Law* (p. 108), Cohen discusses this warranty. Basically, the warranty states that a contractor who bids on the basis of plans and specifications has the right to depend on those documents to accurately indicate the conditions of the job. Further, if actual conditions are otherwise than those described, then the contractor is entitled to proper compensation for any additional costs. One of the leading cases cited is *Hollerbach* v. *United States* (Reference Case 32). In this case, the contractor was to repair a dam. The specifications qualified that the quantities given were approximate, and that the bidder should visit the site to determine the nature of the work. However, the specifications then went on to specifically describe the material which would be found in the dam. These materials were generally described as broken stone, sawdust, and sediment. When the contractor proceeded with the work, he found that the backing was made up principally of sound wooden cribbing of logs filled with stone. The cribbing was so sound that removal was much more expensive that the contractor had anticipated.

The government held that the specifications had been approximate (per statement), and that the contractor was supposed to visit the job site. However, that court held—and many have held since—that a contractor site visit as a prerequisite is not a bar to a claim for unforeseen conditions. Further, even if a contractor does visit a site, it is not contemplated that he will be required to take borings or make unusually extensive explorations that are more in the province of the owner and his designer.

Cohen cites another long established decision: *Christie v. United States* (237 U.S. 234; 1915) which discusses the question of soil borings. The specifications for construction of locks and dams provided that "the material to be excavated, as far as known, is shown by borings, drawings of which may be seen at this office, but bidders must inform and satisfy themselves as to the nature of the material." The borings showed gravel, sand, and clay but no other materials. During excavation, the contractor encountered large stumps below the surface of the earth, as well as buried logs which were cemented together with sand and gravel. The penetration of this material during the boring phase had been difficult and it turned out that the government engineers had continually moved to areas where the rig would drill through. The court found that even though there was no ulterior motive by the government engineers in boring in easy locations, this did not shift the responsibility for the difficult foundations work over to the contractor.

The owner has two basic choices. If he is to provide information in the plans and specifications, then he must stand by that information. If the actual situation proves to be more difficult, then legal precedent indicates that the owner will have to pay for the additional expense, whether it be because of delay, additional equipment, or additional work.

On the other hand, if the owner chooses to be cautious (or devious), he may choose to provide little or no information—shifting the entire responsibility to the contractor. In such a case, the owner who discloses less than he knows because he is afraid that it is inaccurate will at least pay whatever risk factor is introduced into the contractor's bid. In this situation, the courts would find a contract enforceable but the prudent contractor will have put in a substantial amount to cover the uncertainties. Many of the bids that far exceed the owner's estimates for major projects, such as dams and highways, are a direct result of timidity on the part of the owner in refusing to limit the risk of the contractor.

The owner who knows that a subsurface situation is difficult and deliberately withholds the information, may well find that he has a responsibility because of deliberate or constructive fraud. Clearly, the owner should be willing to tell all he knows or thinks he knows about the site. The courts have found that the owner and his designer, having much more time to examine the situation, enjoy a position of superior knowledge. Accordingly, the courts inevitably favor the contractor who is required to bid upon the basis of plans and specifications prepared by others.

In cases of misrepresentation or constructive fraud, the general factors that must be present, include the following:

1. The plans and specifications must make a misrepresentation of facts.
2. The fact misrepresented must be a material one.
3. The misrepresentation must have been made knowledgeably. (If the misrepresentation is not willful it will be constructed to be willful if the background, information, and experience of the maker would have normally led him to an opposite presentation of the facts.)
4. The owner or his agent must have induced the contractor to rely upon the misrepresentation.
5. The contractor must have relied upon the information as given to him.
6. The contractor's belief of the information must have been justified. (i.e., it cannot fly in the face of his experience and knowledge.)
7. The misrepresentation must have caused actual damage.

The contractor who relies upon plans and specifications and then discovers a misrepresentation before completion of the contract may choose one of two paths. He may continue the project, and then enter suit to recover additional costs. He has the alternative of refusing to continue the work on the basis that the misrepresentation constitutes a breach. (*United States* v. *Spearin*, 248 U.S. 132; *McConnell* v. *Corona City Water Company*, 85 P. 929, Cal; *Lentilhon* v. *New York*, 185 N.Y. 548; and *Carroll* v. *O'Connor*, 35 N.E. 1006).

Evidence of an actual fraud or misrepresentation is often difficult to produce. Ironically, constructive misrepresentation or fraud is often much easier to identify, for instance, if an owner had borings taken that would have disclosed a difficult situation, but inadvertently failed to provide the information to the contractor, whether intentional or not. Soil borings are often inaccurate because of failure to promptly locate the boring hole and other factors. For this reason, it is not unusual for an owner to be uneasy about furnishing the information— fearing that it might be inaccurate.

Performance Specifications

Differences, errors, and omissions in plans and specifications intended for use in competitive bidding are readily identified, and are capable of evaluation in terms of delay and/or cost. In design-build situations, performance specifications have been utilized because the designer is also the builder, and there is less need for definitive identification. The use of performance-type specifications has also increased in open bid-type plans and specifications. One reason is the desire to permit the bidder to offer more alternatives in terms of systems which could meet the performance requirements of the owner. Also, most specifications have performance criteria in mind when they delineate definite restrictive specifications. The use of a performance specification allows the owner (and the bidder) the opportunity to offer innovative thinking which may provide better value for the dollar.

In *Clark v. Ferro* (Reference Case 16), the owner purchased a tunnel-type kiln to improve his production. As part of the purchase specification, the design-builder guaranteed to meet very specific production criteria. Among other things, the contract specified that production would reach 5000 sq. ft. of 6 in. by 6 in. tile per twenty-four hours. However, the thickness of the tile was omitted, and this was a significant factor, since approximately 33 percent more tile of ½ in. thickness could be loaded on each car than of tile of ¾ in.—and both are standard thicknesses. However, evidence indicated that ¾ in. tile was the type produced by the owner prior to installation of the tunnel kiln, and evidence further showed that an officer of the design-build firm had visited the plant on numerous occasions and was aware of this.

This was a case of ambiguity of specification through omission. As a result of the ambiguity, the court permitted the presentation of parol evidence on the various factors which led up to the culmination of the contract. (Normally, a contract must be evaluated on its own merits, and represents the complete understanding between the parties at the point in time at which they signed the contract.)

The subject case was one in which the hazards of over-generalization are evident. Inaccurate, loosely defined, poorly prepared plans and specifications can be harmful to either party to the contract—and more often to both.

Errors and Omissions

In *Legal Pitfalls* (p. 47), Walker and Rohdenburg note: "The preponderance of court decisions in the majority of states indicate that the architect or engineer does not guarantee perfection in his plans and specifications, nor does he guarantee that a satisfactory building will result from his work. . . . The mere fact that an architect or engineer makes an error is not in itself evidence of negligence, so long as he has exercised reasonable care."

The authors cite cases where designers have been found negligent for routine judgments, such as relying upon the advertising claims of a manufacturer as to adequacy of a product. The basic premise is commonsense—the architect and his engineers are not supermen. They are required under their professional canons and the law to do a reasonable and diligent job for their client. They are not, however, expected to be infallible.

Generally speaking, the designer receives a fee on the order of 5 percent of the value of the structure for its design. If he is to take the risk, or conversely to guarantee, that the plans and specifications must be perfect, then he would have to be compensated for the taking of that risk. Generally speaking, it is more sensible for the owner to assume that risk. (The owner assumes such a risk with the backstop that the law will find a negligent designer liable for his mistake.)

The owner who capriciously attempts to enforce infallibility upon his designer will constrain the design, raise his costs by forcing the designer to be overly conservative, and will develop a barrier of self-interest between himself and his designer, who is usually his privy counsellor during the budgeting and design phases.

If an owner cannot expect a perfect building, what can he expect? The custom of the trade indicates that problems due to the plans and specifications on the order of 1.5 percent of the construction costs (more or less) should be anticipated by the owner and absorbed by him, if necessary. Similarly, the knowledgeable contractor will recognize the probability of minor coordination problems and errors and would do well to absorb the ones that are of limited scope.

In negotiated work, where the architect-engineer is often a factor in the selection of the contractor, the contractor is much more ready and willing to absorb the cost of minor errors and coordination problems. In low-bid, fixed-price work, the incidence of this type of problem is generally frequent but of low cost and cost recovery is generally difficult. For those isolated instances that are clear and for which cost can be identified the contractor has a legitimate claim, and the owner should be ready to settle it.

The owner should view the discovery of errors and omissions for which he has to undertake change orders with his contractor from two viewpoints. The first is the omission that does not really cost the owner additional monies beyond that which he should have paid. This omission is discovered early enough to allow its incorporation into the work without requiring any destruction or renovation of already completed work. The second category is much more difficult. This type of error requires reworking, or use of more expensive approaches to accomplish a required feature.

The courts have not been sympathetic to the owner who attempts to unreasonably press for items that were inadvertently omitted. In *Nathan Construction v. Fenestra* (Reference Case 44), the suit involved a counterclaim of almost $400,000 in damages based upon the inability of a curtainwall system to meet the obligations to the building owner in regard to the performance characteristics of the curtainwall. The court found for the window wall firm which showed that it had tested its system, and detected no infiltration of air or weather. The owner, in pressing for a higher level of quality, was found to be unreasonable by the court. The court found that the intent of the parties was not such that the building was required to be absolutely water and weather tight. Further, there was no agreement that Fenestra would receive nothing if that high standard was not met.

In *County of Tarrant v. Butcher and Sweeny* (Reference Case 19), the owners attempted to require a literal compliance with plans and specifications. However, their architect-engineers had allowed a number of reasonable changes. The court agreed that the contractor had deviated from the plans and specifications. However, evidence was presented to show that the owner's agent had approved these changes in accordance with the contract, and that the changes were not inconsistent with the purpose of the building.

Quality of Plans and Specifications

As the architect and/or engineer develops a design, he has the problem of transposing all of his thoughts into the plans and specifications. The goal is to transmit, in a clear and concise fashion, the intent of the design. It is quite common that the effort will fall short in some cases, causing confusion and/or leaving the owner open to a claim for added scope or extra work, on the basis of quantum meruit. There are cases, too, where the designer says too much and there is overlap. In these cases, ambiguity develops and imposes a different set of problems.

In the situation of ambiguity, the designer often believes that he has the prerogative to direct the contractor to utilize the interpretation that he (the designer) had always intended. The courts do not agree. In *Rosenman* v. *United States* (Reference Case 51), the court stated: "Although the specifications and drawings may have been clear as a bell in the mind of [the] architect, it is not the subjective intent that is the legal determinant . . . rather, it is the representations of the specifications and drawings themselves." The court went on to note a well-defined principle of law: "When the government draws specifications which are fairly susceptible of a certain construction and the contractor actually and reasonably so construes them, justice and equity require that the construction be adopted."

This legal hazard, implicit in any situation where the plans and specifications may be variously construed, is often ignored or unrecognized. Further, the general conditions section often contains exculpatory clauses or language through which the designer hopes to be able to impose his intent, even in the absence of definitive plans and specifications.

If the quality of the plans and specifications is such that an area of ambiguity does exist, the question of legal responsibility can become quite difficult. In *Reid* v. *Fine* (Reference Case 50), the contractor sued because the owner refused to make final payment for an air conditioning and heating system. The court found that the contractor had performed an unauthorized deviation from the plans and specifications. However, the contractor presented evidence that showed that the plans were deficient in a number of areas. The ducts from floor to floor could not be installed as described on the drawings because of an interference by existing electrical conduits. Further, the room which had been designated to contain the HVAC equipment was not large enough for the equipment specified. The contractor advised the designer that he would be unable to install the work. Based upon informal concurrence by the designer, the contractor made changes in both the equipment and the methods of routing same to remedy the situation. However, the resulting HVAC system was approximately fifty tons lower in capacity than that required, the primary air handling was below capacity by almost 8000 cfm and a number of other instances were cited where either capacity or quality was less than that required. The contractor lost his suit, principally because he had not proceeded properly upon determination of the problems. The owner had been left out of the dialogue regarding the problems, and was awarded a suitable adjustment in contract costs to compensate for the performance of the contractor.

Ambiguous Plans and Specifications

Although the law, as stated in *Rosenman* v. *United States* (Reference Case 51), is generally in favor of the contractor—or at least the contractor's choice of interpretations if two reasonable interpretations (or more) can be drawn from a particular set of plans and specifications—the contractor should not be complacent in this position. In *Meyers* v. *Housing Authority of Stanislaus County* (Reference Case 41), the court found that the drawings were definitely ambiguous. Nevertheless, the trial court and the appeals court ruled against the contractor. The contractor had bid on two housing projects. Part of the sewer and drainage lines shown on the drawing (and necessary to connect the dwelling units to the existing utility mains) extended beyond limits that were shown variously as contract limits, property line, and project limits shown on the plans. The contractor contended that the drawings thus limited their responsibilities to the area within the designated boundaries.

While the court found that the drawings were definitely ambiguous, they also noted that the drawings constituted only one document in an integrated contract. Since all documents that are part of the contract must be construed together, the drawings were interpreted by the court in the light of the specifications. In the specifications, several systems were delineated that were to be done by others at no expense to the contractor. These exempted systems did not include the connection to utility mains. The court interpreted failure to include "off-site" plumbing in this itemization as meaning that it was included in the work.

Clearly, the specifications in this case were not clear enough, while the drawings were definitely ambiguous. The owner won by a slim hair. During reviews of plans and specifications, the design team and the owner's representative should review the drawings from the viewpoint of the contractors who are going to bid on them. This is particularly important in a project that is subdivided into a number of contracts. Clear delineation must be made of those areas that are "not in contract," or "by others." Further, in reutilizing the same sheets for different contracts, it is preferable to renumber the sheets by using reproducible master copies to avoid any confusion. Failure to do so can produce a small economy in drawing preparation at a great expense to the owner and/or the designer.

In *New England Foundation Company* v. *Commonwealth* (Reference Case 45), a more classical, ambiguous situation was involved. The contractor was required to install more than 4000 cast-in-place concrete piles with a safe working load capacity of twenty tons. The specification described a method of testing to validate the safe capacity of a typical pile. The specification also gave a pile driving formula (similar to the Engineering News Record formula). Each pile was driven according to the formula. A load test was conducted after 4,325 piles had been driven; unfortunately, this test indicated that the piles would not hold a twenty-ton load within the criteria. The owner insisted on the driving of an additional number of piles to make up the deficit in load capacity.

The contractor sued for the cost of the extra piles, claiming that they were extra time and extra work. The court agreed with the contractor that given two methods of determining the pile capacity, the contractor had the prerogative of assuming that the formula would meet the specifications.

It is a recognized legal principle that an ambiguity will be resolved against the party who drafted the specification. If there are two reasonable interpretations, the contractor's interpretation will prevail over the designer's interpretation, with the exception of design-build situations. Since the designer is the owner's representative, this, in effect, means that the contractor's position will prevail over the owner's position.

Citations and quotations to this effect were listed in the *Egan v. City of New York* (Reference Case 21) brief as follows:

In Camarco Contractors, Inc. *v.* State of New York *(40 Misc. 2d 4S6, 491, 243 N.Y.S. 2d 240), the Court said: "The court is bound to resolve an equivocal provision of the contract or the interpretation thereof against the one who drew it. That is fundamental law."*

In Heating Maintenance Corp. *v.* State of New York *(206 Misc. 605, 134 N.Y.S. 2d 71), the Court of Claims said: "The State prepared the entire contract on its own forms and all reasonable doubts as to the meaning thereof are to be resolved against it, as it is responsible for the language used and the uncertainty thereby created."*

In Frye *v.* State of New York, *192 Misc. 260, 78 N.Y.S. 2d 342, the Court of Claims repeated the rule of law that where there is an ambiguity in the contract, the same must be resolved against the State which prepared it, and said:*

"In construing the contract in question, the same rules of construction are applicable as between individuals. . . . If the language used is capable of more than one construction, the Court must resolve all doubts against the person who uses the language and most beneficially to the promisee."

In Evelyn Building Corp. *v.* City of New York *(257 N.Y. 499, 513), the Court of Appeals said: "The contract in question was prepared by the City, and, in case of doubt or ambiguity must be construed most strongly against it."*

Exculpatory Clauses

A standard designer's ploy is the inclusion of exculpatory clauses in the general conditions or boiler plate section. These clauses seek to excuse errors, omissions, or other problems which may evolve from the plans and specifications.

Some typical exculpatory clauses follow:

The survey, and in particular the elevations and contours are furnished as information to the bidders. Bidders shall verify survey information, and the owner assumes no responsibility for the accuracy of the survey as furnished.

Data logs shown in the plans are for information only, and the contractor is warned that reliance on this information shall be at his own risk, and that neither the owner nor the engineer shall be liable for errors.

Contractor shall be responsible for interpretation of subsurface soil conditions as described in the engineer's boring data. Further, all soil information, including boring data, is for information only and shall not be considered part of the contract documents.

The contractor shall visit the site and shall satisfy himself as to actual site conditions. Contractor shall verify all existing dimensions, and owner assumes no responsibility for variation in said existing dimensions.

Whenever provisions of any section of the plans and specifications conflict with any union, trade association, or agency that regulates work described, the contractor shall make necessary arrangements to reconcile any such conflict without recourse to the owner, and without delaying the progress of the work.

It is the intent of the plans and specifications to produce first class quality work. The contractor shall request an interpretation in any situation that would prevent the placing of first class work. Should such a conflict occur in or between the drawings and/or specifications, the contractor is deemed to have estimated on the more expensive way of doing the work.

It is the intent of the contract documents to provide for complete installation of all portions of the work. All items, materials, and equipment are to be furnished and installed complete and ready for operation or use. The contractor will be deemed to have based his bid on a complete installation.

Where additional or supplemental details or instructions are

required to complete an item, contractor shall request information from the architect. No work that depends upon this information shall be installed or fabricated without the written
approval of the architect. Further, the furnishing of the data
required shall not be the grounds for a claim for extra work.
Contractor shall be deemed to have made an allowance in his
bid for completing such work consistent with adjoining or similar details and/or the best accepted practices of the trade,
whichever is more expensive.

Where the scope of the work of this contractor in the plans
and specifications requires supports, connections, or installation of any group or group of items furnished by other contractors, the omission of a given item from the drawings of this
contract shall not relieve the contractor from the responsibility
for installing, connecting or supporting such item at no increase in contract cost.

Wherever additional materials or work not shown or specified is required to complete the work in accordance with the
obvious intent thereof, the contractor shall provide these materials or work at no additional cost to the owner.

One of the classic cases in the interpretation of exculpatory
language in specifications is *MacKnight Flintic Stone Company
v. City of New York* (Reference Case 29). The plans and specifications had been prepared by the city, and inspection work
was by the city. As part of its work for the completion of a
district courthouse and prison for the City of New York, the
contractor was to furnish "all materials and labor for the purpose to make tight the boiler room, coal room of the court house
and prison." The design documents contemplated a water
problem since the floor of the boiler room was twenty-six feet
below curb level. The specifications described in detail the
manner in which waterproofing was to be accomplished.
Further, the specifications required that the facility was to be
turned over to the city "in perfect order and guaranteed absolutely waterproof and damp proof for five years." There were
leaks and the city refused to pay for the work.

The contractor brought suit on the basis that he had followed
the specifications exactly, and that nevertheless leaks had developed. The court agreed with the contractor. It noted that the
construction contract was an agreement not simply to do a
particular thing, (i.e., waterproof the basement), but to do it in a
particular way and to use specified materials in accordance
with the design. Accordingly, in the failure of the specific design, the contractor could not be held accountable for the more
general requirement to waterproof the basement. In fact, the

court went on to say, the contractor would have been in error if he had followed his own alternate work plan (which he had presented).

Codes and Regulations

It is implicit in a contract that it shall be legally constituted, including an implicit agreement that the contract shall neither request nor allow any illegal activity. Often a general conditions clause is included to the effect that all actions under the contract shall comply with applicable rules and regulations of governmental bodies and agencies.

This approach is reasonable, in that, the contractor is to obey the laws of the locality, county, state, and federal government. Specifically, in construction, the laws of the federal government include the regulations promulgated by the U.S. Department of Labor under the Occupational Safety and Health Act (OSHA). A contractor's failure to be cognizant of these generally distributed rules and regulations is not an acceptable defense.

However, the expectation that the contractor shall meet the rules and regulations of the governing building codes goes a step further. On occasion, the contract general conditions include language similar to the following:

> The latest requirements of the National Electric Code shall govern the work specified under this section. In case of conflict between the specifications, drawings, and/or the National Electric Code, the more stringent requirement shall prevail.
>
> The contractor shall be required to comply with applicable regulations, rules, and requirements of the New York City Building Code and the requirements of all other authorities having jurisdiction. The latest editions or revisions will govern, and where conflicts occur, the more restrictive requirement shall be deemed to govern.

While on the face of it, an experienced contractor in an area or a trade would be expected to be familiar with the governing codes, the courts have found it unreasonable to expect the contractor to undertake a detailed comparison of the design plans and specifications with the appropriate codes in the limited time available for bidding. To the extent that the governing codes and the plans and specifications conflict, the courts find the situation to be one of ambiguity, and rule in favor of the contractor.

In *Blount* v. *United States* (Reference Case 8), the court recognized that contractors are businessmen. Further, they specifically recognized that contractors are usually pressed for time during the bidding phase. The court defined the contractor's obligation as follows: "They are obligated to bring to . . . attention major discrepancies or errors which they detect in the specifications or drawings . . . but they are not expected to exercise clairvoyance in spotting hidden ambiguities in the bid documents."

In the case of *Green* v. *City of New York* (283 App. Div. 485, 128, N.Y.S. 2d 715; 1954) the case involved a contract where the specifications permitted the use of plasterboard partitions in bathrooms. However, in the general conditions, there was a statement that the contractor would have to comply with the rules and regulations of the state. Further, it provided that: "This rule shall take precedence over any requirements of those specifications where a conflict occurs." The Department of Housing and Building of the State of New York ruled that plaster over lath was required by the Multiple Dwelling Law in partitions enclosing bathrooms.

In the suit, the court ruled against the city on the basis that: "It could not be expected that the bidders would examine the various laws and building codes as to each item specified to see if the codes required some different method of construction. Such procedure would make the bidder's interpretation of the law, rather than the specifications, controlling. It would make the specifications so indefinite and uncertain as to destroy the validity of any contract awarded pursuant thereto."

In the *Town of Poughkeepsie* v. *Hopper Plumbing & Heating Corp.* (Reference Case 55), a somewhat different situation arose. Two school districts had awarded contracts to Hopper Plumbing and Heating for plumbing work in new elementary schools. The town entered an action to prevent performance of that work until the plans had been submitted for a plumbing permit. This would be in keeping with the town plumbing code and ordinance requiring that all new plumbing work be inspected. The commonsense question would be one of public interest, specifically, public safety. However, the legal evaluation requires interpretation of the status of the two school districts. The court found that under the Education Law of New York State which required approval of the plans and specifications by the Commissioner of Education indicated that the New York State legislature had preempted the area of review from the local jurisdiction and vested it exclusively with the state. Similar exclusions occur in federal and state work for projects that occur within local jurisdictions. In essence, the local site is generally considered to become a federal or state reservation. (There are often specific exclusions to the exclusion itself and each case must be examined on its own merits.) The guiding principle continues to be that the contractor has the right to rely upon the specific information in the plans and specifications, and is not called upon to identify those areas of overlap or ambiguity with existing regulation. Where such ambiguity or overlap occurs, the owner is responsible if the resolution imposes additional expense.

Once again, the contractor must be alert to maintain his rights and prerogatives. In *Reetz v. Stackler* (Reference Case 48), a contractor was to provide an acoustical ceiling in a bowling alley. Three of the general conditions invoked exculpatory language in terms of building codes and laws. The town building department advised the contractor that a two-hour fire rating would be required for the ceiling. A change to the contract was executed to that effect. After completing the work in conformance with the building department instructions, (which was made a change), the contractor submitted a claim for extra work citing the fact that the installed work was more expensive than that described in the contractual plans and specifications. However, the court found that the contractor had assumed the specific obligation of erecting the more expensive ceiling by agreeing to the form of the contract rider as it was presented.

Summary

The general position in regard to plans and specifications, their completeness and quality, is summarized in the following from *United States v. Spearin* (248 U.S. 132, 136, 137, 39S. 3c. 59; 1918):

If the contractor is bound to build according to plans and specifications prepared by the owner, the contractor will not be responsible for the consequences of defects in the plans and specifications. . . . This responsibility of the owner is not overcome by the usual clauses requiring builders to visit the site, to check the plans, and to inform themselves of the requirements of the work.

The duty to check plans did not impose the obligation to pass upon their adequacy to accomplish the purpose in view.

Chapter Five · The Architect and Engineer in the Field

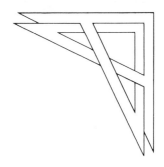

With the award of the construction contract, the role of the designer undergoes a dramatic change, both legal and psychological. In most instances, the arrangements for the construction phase are made at the same time as the selection of the architect or architect-engineer for the design, although an increasing number of owners are making this contractual arrangement for the construction phase an option. This permits the owner to consider the effectiveness of the working relationship during the design phase.

Design firms are selected on many bases in which in addition to the designer's professional skill includes social, business, and/or political considerations, mixed in with good fortune and good timing. Whatever these factors, the controlling ones are generally very much oriented to the preconstruction or design phase. Some design firms are well known for their good coordination and administration abilities during the design phase, but this is usually a secondary consideration in design selection. A firm known for pedestrian design but good building skills will usually not pass the screening for design selection. (This type of firm does exist, and some are having combined assignments with more creative design teams that enjoy a less successful field reputation.)

There are an unlimited number of combinations of skill and factors that could be discussed. It is clear, however, that those factors that encourage the selection of an architect/engineer for the design of a project are different from those that make him a skillful administrator during the construction phase.

Contractual Relationships

The legal relationship between the owner and the architect/ engineer in the field is generally a continuation of the basic design contract. The standard American Institute of Architects' contract allocates 25 percent of the full design fee for field involvement. Many owners negotiate a design fee at a level less than that recommended by the AIA, a practice that will probably become even more widespread after the recent federal antitrust action against the various professional design organizations. Many owners, even after negotiating a lower professional fee than that suggested, seem to expect a project management activity on the part of the design team—looking for something for nothing. The basic funding, even at full fee, allows the design professionals to maintain contact with the project, review shop drawings, make design interpretations, and conduct or attend periodic job meetings. The fee is tight for the accomplishment of these traditional roles. Generally, if the owner requires full-time resident field supervision, a supplementary fee will be negotiated.

In rationalizing supplementary fees, this phase of the design team effort has been called supervision of construction. That term has very definite professional and legal connotations, and much more careful language is now being utilized, since it is really the contractor who supervises the construction. The architect/engineer field representatives perform a monitoring function for quality control, confirmation for the amount of work in place, site progress, and the general level of site activity.

The reality of field construction is that each of the major parties (owner, architect, contractor) has his own areas of self-interest to protect. This triangle can produce some interesting permutations and commutations.

The contract between the owner and the architect/engineer generally describes what the designer will do in the field and how he will be compensated for that professional activity. The contract between the owner and the contractor defines what the contractor will do. The architect is described (typically) as the owner's representative (or one of them, if a construction manager or project manager is also assigned).

The general conditions and special conditions (Division 1) of the specifications delineate the manner in which the architect will perform as the owner's representative. The architect/ engineer is usually described as the sole interpreter of the intent of the plans and specifications. The general conditions/ special conditions also describe the manner in which the architect/engineer will review and approve (or reject) shop drawings, samples, pay requisitions, and other submissions from the contractor to the owner.

As the owner's representative in the field, the architect is often limited in his authority by the contract between the owner and the contractor. This imposes a standard bureaucratic environment within which the architect/engineer can say no to a request or submission, but cannot necessarily say yes. Thus, in Reid v. Fine (Reference Case 50), the contractor lost his claim for extra work that had been tentatively approved by the designer on the basis of the contract limitations on the designer's authority to sign changes to the contract.

The appeals court discussed this authority of the architect in terms of his activity as an agent of the owner in the field:

"Thus, it is clear that the authority of the architect and the engineer to act as agents of the defendants was of limited scope confined to those areas set forth in the contract. . . . It is equally clear the changes in the work . . . could only be made on the written order of the [owner]."

Privity of contract was a key issue in the case of Aetna Insurance Co. v. Hellmuth, Obata and Kassabaum, Inc. (Reference Case 1). In this case, the contractor was in trouble from the start of the job for the construction of a plaza at the St. Louis Municipal Airport. Early in the job, Aetna, the bonding company, was required to assist the contractor, and ultimately to take over his work. The architect (H.O.K.) had a contract with the city of St. Louis to perform "general supervisory services and advice during the construction period." In undertaking the performance bond, Aetna knew that H.O.K. was the "engineer or architect in charge of work" as described in the contract between the contractor and the city.

There were a number of premises regarding the performance of the supervisory aspect by H.O.K. that were criticized by Aetna. Aetna, in effect, held that had H.O.K. done their job properly, the contractor would have been forced to do a better job, resulting in fewer deficiencies that had to be corrected by Aetna. Both the appeals court and the trial court found that: "Plaintiff [Aetna] failed to demonstrate by substantial evidence that Defendant [H.O.K.] breached any duty owed to Plaintiff which would create liability on Defendant." Both courts found that the contractual connection was between the city and the architect (H.O.K.). Thus, there might have been an action by the city if any direct damages or losses had been incurred by the city as a direct result of the architect's actions or inactions in supervising the contract.

The court discussed the law of privity, pointing out that the lack of a contract between the surety or the contractor and the supervising architect did not necessarily bar a recovery for loss occasioned by the architect's negligence. This led to a discussion of the supervisory responsibilities of a design professional in the field.

Supervisory Responsibilities in the Field

In *Herbert* v. *Aitken* (Reference Case 30), which was decided in 1890, the court discussed the responsibilities of a supervising architect. The court held that the architect was not the insurer of the work, and that he could be bound only: "to exercise reasonable care, and to use reasonable powers of observation and detection in the supervision of the structure. . . . The only question that can arise in a case where general performance of duty is shown is whether, considering all the circumstances and peculiar facts involved, he has or has not been guilty of negligence. This is a question of fact, and not of law."

In *Aetna* v. *Hellmuth, Obata and Kassabaum, Inc.* (Reference Case 1) many years later, the courts continued to hold generally the same opinion. The court in this case elaborated on the responsibilities of professionals:

An architect whose contractual duties include supervision of the construction project has the duty to supervise the project with reasonable diligence and care. An architect is not a guarantor or an insurer, but as a member of a learned and skilled profession, he is under the duty to exercise the ordinary, reasonable technical skill, ability, and competence that is required of an architect in a similar situation. . . . Whether the required standard of care was exercised presents a jury question.

The court also discussed in detail the problems involved in establishing the standard of care which is required within the design profession. The court quoted the law of torts that points out "professional men in general . . . are required not only to exercise reasonable care in what they do, but also to possess a standard minimum of special knowledge and ability." Often, in evaluating professional standards, laymen are incompetent to pass judgment on questions of technique, but with the qualification that when the matter to be evaluated is within the common knowledge of laymen (example, "where a surgeon saws off the wrong leg . . . ") it has been "held that the jury may infer negligence without the aid of any experts."

In *Regan v. Parsons, Brinckerhoff, Quade, & Douglas* (Reference Case 49), a contractor was damaged extensively by flooding in a tunnel caused by an adjoining contractor. The design engineer (P.B.Q. & D) was also supervising engineer in the field for the owner. The contractor Regan alleged the engineer to be responsible for leaks around a temporary wooden bulkhead because Parsons had approved the structural soundness of the plans drawn and submitted by the adjoining contractor who was responsible for the bulkhead.

In the contract documents, P.B.Q. & D. was designated as owner's representative with certain authority to supervise and inspect the work so that the ultimate permanent result required would be achieved. However, the court found that the document did not impose on the engineer, not a party to the contracts, any duty towards the contractors or their personal property.

The court found in favor of the engineer pointing out that the express provisions of the contract did not support a theory invoking a duty on the part of the engineer to insure that one contractor's negligence would not damage the property of another contractor. The court indicated that there is not an implied continuing duty to inspect temporary details of construction. However, the court noted that it is possible: "for an engineer to assume such sweeping duties of supervision and control over all details of construction that nothing else appearing, he may be held to have assumed a duty to parties outside his contract." This latter is certainly a caution to design professionals in the field who would become overly involved beyond their legally constituted scope.

In a similar case involving temporary structures (*Olsen v. Chase Manhattan*, 9 N.Y. 2d 829, 175 N.E. 2d 350; 1961) a construction worker on the night shift was injured by the collapse of a temporary platform built to hold air compressors. The contractor sued both the owner and the architect/engineer. In regard to the architect/engineer, the court found that their supervisory function was only to insure performance of construction in accordance with the plans and specifications, and to insure that standards of safety were met for the permanent construction in regard to adjacent structures and buildings. The safety of temporary structures and platforms was found to be an area beyond the scope of their professional supervision.

In *County of Tarrant v. Butcher & Sweeney Construction Co.* (Reference Case 19), the county sued for damages caused by negligence on the part of the architect in failing to provide for expansion joints in the brick veneer walls. The jury agreed that the architect had failed to use the proper degree of care in regard to minor items and allowed damages of $700, but refused the county claim of $128,722. Evidence showed that the engineer working for the architect had approved changes without the approval of the county. However, the jury found that these changes were minor in scope, did not involve extra cost, and were not inconsistent with the purpose of the building. Further, although the county had not made a formal approval, informally, their inspector and engineer knew of the deviations. There was no prompt complaint made. In essence, the designer was found guilty of exceeding his authority, but the finding was mitigated by limitation of his damages to a relatively small portion of that claim.

Interpretation of Design

One of the important roles which the design professional carries into the field is that of interpretation of his design. Most of the requests for interpretation involve clarification, and neither claims nor delay result.

Justin Sweet, in *Legal Aspects of Architecture, Engineering, and the Construction Process* (p. 532), makes the following observation in regard to the design professional's authority to interpret: "There is no unanimity on the finality to be accorded decisions of the design professional, even where the contract language 'appears' to make his decision final. Most courts have accorded finality to determinations by the architect or engineer which, even if erroneous or even negligent, were honestly made." This situation was addressed in *City of Lawton* v. *Sherman Machine & Iron Works* (Reference Case 14) where the contract bound all parties to the condition that "the City engineer shall, in all cases . . . decide all questions which may arise relative to the execution of the contract on the part of the contractors. . . . " The court found that the approval of an engineer designated in this manner is binding on the parties. However, the finding can be overturned by a determination of actual fraud, or of such gross errors or mistakes as to constitute a constructive fraud.

Although the contract may state that the decision of the architect or engineer is final, the courts may find otherwise if required or requested to review a decision. Naturally, judicial review is an involved process, and not requested lightly. In making the review, the courts give more leeway to the contract that permits judicial review, in particular, arbitration. Further, when the review is made, it can be either a review of the authority to make the decision, or of the entire process itself. Again, where the contract is properly structured, the courts are inclined to accept as binding the finding of the designated architect or engineer, particularly if all of the parties involved have had an opportunity for a hearing.

The design professional called upon to interpret plans and specifications that he has prepared is in a difficult position. He would like to avoid a finding of either error or omission in the documents, since any significant finding could result in an action by the owner against him. Thus, where ambiguous language occurs, the design professional could be expected to find that his interpretation runs in the same path that it did during the design period. Sweet also notes (p. 529): "It is difficult for a creative person to step away from his work and make honest judgments about its clarity and accuracy. . . . It is hard for the design professional to put himself in a position of absolute neutrality in interpreting the contract documents."

In terms of delay, the danger inherent in the interpretative responsibilities of the design professional in the field is that a dispute could be set off wherein the actual error or omission (if any) would involve a relatively limited scope, but the impact upon the job progress would be substantial with delay costs many times that of the specific area of dispute. Without an overview perspective, such as that which a project manager might have, one or more small disputes might well mushroom into a major confrontation.

This occurred in a case in which the architect issued a number of controversial design interpretations. In one of his directives, he insisted that the contractor provide a high quality electric outdoor clock in a school courtyard. The clock was not mentioned in the specifications in any division, including electrical. It was not shown in the electrical schematics. In fact, the only reference to the clock in the plans and specifications was its appearance in one architectural elevation. In another example of this architect's actions, he demanded that an entire television closed circuit conduit system be installed despite the fact that the only reference to television was the appearance of television outlet boxes on the architectural drawings. No electrical schematic was included. These instances were typical of many relatively small areas wherein the architect continually found in favor of his own version of what the project should contain.

Finally, the contractor refused to proceed beyond one point involving waterproofing of a swimming pool until the architect gave him written instructions clarifying which portion of the work would be included as a change order. (In this particular area, the architect had revised the drawings after the contract introducing a number of substantial changes that had never been confirmed in writing.) In this one area, some 171 days of delay occurred while this dispute continued. Ultimately, all parties lost because of this delay. However, the contractor had been pushed beyond the specific situation as it related to that one change, and felt that as a policy, a stand had to be taken to resolve the arbitrary manner in which the architect exercised his field supervisory powers.

Liability of the Architect Engineer

The architect/engineer is responsible to perform professionally, and in a manner in which a reasonable and diligent professional would perform. In Reference Case 33, an architect insisted that a subcontractor be discharged by the prime contractor as a result of a dispute between the architect and the subcontractor in regard to the number of workers required to complete the subcontract work on schedule. This directive was issued by the architect without any form of hearing, or even contact between the architect and the subcontractor. The judge stated: "This amazing directive was issued by the architect's office without notice to the plaintiff and without giving the plaintiff any opportunity to be heard orally or in writing, formally or informally. This action on the part of the architect's office was contrary to the fundamental ideas of justice and fair play."

Clearly, the court was in the mood to find some form of damage against the architect. However, the subcontractor did, in fact, leave the job for other reasons as described in Reference Case 33, and the court concluded that no damages had occurred, even though the architect's action had been arbitrary and unreasonable. Note that the action was between the subcontractor and his prime contractor, for the basic legal reason that there was no privity of contract between the design professional and the subcontractor. Beyond the question of privity, the law may accord some level of immunity from liability to persons exercising quasi-judicial functions.

In *Lundgren v. Freeman* (307 F. 2d 104, 9th Cir.; 1962) a school district terminated a contractor's contract at the advice of their architects. The contractor sued the school district for damages resulting from wrongful termination, and also brought action against the architects. The court found that the architect could have been acting in one or more of three capacities: agent of the owner; quasi-arbitrator; or in his own interest. As an agent, he would not be liable unless the principal (i.e., school district) failed to pay on any judgment against them. (In that event, the school district, in turn, would have to sue the architect to recover the damages incurred as a result of the actions of the agent. Even then, any such action would have to be proven to be the result of willful and intentional misconduct by the architect.) In the second case, if the acts were as a quasi-arbitrator, the architect would be immune if the decisions were made in good faith. Finally, the architect could be held liable for damages that were resulting from actions outside of the role as agent or quasi-arbitrator. However, the contractor would have to show that these acts were, in fact, beyond those two roles. (This was an appeal, and the court did find that the trial court was in error in dismissing the charges against the architect. The reviewing court held that the contractor should have had the opportunity to pursue the situation judicially.)

Advice to the Owner

In addition to the role of interpreter of the design, the designer in the field has an advisory role to the owner. This role includes continuing commentary on routine, but important, matters, such as shop drawings, change orders, requests for time extensions, and other normal contractual matters. In addition, the owner normally seeks the designer's advice on all unusual matters that occur.

Shop Drawings. The area of approval on shop drawings, samples, and materials is one of the most substantive ones involving the designer during the field phase. This work takes a tremendous amount of time, and is fraught with legal implications for the designer. Accordingly, he does not approve these items capriciously. In fact, it is usual for the architect to have an approval stamp that includes a disclaimer to the effect that the shop drawing has been reviewed and either no defect has been noted, or those that have been noted are identified on the drawing. However, the disclaimer goes on to say, these notations are not necessarily complete, nor do they remove the requirement that the contractor meet all appropriate scope and requirements of the contract, as well as all standard safety practices.

In the case of *Day* v. *National Radiator Corp.* (241 La. 288; 1961) a family sued to recover damages for the death of the husband, a construction worker, as the result of a boiler explosion. The shop drawings for the boiler involved had been reviewed by the architect.

As part of their contract with the Louisiana State Building Authority, the architects were to exercise "adequate supervision of the execution of the work to reasonably insure strict conformity with the working drawings, specifications, and other contract documents. . . . This supervision was to include, among other things, . . . inspection of all samples, materials and workmanship, . . . checking of all shop and setting drawings, . . . frequent visits to the work."

The architects retained a consulting engineering firm to prepare the plans, specifications, and field supervision for the mechanical and electrical systems. The architects admitted that they had relied on the consulting engineer's technical ability for the installation of the mechanical and electrical equipment of which the boiler that exploded was a part.

The plans and specifications included requirements for thermostats, temperature and pressure relief valves, and stated that drawings should show construction details and dimensions. In the section of the contract specifications entitled shop drawings, the section specifically provided: "shop drawings marked 'approved as noted,' are assumed to be approved for fabrication or placing orders."

The HVAC subcontractor submitted brochures and shop drawings regarding the boiler in question. After installing the hot water system, the subcontractor, to check his own work, lighted the boiler for a preliminary test. The explosion that ensued resulted in the death of the employee. This preliminary test was made without informing either the architects or the consulting engineers that the hot water system was ready for inspection, and did not request any of these persons to make an inspection before the explosion. Testimony made it clear that the explosion was inevitable since the boiler was not equipped with a pressure relief valve.

The court recognized certain realities. The Louisiana State Building Authority attempted to impose on the architects the obligation of supervising the installation of the hot water system. The building authority held that the architects had breached this obligation because they were not aware that the system was being installed and that they had not inspected the system during installation or after completion—and claimed that this constituted negligence. The court stated:

The narrow question here presented is whether the architect's contract with the owner imposed upon him the duty to be aware that the boiler was being installed by . . . the plumbing subcontractor, and whether they were required by their contract to inspect the hot water system, of which the boiler was a part, during installation and before the boiler was tested by the subcontractor. . . .

We do not think that under the contract in the instant case the architects were charged with the duty or obligation to inspect the methods employed by the contractor or the subcontractor in fulfilling the contract or the subcontract. Consequently, we do not agree . . . that the architect had a duty . . . to inspect the hot water system during its installation, or that they were charged with the duty of knowing that the boiler was being installed.

In regard to the question of shop drawings, the court held: "We finally considered the question of whether the architects were negligent in approving . . . shop drawing[s] or brochure[s] which did not specify the pressure relief valve for the boiler, and, if this was negligence, whether such negligence was a proximate cause of the accident. . . . It is to be noted that according to the specifications, a shop plan 'approved as noted' was assumed to be approved for fabrication or placing orders." The court went on to note that even if the shop drawings had been complete and proper in this case, the HVAC subcontractor did not follow even his own initial submittal.

There is additional law in regard to the approval of shop drawings. The purpose of this illustration is to demonstrate the serious nature of the approval. In a typical project, the designer is called upon to approve literally hundreds, if not thousands, of shop drawings. With the serious potential of any failure, there is a natural tendency for the designer to proceed very slowly in the approval cycle.

Even though, in the above case, the note indicated that approval was for the purpose of placing an order only, simple economics dictate that shop drawings should be reviewed on a one-and-done basis, if at all possible (although this is unusual). The net effect in terms of delay is to cause potential delay, or actual delay by failure to expeditiously pass through shop drawings.

One approach to the establishment of priorities for reviewing shop drawings is to key them into the approved project schedule. Some owners even call upon the contractor to identify those activities on the CPM or PERT schedule, which are affected by shop drawings. This information is used to set priorities for shop drawing review. The tradition in the trade is a claim that shop drawings will be returned within two weeks. The actual mailing, handling, and return time is usually one week or even more. The basic reality to the tradition of the trade is that shop drawings are *not* returned within two weeks. Use of proper coordination techniques and thorough expediting of all shop drawings can be used to move those that have direct field impact in terms of delay.

Another psychological problem that occurs in shop drawing review is the propensity of both the designer and, where he is directly involved, the owner to exercise a bureaucratic-type review on the shop drawings. Where the design does not meet requirements, the designer and/or owner, through their staff, tend to make detailed comments and remarks that really do not advance the situation. Further, the reviewing staff is generally not project-implementation oriented, and really does not know which drawings should be moved ahead of others. Often the reviews are sequenced in order of the receipt time (which presumes that the contractor had a reasonable order of priority when submitting the drawings), or is done on the basis of those drawings that the reviewer is most interested in. Since the shop drawings first submitted are often those that arrive first, the two approaches result in reviews on an arbitrary or random basis in terms of actual field priorities.

Apart from the random nature of the voluminous shop drawings review, a designer may attempt to impose his will in limited and specific areas by delaying the approval of shop drawings. This is countered by the contractor's typical ploy of resubmitting the same disapproved shop drawing with little or no change, in hopes that the designer or owner will ultimately go along with it. In fact, these two effects often operate in tandem to the detriment of the entire job progress. During litigation, it is not always easy to separate the cause from the effect.

In view of the high cost of delay, the designer should be aware of the possibility of imposing upon the owner a greater cost by his attempts to control a relatively minor cost area. This does not say that the designer should give in to any demand of the contractor. However, in the event that a contractor attempts to impose his will, or to bend or break the contract, the designer would be well advised to inform the owner in writing, and in certain cases, to recommend that the contractor be allowed to exercise his options, rather than risking delay of the entire job. The question can generally be reduced to dollars and cents, and it is the owner who should decide, since it is generally the owner who pays the entire bill.

Time Extensions. The general conditions call upon the architect and/or owner or construction manager to approve any requests for time extensions. This is an area that must be carefully considered. However, it is not unusual for a designer to advise the owner not to authorize a time extension, even when one is clearly allowable. The basic premise, apparently, is that the contractor should not be given too much of a time frame within which to operate. In a sense, this is the old carrot-and-donkey rule, or a paraphrase of Parkinson in which it is assumed that the contractor will expand his time frame to meet any amount of time offered to him. The paradox is that the situation described is one in which the contractor has the time coming to him. Where this is the case, the designer often loses track of the fact that delays were imposed upon the project by the owner—often through design changes or design omissions. In giving a time extension, the designer carves out the extension not only for the contractor, but also for delays accruable to the owner or his agent (i.e., designer).

There is a school of thought that says that delay does not occur until it has been experienced. Thus, New York City is bound by its rules as expressed by the city comptroller's office to withhold all time extensions until the end of the project, when the actual delay can be identified. Nevertheless, New York City requires contractors to give immediate and due notice of any delays for any reason during the course of the job.

Experience indicates that in the early phases of a contract, most contractors are optimistic and, if they must request a time extension, they still hope to finish the job on time. In this early portion of the project, time extensions are usually accepted at no cost to the owner, and at the request of the contractor. Often, by the end of the project, the contractor does not choose to accept time extensions, now having in mind a claim against the owner for the cost of extra time incurred.

Negotiating Change Orders. In negotiating change orders, some designers/construction managers see fit to avoid the question of time extensions. As noted, in New York City, there is no choice since time extensions cannot be issued until the actual delay is noted. This is an unfortunate and archaic approach. It pushes off delay so that it must be considered in a lump. The courts have generally found that this "lumping" approach is unacceptable, and in the absence of a relatively clear-cut definition of the cause of delay that can be attributed to one party or the other, the courts have chosen not to allow delay claims.

In the negotiation of change orders where the designer presses to give no additional time, or where the contractor fails to ask for additional time, it might appear that the contractor is forfeiting his claim for such time. In fact, in many cases, the counsel for the owner has assumed that the contractor cannot come back and claim the time impact for the change order, whether deserved or not. The courts, however, have taken a broader view of the matter. Where no time was requested for the change in itself, taking the project in its broader context, the court has been willing to entertain a claim for delay. For instance, where only one change order was imposed through the life of a contract, the court might well hold that commonsense would indicate that this change could have been worked into the overall with limited impact. On the other hand, where several hundred change orders are imposed, even though few or even none were on the critical path, the court might hold that the very level required an increase in the span of management of the contractor, and that his resources were taxed, thereby setting up a situation wherein he was actually delayed by the owner's changes.

Experience indicates that an ostrich approach (i.e., the owner burying his head in the sand) fails most of the time. Where procedures and laws permit, it is much more reasonable to evaluate time impact on either the individual change order or by groups of change orders over a calendar period of time. The use of the contractor's network for evaluation of the impact of these changes can be quite effective. Also, it should be remembered that where delay is inevitable (as a result of causes that can be defined), it is much better to admit the delay and to apportion the cause of it in a timely fashion. This solves problems much more readily, often avoiding litigation. Failure to evaluate and appropriate delay on an incremental, realistic, and timely basis can result in the accrual of large amounts of delay that are unacceptable, and causing polarization that could well lead to litigation.

The overzealous designer does not earn any additional fee for pressing the owner's rights beyond equitable limits. Further, he really is not doing the owner a favor. The owner will ultimately pay, in most of the cases, and the best advice is to evaluate fair payment for fair delay, rather than letting situations build up to the point where the owner incurs a much greater jeopardy then he realized.

Progress Payments

A major role of the designer is the approval of progress payments. Where there is a construction manager, he often approves in tandem or series. Traditionally, the designer has been required to sign a certificate with each progress payment, usually on a monthly basis. The right of review of payment is a very powerful weapon on the owner's side. Failure to approve payment in an equitable fashion, to pay the contractor for work in place, can be considered a very definite breach of contract.

In *Shine v. Hagemeister* (169 Wisc. 343 172 N.W. 750; 1919), a heating installation was not completed within the contract time, and a new concrete floor for the basement heaved and broke during extreme cold weather. The architect withheld the last certificate of payment to the heating subcontractor. The court held that this was beyond his authority as follows:

The architect clearly attempted to pass upon a matter not submitted to him by the contract. . . . His powers were simply to issue certificates for "work done and materials furnished upon premises." . . . A refusal to award a certificate because of matters entirely outside of the submission is necessarily a mistaken and arbitrary refusal and amounts in law to a fraudulent refusal, even though made in entire good faith. . . . The plaintiff's work having been done and the materials having been furnished, the certificate was due and the question whether the plaintiff's delay in installing the apparatus caused breaking of a floor which another contractor had put in was a question to be fought out between the parties after the certificate was given. The architect mistook the scope of his duty, and because of that misapprehension refused the certificate.

In another case, *Arc Electrical Construction Company Inc. v. George A. Fuller Co.* (Reference Case 2), the architect approved the first eight monthly requisitions totaling approximately $1.4 million. However, the next month, the architect did not approve the requisition even though the general contractor had already approved it. Four more monthly requisitions were submitted, all of which were refused by the architect. The case does not bring out the area of disagreement between the architect and Arc. However, Fuller, on the insistence of the architect, cancelled Arc's contract. This despite the fact that Fuller was unable to show any defects in Arc's performance. Prior to the cancellation of the subcontract, Arc was in a difficult position and unable to recover the amounts held up without suit. However, upon cancellation, Arc had a clear-cut opportunity to claim for the value of the work in place, and did so successfully.

In this case, and its hearing in the lower court, the architect was clearly in jeopardy of a claim for arbitrary action in withholding approval. For as the appeals court noted: "It is undisputed that the work had, in fact, been substantially performed by Arc, and the fact that an architect, for some undisclosed reason, had failed to approve the work would not prevent the plaintiff from receiving compensation for his labors." If the five delayed payments were on the same order of magnitude as the eight requisitions that had been approved, the amount withheld would be on the order of $1 million. At reasonable interest rates, for a time lapse of four years, (the time between the commencement of work and the final judgment), the cost in interest alone could easily have been $250,000—a figure that the recalcitrant architect might well have been liable for. The failure to pay the contractor may require him to slow down his operations. Thus, the indirect cost of delay to the contractor and the owner mutually could exceed the cost of simple interest.

Summary

During litigation, the design professional has many hours to look backward over his actions. He finds it difficult to step forward and stongly defend a position too vigorously, since he may by his own admission show that he overstepped his authority. Further, during litigation, he is at best being paid on a daily basis. He probably won't win additional fees or assignments; further, he stands to lose reputation, business, his own funds, his own valuable time, and even his professional insurance.

Chapter Six · The Owner

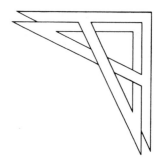

The owner's position rarely gets any stronger than it is at the start of the construction contract. He is still on budget, he has a design, and he has established a schedule based upon his needs. If properly structured, the contract is a very strong one, as discussed in chapter 3, "Construction Contracts". It attempts to give the owner a maximum of prerogatives, while holding him harmless from as many of his own actions (or lack of action) as is possible.

During the construction stages, inevitable, and often unforeseen, problems arise. The schedule tends to become expanded, while the contract tends to increase because of the additional costs of unforeseen conditions, delays, and out of scope work.

The realistic, experienced owner expects some delay and to pay more than the base contract price. Cost is generally better controlled than time, with an acceptable cost increase range on the order of 5 percent. (In many public situations, the executive in charge, such as the commissioner of public works, may authorize changes up to an aggregate of 5 percent without additional approval).

Time overruns tend to be much higher in terms of percentage of the time specified. This causes hardship to all parties. The contractor's overhead increases, while the owner's costs for lack of availability of required space can range from loss of rental to loss of contracts because of lack of production facilities.

Over the years, it has been a general practice to forgive and forget delay. However, as the cost of time extensions continues to increase, it is no longer reasonable to ignore these very real costs.

Responsibilities

Walker and Rohdenburg (*Legal Pitfalls*, p. 123) state a general rule: "An owner who undertakes to erect a building, and employs a competent architect and a competent contractor, is not responsible for an accident caused by failure of the contractor to follow adequate plans or the failure of the architect to properly plan or supervise the work."

This rule stems from precedents such as *Burke v. Ireland* (Reference Case 10) wherein an owner was sued because of the collapse of a building under construction. The collapse was serious, with some fifteen people losing their lives. The court relieved the owner from liability reasoning that "the owner was not competent himself to plan the building which he desired to erect. He was not competent to construct or superintend the construction. . . . It was his duty to devolve these things upon persons possessing sufficient knowledge and skill to accomplish the result intended. . . . he took all such measures to construct the building that any reasonably prudent man would under the same circumstances."

However, the same insulation does not accrue to the owner in cases where the injury is one of cost through delay. For instance, in *Bentley v. State* (Reference Case 4), the State of Wisconsin employed an architect to prepare plans and specifications for an addition to the state capitol building. The work was well advanced when part of the structure collapsed. The contractor was required to restore the damage, but then sued the state for the additional costs (probably including delay). The court ruled that the specifications were faulty, and therefore the architect was at fault. Further, the court found that the state was responsible for its architect stating: "What was thus done, or omitted to be done, by the architect, must be deemed to have been done or omitted by the State."

Although not cited in cases, it is probable that the court recognizes to some extent as a factual background, the experience level of the owner. Thus, the owner of a one-time building, such as a hospital or church, fulfills his obligations when he contracts with competent people to design and construct. This discharges the responsibilities of the normal person or organization.

The experienced organization that builds many times, such

as a governmental department of public works, cannot so readily discharge its obligations. If it has professional staff capability to recognize problems that the inexperienced owner would not recognize, then this fact potentially becomes material. The increasing popularity of approaches, such as construction management, which make available additional field experience to the inexperienced owner, may tend to wash out this distinction.

The owner has to expect to pay for every reasonable cost on his project, even when unforeseen. In *Cauldwell-Wingate* v. *State of New York* (Reference Case 12), the construction company, Cauldwell-Wingate, was on a phased contract, responsible for the superstructure. The foundation contractor had anticipated an easy demolition job until he discovered many unanticipated subsurface conditions. The contractor was issued a change order for his work, including a nine-month extension. The superstructure contractor successfully sued for the cost of delay including escalation in salaries, and in the cost of materials. In addition, he was able to claim additional costs for a two-stage work plan that was more expensive than his previous one-stage plan. Further, the nine-month delay pushed more of the work into winter season, and the contractor successfully sued for additional costs of winter work. Another factor allowed was the cost of storage of materials.

The court, in effect, stated that the contractor had the right to rely on the start schedule that the owner had given. Further, while the failure to provide sufficient subsurface information was not deemed to be negligent, responsibility for furnishing this information would clearly have been that of the owner (or of his designer, who would have been compensated separately for the subsurface exploration).

Schedule

The owner sets the schedule for the work, utilizing advice from his designer and other confidants, but generally undertaking establishment of the schedule himself. The typical schedule is a tight one, either intentionally or accidentally. The intentionally tight schedule is a reflection of the requirements that the project will fulfill for the owner. (Often by the time that the design is completed, much of the time originally available has been utilized in the preconstruction stages.) The accidentally short construction schedule occurs when the owner is not knowledgeable or realistic about the time necessary to construct the project at hand.

While the schedule is the statement of the owner's requirements, it also sets the base and time frame for the contractor's work, and, therefore, the base for any allegation of delay, and claims springing therefrom.

In *Gasparini Excavating v. Pennsylvania Turnpike* (Reference Case 26), the court recognized that the owner had an obligation to provide a "predetermined program." Further, failure to provide such a program was, in effect, the main cause of interference with the contractor's ability to work, and the court accordingly allowed delay damages to the contractor for a five-month delay that resulted when a preceding contract was not completed.

In *Kiewit v. Iowa Southern Utilities* (Reference Case 35), the contractor claimed that a construction schedule furnished by the owner was binding in terms of its milestone dates, as well as the end date. Iowa Southern had provided a complete construction schedule as part of the specifications to provide all contractors with the basic idea of when the various phases of the work would start. The completion date was clearly of the essence, and was so stated in the contract. The schedule also showed intermediate milestone dates that showed the interrelationship between several contractors. There was no express provision in the contract to make these milestone dates binding. Thus, the court held that the schedule as prepared by the owner for the completion of the elements of construction was not binding on the owner.

The court in the case of *Bethlehem Steel v. City of Chicago* (Reference Case 5) found that the interior milestone date for erection of steel was definitely binding upon the steel contractor (Bethlehem) and enforced the application of liquidated damages in the amount of $52,000. This finding for the city was binding despite the fact that the overall contract was completed on the day scheduled by the city. Bethlehem contended that, therefore, the city had not suffered actual damage.

In *Consumers Construction Co. v. Cook County* (275 N.E. 2d 697; 1971), the county argued that the requirement to complete the base contract within 210 calendar days was placed in the contract for the benefit of the county, and could not be used by the contractor as a base for delay damages. The trial court agreed with the county position and found that the delays in completion of the contract did not give the plaintiff contractor a right to recover damages, even if these damages were caused by the defendant or his agents. The appeals court ruled against the trial court stating:

The issues of determination of the party for whose benefit the time limitation was included in the contract actually bears no relationship to the legal basis of the plaintiff's claim. In the case at bar, the lengthy specifications provide that the right of the plaintiff as contractor to proceed shall not terminate because of any delays in the completion of the work due to unforeseeable causes beyond the control and without default or negligence of the plaintiff.

Plaintiff takes the position that by necessary implication, arising from the very situation of the parties, it was the duty of the defendant as owner to take reasonable steps to avoid frustration of plaintiff's efforts by lengthy delays for which plaintiff has no responsibility. This contention is strongly supported by cases decided in this and other jurisdictions.

Based on these authorities, we hold that in a public works contract, such as involved here, where material delays arise without fault of culpability of the contractor, he may at his option either terminate the work or complete performance of the contract. In addition, we hold that where the owner bears responsibility for the delay, the contractor has an action against the owner for such damages as reasonably and proximately resulted from the delay."

In *Taylor-Victor Steel Construction Co. v. Niagara Frontier Bridge Commission* (261 App. Div. 288, N.Y.; 1941; affirmed 287 N.Y. 669), contractor claimed a breach of contract due to delay by another contractor. The plaintiff was under contract to construct steel superstructures for two bridges over the Niagara River. A separate contract had been let for the supporting foundation substructures. The specifications included a schedule of completion dates for the different parts of the substructure. Based upon this schedule, the structural contractor had anticipated completion in fourteen weeks. However, the actual completion time required thirty-seven weeks. Specifications included a no damages for delay clause.

In starting his portion of the work, the structural contractor requested a postponement of the commencement because he recognized that the foundation structure operation for piers and abutments were being hampered by winter weather. That contractor had also encountered unexpected conditions below the surface. The commission had insisted that the superstructure be started.

The courts found against the steel construction company describing the schedule as the engineer's best judgment as to time at which substructure would be ready. Although this judgment was incorrect, there was no interruption or interference with the actual progress of the structural steel erection. Therefore, the court held that the provisions of the contract for no damages for delay precluded a damage claim.

This case, described in *Public Construction Contracts and the Law* (Cohen, p. 238), is one in which the owner's representatives were not held accountable for milestone dates set within the overall contract schedule. Based on the evidence, the court did find that the engineers had used their best judgment prior to the contract, and apparently took all reasonable steps to expedite the work in the field. Therefore, the problems encountered were not considered to be interference by the owner, and the weather and subsurface conditions were held to be unforeseen conditions.

In a similar case, *Shore Bridge Corp. v. State of New York* (186 Misc. 1005, N.Y.; 1946; affirmed 271 App. Vip. 811), the contractor sued the state for delay of one month. The contractor proved that the state had delayed his operation through delay and its driving of test piles. During this time, the contractor's equipment at the site was completely idle. Despite the delay, the contract was completed on time.

The contractor claimed that his progress schedule had been arranged to complete one month before the specified completion date, and therefore, the month of delay had imposed damages upon him in the form of the idle equipment time, as well as additional overhead for the final month of completion. The court held that in each contract there is an obligation that neither party will interfere or impede the progress of the other party. Therefore, on the law, the delay could be found against the state if the facts supported it.

Time of delivery of a construction project is a key factor to the owner. In terms of cost of the project, it is important to the contractor, also. Therefore, the contractor must have some definite opinion as to the overall length of the project if he is to make a meaningful bid. Some of the contractor's overhead can be spread throughout the job. However, there will inevitably, be additional costs to the contractor in terms of price escalation due to wages and a basic overhead cost that is tied to the length of the job, rather than to the specific level of field activity. Therefore, the contractor must include some contingent amount to cover his risk or exposure due to an extended contract. If he is to be the successful bidder, these contingencies cannot be extravagant.

The owner who includes only the completion date in the contract has very little control during the progress of the job. In order to establish feasible schedules, many owners are turning to a preconstruction evaluation by their staff, consultants, or the construction manager, if assigned. The purpose of this pre-bid analysis is the development of a construction plan by knowledgeable people that can be used as the basis of the owner's schedule. The preconstruction study may well inform the owner that a reasonable contractor under normal circumstances cannot meet his dates. The owner would then have a number of alternatives. One of these would be to describe the contract time as a tight one, and insist that overtime be programmed into the project on a preset basis, such as six or seven days a week. Another approach would be the requirement that the contractor work double shifts. There are, of course, severe budget impositions as a result of this type of measure. Also, the measure would have to be evaluated in terms of area work practice. Some labor unions require full premium for double shift, while others impose only a nominal increase. Some areas will not work on this accelerated basis, regardless of salary premium. Another alternative is for the preconstruction schedule study team to establish a phased projected series of dates at which parts of the project could be taken over. Often this meets the owner's true requirements. If this is the case, the phasing is made part of the contract, and no additional cost is programmed into the project.

When a preconstruction evaluation of this type has been made, there are two basic approaches that the owner can take. One is to state that such a study has occurred, and that, therefore, there is a practicality to the dates required. This contractual clause usually goes on to state that liquidated damages are based upon reality and will be imposed. The second approach is to furnish the study to all bidders or make it available (similar to soil borings).

In the first instance, the scheduling information given to the contractor is once again only a narrative statement. The owner does not include the results of the study as part of the contract documents. The recommended approach is to include at least a summary network and/or computer run in the network for use by the bidding contractor. This section can be marked information only. However, it gives the contractor a rapid method of evaluating one way in which the project can be accomplished. (The scheduling information should be conditioned in that manner also. The network does not insist that the contractor perform the project in this specific manner, but suggests that this is one way of doing it. The owner is, after all, attempting to buy the innovative thinking of the contractors as one of their basic skills.)

In most cases, bidding contractors do not make a serious evaluation of the contractual time requirements, unless they are unusually and obviously stringent. Even in this case, the contractor who includes a condition in his bid response will definitely be found nonresponsive by public agencies, and will probably be found nonresponsive by private organizations. The effect is to reject the bid of the contractor who has questioned or conditioned the time frame. Therefore, most contractors will not do so, but may offer their concern after award of contract. The experienced contractor knows that there will be unforeseen conditions and unexpected situations for which time extensions will be allowed. He also expects changes on the part of the owner and anticipates that the owner will either relax the end date, or that if need be, he (the contractor) will be able to successfully handle any delay claim on the part of the owner. Further, liquidated damages have traditionally been set too low by owners who are unaware that their claim for damages is limited by the liquidated damages.

The preconstruction schedule can be used to develop something more than an end date. By the network evaluation, key milestone points can be identified. The analysis really tells the owner that if certain things do not occur by certain stages of the contract, there is no way in which the end date can be met. Therefore, the section on scheduling can establish these milestones as specific days following the notice to proceed.

Under normal contract procedures, the owner has only the end date as a contractual requirement. There is usually general language to the effect that the contractor shall keep on schedule. However, the contractor, when running behind schedule, can always allege that he is going to put more work force on, will work overtime when required, or that he is bringing more subcontractors on to the project. There is no definitive means of establishing that he has failed to meet his contractual obligations.

The establishment of the milestone as a contractual requirement helps insure the owner of a means of controlling progress, and gives a definitive area in which to require performance by the contractor. The contract language should include some flexibility, permitting the owner to adjust milestone dates if a contractor can demonstrate a realistic means of readjusting. Such requests should be in writing, and require the signed concurrence of the owner.

Typical milestone points include: completion of foundations; completion of structure; close-in and watertight; start of temporary heat; complete basic air handling system; complete permanent heat; complete lighting system. Milestone dates can also be established by area. Thus, in a hospital, certain areas may be designated for acceptance by the owner in stages. A typical initial area is the ambulatory care and staff administrative spaces. If the owner intends to take phased occupancy, the decision should be made early in the design phase, so that the layout of the facility reflects the incremental occupancy intended. Also, the mechanical and electrical systems may require controls by local area. The zoning by areas is generally a favorable factor for building operation and maintenance.

Coordination by Owner

Long experience in the construction industry clearly demonstrates that the owner who practices laissez-faire during the progress of his project is an owner who can expect to take over the project much later than he had hoped and probably at a cost beyond budget. Worse than this, he may well face a claim from his contractor for the delays that the contractor himself incurred.

The knowledgeable owner recognizes that he must be involved in his project, either through his own staff or by retaining a construction manager if he does not have the staff available. This involvement is not without risk. For instance, in the case of *Kiewit v. Iowa Southern Utilities* (Reference Case 35), the contractor attempted to use the interim dates in the schedule against the owner. Since these were not imposed as contractual milestone dates, the owner was able to avoid claim on the basis that these claims were just advisory. In the recommended approach wherein milestones are used, and are contractual, the owner will have to take care that he meets his obligations. (Conversely, if during the contract, the owner is unable to meet his obligations, then he should make the appropriate contractual adjustments that absorb any damage to the contractor.)

In *Hammermill Paper v. Rust Engineering* (Reference Case 28) the case involved a knowledgeable owner who was very actively involved in coordination of his contract. Further, the defendant was a well-known, design-build organization with an excellent reputation. The situation would seem to have been the best combination. The situation arose in which a long brick curtain wall collapsed. The owner claimed that the collapse was because of faulty and negligent construction, while the contractor claimed that excessive rains had caused the collapse. The contractor in defending indicated that they had been so controlled on the job as to become "an employee agency under the direct control of Hammermill," and therefore, since Hammermill was in charge, they were at fault, having retained control and responsibility.

The court did not agree, saying: "Nowhere in the agreement is there any specific language which gives Hammermill the responsibility for final approval of the design and specifications to be supplied by Rust, nor any indication that Hammermill, following the guidelines of such design and specification, was to supervise, inspect and approve as the work progressed. . . . Hammermill was interested, primarily in the result, and secondarily, in keeping an eye on the costs incurred. . . . The fact that Hammermill retained control necessary to supervise and exercise direction over the costs feature of the work; that it secured the necessary work permits and that it retained the right to add or subtract from the work to be done, does not convince us that Hammermill thereby occupied the status of an employer of Rust. Naturally, Hammermill was interested in the results and the cost of obtaining such results, but the indices of such interest as delineated in the agreement do not constitute a responsibility for the manner in which the work was to be done by Rust. Rust was a specialist, and possessed expertise in the construction field. . . . between the parties, Rust and only Rust, had the necessary skills to perform the required work. . . . We fail to find . . . that Hammermill was insisting on retaining and reserving such a broad scope of control as to deprive Rust of the freedom of decision that [they] would normally employ as an independent contractor."

This case goes far to delineate the prerogatives of owner's interest, and thereby owner's coordination, which can and should be retained by the owner.

State laws in many of the states including Pennsylvania, New York, and New Jersey, require that state and local government agencies utilize separate prime contractors on each project. The law usually requires that there be at least four prime contractors, and sometimes more depending on the dollar size of certain special segments, such as elevators and escalators. The basic premise for the laws has been the idea advanced by the mechanical contractors that the public can get a better buy if mechanical contracts are not loaded with the general contractor's overhead and profit factors. These laws have withstood many attempts to change them.

Generally, government agencies have disliked the additional work imposed by this type of separate prime contract requirement, because coordination between prime contractors becomes the owner's concern.

The federal government, which does not have a separate prime contract requirement, has done much to develop the concept of construction management, wherein a construction manager is in charge of many separate prime contracts. There is a close analogy to the role of the general contractor and his subcontractors. However, the overhead loading under the construction manager concept is not as great. The construction manager is guaranteed a fair profit return for his time and cost exposure. In order to keep his fee at a reasonable level, he is not exposed to risk. In essence, the owner takes all the risks including coordination problems, and thereby avoids the insertion of large risk premium costs in the contractor contingencies.

Many state and local government organizations that are subject to separate prime contractor requirements have followed the lead of the federal government in the use of construction managers. The concept is within the separate prime laws, and establishes appropriate staffing and manpower to perform the coordination function imposed. In *General Building Contractors v. County of Oneida* (Reference Case 27), the state and their architect attempted to impose a responsibility for coordination upon the separate prime contractors rather than upon the owner. In this instance, the Association of General Contractors were in the unusual position of defending the separate contract law.

The specifications attempted to shift a number of coordination responsibilities to the general contractor prime. While the general contractors are accustomed to handling these areas in a normal general contract situation, the plaintiffs objected to the work in this manner on a state job. The special conditions part of the contract called for the general contracting prime to submit a satisfactory progress schedule for all of the prime contractors; to review and check all shop drawings (for all contractors); to insure conformance with the intent of the drawings and specifications and for contract requirements; and to be "fully responsible for the fitting of all work."

The court found that this imposed upon the general contractor: "responsibilities and obligations as to supervision and coordination not envisioned by the statute and which should be borne by the owner and/or the architect."

The court went on to quote Section 101 of the General Municipal Law requiring separate prime contracts and said that "while the statute is silent as to whether the municipality may assign the work of such supervision to the successful bidder, it appears to this court that had the legislature intended such assignment where separate bidding is required, it would have so provided. . . . The State recognized the increase in administrative problems imposed upon it by the multiple bid contract system, but accepted this burden in view of the overall savings."

The same group of contractors tested the law again in *General Building Contractors* v. *City of Syracuse* (40 A.B. 2d 584, 334 NYS 2d. 730; 4th Department; 1972) wherein the court stated: "bid specifications insofar as they require the general contractor's superintendent to correlate all the work on the job, the separate prime contractors to coordinate their work schedules with that of the general contractor, and hold the general contractor responsible for setting the pace of the job and for all the work in place are violative of Section 101 of the General Municipal Law."

Various variations on the attempt to assign the coordination and supervisory responsibility in separate prime law states have occurred. The Division of Building Construction in New Jersey successfully assigned contracts for building systems, (partitions, ceilings, structural steel, and other systems) purchased for the state colleges at Stockton and Ramapo to the successful separate prime general contractor. However, the state still awarded separate prime contracts for plumbing, HVAC and electrical work, so that the concept was still within the requirements of the New Jersey statutes.

In private work, an owner can assign supervisory and coordinating duties, but the contract must be carefully constituted so that risk is identified, and taken appropriately. In the face of intangible contractual wording, a number of contractors may include funds to cover coordination risk, so that the owner may pay several times.

In *Forest* v. *State* (Reference Case 24), the plaintiff was the separate prime electrical contractor at a state hospital. Other contracts were for general construction, heating, sanitary work, refrigeration, elevators, and food service equipment. Work was to be completed in approximately thirty months. The electrical contractor finished his work approximately two years after the contract date. He claimed that the state had unreasonably failed to coordinate the work of other contractors, specifically noting delays in the construction of walls, ceilings, painting, elevators, plastering, hung ceilings, ceramic tile, all of which were preliminary to his work.

The state was also to provide two material hoists and one for workmen. After the hoists were removed, only the elevator remained for men and material. This caused delays. Evidence indicated that "the general contractor was quite indifferent to its obligation to properly man, supervise, and coordinate its work . . . and that the State was lackadaisical and indifferent to the many and continuing complaints of the claimant." The court found that the state had a very casual attitude toward the delays. Further, it failed to exercise normal management control, holding only seven job coordination meetings over the life of the job. The court found that the state had a duty to coordinate the project, and failed in that duty.

The owner should set up definite procedures for field coordination activities by his staff or his representatives, including the design team. In *Dudar* v. *Milef Realty Corp.* (258 N.Y. 415; 1932), the owner's superintendent directed the contractor's foreman to start work on a certain floor. The owner's representative said that he would notify the hoist engineer not to operate the hoist above the eighth floor which was in a danger zone where men might be working in a vulnerable position. The owner's representative failed to carry out that assurance, and the plaintiff was injured. The court held that when the owner assumed some measure of direction of the work, he could be held responsible for negligence in not performing in accordance with assurances made by his representative.

In a broader sense, an owner giving directives or directing the activities of the contractor may be found in breach of the basic contract. Depending upon the circumstances, a contractor may be able to sustain a claim that he was no longer allowed to perform the project in the manner in which he had originally perceived that he could, and that therefore, the owner should be responsible for all costs above and beyond those contemplated by the contractor in his bid or estimate. If sustained, such a claim would be effective probably only for the excess costs in the period subsequent to the breach. However, since most project cost breakdowns are front-end loaded, the contractor could receive his entire profit, and recover additional profit in costs through the breach claim.

For this reason, an owner is well advised to be very careful in the manner in which he or his representatives carry on a dialogue with the contractor, and to enter into directed action only when absolutely necessary.

Owner Interference

The courts have held that interference by the owner is cause for claims or losses due to delay by the contractors. One of the most common owner interferences is failure to provide a working area. In *Schunnemunk Construction Company* v. *State of New*

York (116 Misc. 770, N.Y.; 1918) the contractor could not continue his work because the state failed to provide the necessary right of way. The court stated: "The issue is whether the State has violated the contract by interfering with and interrupting the claimant in its performance of the obligation." The decision held that a builder whose work progress was interrupted by an owner, even unintentionally, could recover damages caused. Other appropriate citations include: *Brennan Construction Co. v. State of New York* (117 Misc. 116; 1921); *Carr Auditor, et al. v. State* (127 Ind. 204; 1871) *Hartman v. Greenhow* (102 U.S. 672; 1880) and *Grogan v. San Francisco* (18 Cal. 590; 1861); *State v. Feigel* (178 N.E. 435 Ind.; 1931).

However, in another case, *Connelly v. State* (120 Misc. 854 N.Y.; 1923), a contractor claimed for delay damages against the state because of delay in the right-of-way transfer. The court found against the contractor because he had prior knowledge of the delay in acquisition of the right of way.

Yet in *American Bridge v. State of New York* (245 App. Div. 535; 1935), the plaintiff was the fabricator of the superstructure for a bridge. The foundation contractor for the state was delayed. Despite this delay, the steel was fabricated and had to be stored out of doors for a long period of time. Despite the prior knowledge on the part of the plaintiff, the state was held liable for a claim for the additional work required in repainting the material. However, in this case the state had ordered the fabricator to proceed with the fabrication even when they knew the delay would be of long duration. The distinction between this case and *Connelly v. State* is one of direction that constituted active interference on the part of the state.

Although many contracts have clauses stating that the owner will not be liable for damages due to delay for any cause, the courts have generally found that active interference on the part of the owner constitutes a breach of contract, and thereby opens the way for the contractor to claim for damages. This was the finding of the court in *Cauldwell-Wingate v. State of New York* (Reference Case 12).

However, findings of the courts are not always consistent. In *United States v. Blair* (321 U.S. 730; 1944), there were a number of contractors on the same work site. The general contractor was held responsible for completion of the work except for situations that might be created by the government. Another contractor caused the delay that the general contractor was not able to overcome. The courts held that the government was not responsible to force performance by the other contractor.

In *Endes Plumbing Corp. v. State of New York* (198 Misc. 546; 1950), the court agreed that a government unit would be liable if the public unit or their representatives interfered with the progress of work or failed to take action to advance it reasonably, but still stated that the government unit would not be automatically liable if delay by one contractor caused another contractor to be delayed.

In general, owners should anticipate responsibility, and act in the field as though they would have to be accountable for their actions. Two cases in which this type of accountability was required follow.

In *Stehlin-Miller-Henes Co.* v. *City of Bridgeport* (117 at 811, Conn.; 1922), the contractor (plaintiff) was the electrical and heating contractor. The contract included a time of the essence clause and stipulated that the contractor was to avoid delaying the general contractor. The reverse situation occurred, and there was a complete delay of three months in the work of the general contractor during which time the plaintiff was not able to complete his work. Further, there was additional delay while Bridgeport engaged another contractor to take over from the original general contractor. The electrical and heating contractor sued for damages due to the delays. The court agreed stating: "An implied contract arose on the part of the defendant to keep the work on the building, whether done by itself or other contractors in such a state of forwardness as would enable the plaintiff to complete its contracts within the time limited."

In a Washington state case, *Byrne* v. *Bellingham Consolidated School District #301* (108 P. 2d 791, Wash.; 1941), the plaintiff was the electrical contractor. The building had been delayed more than ten months increasing the amount of time which the electrical contractor had to be on the job by that same amount of time. The delay was caused by the general contractor. Nevertheless, the court found the school district responsible for the delay stating: "In the absence of any provision in the contract to the contrary, a building or construction contractor who has been delayed in the performance of his contract may recover from the owner of the building damages for such delay if caused by the default of the owner. . . . Such right of recovery is predicated on a breach of what we have already stated is an implied obligation on the part of an owner to furnish to the contractor a building in a state of forwardness sufficient to enable the contractor to complete the contract within the time limit."

Summary

The owner should be well aware that he is the payer, not the payee, in the construction situation. The courts frown on something for nothing. Accordingly, they are willing to award costs (including delay) for the work beyond the scope anticipated by the contract under the legal premise of quantum meruit (Reference Cases 13, 20, and 25). Further, the courts frown upon attempts to avoid payment for substantial performance (Reference Cases 3, 44, and 50). Finally, damages for delay are limited to the cost of the remedy (Reference Cases 16 and 19).

As described in chapter 11, "Damages," liquidated damages are a limited area, also. The owner cannot recover more than the figure that he imposed on the contractor—thus limiting the scope of damages that can be sought. There are exclusions, but they are not easy to establish. The owner should recognize that litigation is effective only to recover part of the costs of an extreme situation. The owner should not enter into litigation for righteous purposes, for if he does, he again becomes the payer, not the recipient of value.

Chapter Seven · The Contractor

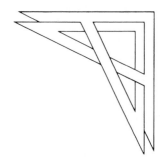

The contractor starts most contracts in the worst position possible. He has agreed to, as a meeting of the minds, a contract that has been unilaterally drafted by the owner and his representatives—particularly the architect/engineer. More than that, he is almost inevitably the low bidder, and is counting and recounting the money that he "left on the table."

Throughout the project, he negotiates, operates, and maneuvers to make the contract work for him, to the greatest extent possible. In almost all instances, the contract does undergo an evolution, forfeiting some of its more preemptive rights, waiving some clauses through performance (or lack thereof), and muting some of the controls that the owner retained (or thought he was retaining).

The courts, viewing the contract as the cornerstone of their interpretation of any claim, resist any overt attempts to change the contract, as in the case of *Bethlehem Steel* v. *City of Chicago* (Reference Case 5).

Method of Construction

While the owner sets the schedule, often including milestones, the contractor has the right to select the method and manner in which he will accomplish the contractual requirements. This prerogative, if changed by the owner, may become the basis for damages, including damages for delay.

One of the classic cases setting the prerogative of the contractor is *Meads* v. *City of New York* (Reference Case 40). In this case, the contractor was given the option in the specifications to either sheath from grade level to the bottom of an excavation, or to pitch back the banks in an open cut. The contractor elected to pitch back. During the work, a slide occurred and the architect ordered the contractor to use the sheathing method rather than the pitch back method henceforth. The contractor protested the change in method but continued to perform as directed.

The court held: "The contract expressly gives the contractor [the right] to choose his method. The architect deprived him of his choice and compelled him to adopt a more expensive one. . . . So long as a contractor produces work which satisfies the specifications, he can, in the interests of economy, choose his own methods."

This prerogative was reaffirmed in *Baker Company* v. *State of New York* (267 App. Div. 712, N.Y.; 1944). The state awarded separate contracts for the construction of a powerhouse, tunnels, and mechanical systems. Plaintiff Baker had the job of installing piping systems and heating equipment. Another contractor had the structure of the powerhouse and concrete tunnels. Baker Company, in preparing their bid, assumed that the construction of the tunnels would be performed in a continuous sequence. The state, however, during construction, permitted the other contractor to build the powerhouse and tunnel in an interrupted sequence. Baker Company protested. Despite the protest, the state permitted the other contractor's sequence to prevail. The contract was completed eleven months late by the structural contractor. Baker claimed that he not only had to build in a sequence not anticipated, but he also experienced additional overhead for eleven months and had water damage to his work in the overrun period of time. The court ruled that the state had interfered with the work of Baker Company and prevented him from using economical methods that he had anticipated he could use.

In *Turner Construction* v. *State of New York* (Reference Case 57), the court found: "The State inspectors were wholly unreasonable in requiring the contractor to cut a large number of brick in the body of the brickwork on the exterior walls of nine buildings. . . . The requirement of the State's inspectors was not authorized by the contracts or specifications and was arbitrary." The contractor had planned to use standard stretchers that could be obtained commercially. The owner was liable for both the delay and the damages thereby.

In *Manhattan Fireproofing* v. *J. Thatcher & Sons* (38 F. Supp. 749, E.D.N.Y.; 1941), plaintiff concrete subcontractor had been promised by defendant general contractor that the site would be delivered in such a manner and in such time so that plaintiff's work could be done in one continuous operation, to be completed by a specified date. The plaintiff was hindered and delayed and allowed to work only spasmodically. Imposing liability on the defendant, the court concluded: "The delay occasioned by the defendant retarded and hindered both the progress of the work and the time within which the plaintiff was able to finish its job. The plaintiff was able to do his work piecemeal at best."

In *Lichter v. Mellon-Stuart Company* (Reference Case 36), the court found that a subcontractor had been harmed by delay caused by the general contractor. Evidence clearly proved that the general contractor breached its contract by causing delays that affected other phases of the overall construction. These delays, in turn, created a situation of unreadiness for the orderly and systematic performance of the masonry work. Evidence showed that the masons had to perform an average of thirteen separate operations on each floor of a ten-story building, where normal procedure would have involved two or three operations per floor. However, the court did not award damages because the claim did not present a basis by which damages due to delay caused by the general contractor could be separated from those delays that were occasioned by unforeseen causes, including strikes.

In *Terry Contracting v. State of New York* (Reference Case 54), the contractor, Terry Contracting, had undertaken the contract to fabricate a superstructure for a precast, prestressed continuous concrete girder bridge consisting of three spans. Terry, in preparing its bid, planned upon a method of fabrication that would involve pouring of the large girders (approximately 145 ft. long) in a horizontal position. This would greatly reduce the cost of casting, as well as increasing the quality of the members.

The contract documents prepared by the state envisioned only pouring of the girders in position, with vertical forms. The state did not object to casting in vertical position but not in final location, but did object to the horizontal casting. Their concern was the stability of the long girders during the transition from horizontal to vertical position, before being moved into location. Testimony indicated that even the vertical casting was an advanced state-of-the-art project. The state and the designers were somewhat concerned, in that Terry had not previously performed this type of work. However, the firm had a good reputation in bridge building, although the other bridges previously had been structural steel.

The engineers and state, in reviewing the Terry Contracting requests for approval of the horizontal casting method, did not reject the approach. However, they indicated that they would not pay progress payments for this work, but would pay only when the individual girder had been successfully rotated to its vertical position. (The state and the engineer were concerned that the methods required to move the very flexible 145 feet long by 14 feet high by 4 feet wide, 250-ton member without overstressing it would be beyond the state-of-the-art and the available equipment.) However, they did not really refuse, they just proscribed a different form of payment. Terry held that this refusal to pay progress payments on the usual monthly basis would preclude their innovative approach. Terry relied on a single paragraph in the specifications that indicated that the method of forming the girders was left to the contractor's discretion. (This same phrase provided that: "the contractor shall, however, submit plans for the forms he intends to use to the engineer for his approval prior to undertaking the making of the forms.") It was clear from the testimony that Terry did, indeed, have to pay a considerable additional amount for pouring in the vertical position. In fact, this was estimated to be over $1 million more on a unit price estimate basis. The court dismissed the cause of action involving the method of construction on the grounds that Terry failed to prove any breach of contract by the state. This finding was affirmed both at the appellate division and by the court of appeals.

Contract Performance

It is legal for a contractor to undertake to do the impossible. For instance, the court in the case of Connors v. Town of Tewksbury (318 Mass. 615; 1945), the court stated: "It does not appear that the plaintiff contracted to do the impossible, but if he had, he could be held to his undertaking."

Williston has stated: "A man may contract to do that which is impossible. . . . the important question is whether any unanticipated circumstance has made performance of the promise vitally different from what should reasonably have been within the contemplation of both parties when they entered into the contract."

In Fanning & Doorley Construction Co. v. Geigy Chemical (Reference Case 23), part of the work included underground piping for Geigy Chemical at one of its plants. The system was designed by a leading consulting engineer. Because of the corrosive nature of the material to be carried in this particular pipe, the specification required that a corrosion resistant stoneware bell-and-spigot pipe should be used with a special caulking material for the joints. The specification required a specific caulking material called Causplit. The general conditions of the contract included an agreement that required that the engineering firm would in all cases determine the acceptability and fitness of the work.

Fanning and Doorley requested guidance from the owner in the installation of the joints, which they did not have previous experience with. The resident engineer actually participated in the mixing and placing of the first joint. He later testified that all recommendations of the manufacturer were carried out at all times by the contractor. The initial joints did not hold water within the requirements of the specification. Two special adjustments, not part of the specifications, were attempted without success. After a month, the manufacturer was asked for field assistance. He replaced the mortar with another having a faster setting ingredient, and recommended the use of space heaters during installation. Two weeks later, a representative of the manufacturer recommended a change in the mix to increase the setting time. He also recommended adding a special sulphur cement around the Causplit. Additional special recommendations were made, such as placing dry ice under the mortar pan. The manufacturer's representative himself tested a joint made under his direction and found that the leakage exceeded specifications. Finally, after three months of constant attempts, the engineer told the contractor to stop work on the pipeline. The court found in favor of the contractor saying that the specifications required the contractor to do work in a manner and to a degree that could not have produced the desired results as originally written. While the information is more current and detailed, the general situation is similar in many ways to *MacKnight Flintic Stone Co. v. the Mayor*, (Reference Case 39).

In *City of Littleton v. Employer's Fire Insurance Co.* (Reference Case 15), the defendant was the bonding company for a contractor. The contract was for construction of two five million gallon water tanks for the city of Littleton. The contractor began constructing the tanks in accordance with the plans and specifications, but during construction, the tanks collapsed. After this collapse, the city and the contractor entered into a supplemental agreement for reconstruction in accordance with the same plans and specifications. However, supplementary instructions were to be supplied by the consulting engineer. After this supplemental agreement, the contractor made numerous request for details without receiving the additional information in writing. Finally, the contractor ended the agreement explaining that the design was faulty. The court held that, had the contractor known the design was impossible at the time of signing the supplemental agreement that impossibility would not be a defense.

However, in reviewing the case, the supreme court found that the consulting engineer did not come to a conclusion as to the cause of the collapse until more than a year after the supplemental agreement had been signed. Therefore the impossibility of construction was an unforeseen factor. The supreme court included in its findings a legal definition of impossibility: "The law recognizes impossibility of performance as a defense to an action for breach of contract. . . . The restatement Section 454 definition of impossibility . . . means not only a strict impossibility but impracticability because of extreme and unreasonable difficulty, expense, injury or loss involved. . . . 'impossible' must be given a practical, rather than a scientifically exact meaning. Impracticability rather than an absolute impossiblity is enough."

In *Blount Bros. Corp.* v. *Reliance Insurance Co.* (Reference Case 7) the question of impossibility was used as a defense for delay as a result of a subcontractor's failure to perform. The contractor was the painting subcontractor for the construction of a nuclear reactor facility. (Reliance was the bonding company for the subcontractor.)

The specifications for the painting project included some unusual wall coverings designed for special performance. The high performance areas were specified in great detail requiring, for instance, several pages of specifications to adequately set forth a Type 10 material. Types 11, 12, and 13 were nonelastomeric, decontaminable coatings for the reactor area. These required ten pages of specifications including six pages describing the method of submitting approvals of proposed manufacturers for these special coatings. Dunbar contended that he did everything possible to obtain approval, exercised due diligence in doing so, and that the fault in securing the approval of certain coatings lay in the specifications designed by the government.

The evidence showed, however, that Dunbar had failed to follow up on any of the schedules or any of the lists of materials and names of suppliers of Types 10, 11, 12, and 13 coatings as required in the general contractor's legitimate directive to do so. Further, rather than submitting the recommended suppliers, Dunbar persisted in submitting an unacceptable paint despite prior rejections by GSA.

In *Vernon Lumber v. Harseen Construction Co.* (Reference Case 60), Vernon contracted to furnish a large quantity of lumber to Harseen. Vernon arranged to purchase the lumber from a mill in North Carolina, but the contract between Vernon and Harseen did not specify the source. The War Production Board assigned higher priorites to the output of the mill to another user, and reassigned the lumber. Vernon attempted to be relieved from performance by indicating that conditions beyond his control had made performance of the contract impossible.

The court found against Vernon. It stated: "The term 'impossible' does not mean an absolute impossibility. . . . 'Impossible' must be given reasonable and practical construction . . . but it is not satisfied by the allegation . . . that the plaintiff sought to procure the lumber 'from its usual and regular channels as well as elsewhere.' " The court noted also that the reply by Vernon did not specifically mention the word impossibility, and that being excused on the basis of impossibility would require the plaintiff to allege impossibility of obtaining the lumber.

In performance of a còntract, many delays are due to an accumulation of day-to-day problems. The range of ability of contractors to manage and coordinate their work falls in the normal statistical distribution ranging from good to poor, with most being average. The owner does not have to prove substandard performance, particularly if he has specified liquidated damages. In this situation, the amount of delay as a measure of poor performance is a matter of fact. The contractor's defense to the amount of delay is generally in identifying those delays due to interference by the owner for reason of poor plans and specifications, unforeseen conditions, or changes imposed by the owner. (A neutral discount from the amount of delay would be those factors beyond the control of either party, such as weather, strikes, acts of God, and other force majeure factors.)

Change Orders

Owner imposed delays due to poor plans and specifications, interference by the owner or his representatives, and unforeseen conditions are discussed elsewhere. Changes or change orders by the owner are one of the major factors alleged in most delay claims as a critical factor in delay. Change orders in value of 5 percent or less of the original contract value are usual, and should be anticipated by the contractor. No similar number of appropriate changes is available as an accepted statistic principally because the number of changes can be disguised by packaging smaller changes into single change orders. Packaging of change orders in this fashion is a poor practice, since it makes the negotiation of change orders more difficult.

In virtually all contracts, the owner retains the prerogative of making changes to the work by the use of clauses, such as:

The Director, at his discretion, may, at any time during the progress of the work, authorize additions, deductions, or deviations from the work described in the specifications as herein set forth; and the contract shall not be vitiated or the surety released thereby. . . . Additions, deductions, and deviations may be authorized as follows at the Director's option:

1. *On the basis of unit prices specified.*
2. *On a lump sum basis.*
3. *On a time and material basis.*

Further, the contractor must accept this additional work as it is within the context of the contract. Although the terms "additional work" and "extra work" are used synonymously, there is an important legal distinction. Extra work involves the requirement for performance of work entirely independent of the contract. *Public Construction Contracts and the Law* (Cohen, p. 121) describes extra work as: "The performance of work and the furnishing of the required labor and materials outside and entirely independent of and not necessarily to complete the contract or something done or furnished in excess of the requirements of the contract, not contemplated by the parties, and not controlled by the contract." (Citations: *Kansas City Bridge Co. v. State*; 250 N.W. 343, S. D.; 1933; *Blair* v. *United States*; 66 F. Supp. 405, Ala.; 1946).

Additional work is the work that can be imposed within the contract documents. It is a change or alteration to the plans or specifications for a number of reasons implicit in the original agreement. These reasons could include, but not be limited to, omissions in the design documents, recognition of better methods or materials to achieve the required effect, resolutions of problems recognized, resolution of unforeseen conditions not anticipated, and similar adjustments within the intent of the original contract.

Within the context of additional work change orders, the owner may impose changes to update the equipment, to recognize different functional requirements, and to otherwise improve upon the design. Changes of this nature could potentially be identified as extra work rather than additional work. As work above and beyond the contract, the contractor may choose to refuse the extra work change orders. However, generally speaking, the contractor will prefer to accept both additional work and extra work change orders if they do not obviously impede his progress in the field, and if they can be negotiated at an equitable figure. In negotiating change orders, the principal focus is upon units of work involved and the cost per unit. Where change orders delete some contract work replacing it with other work, the identification of the exact scope of the change order can be very difficult.

Early cases often combine the right of the owner to make changes and the no damages for delay clause to refuse legitimate damage claims within the contract. Thus, in *Wells Bros. Co. v. United States* (254 U.S. 83; 1920), the contractor was refused a claim for delay damages. The contract was for a federal post office-court house building. Immediately after the contract was signed, the government "ordered and directed" the contractor not to order the limestone specified in the contract because a change was anticipated. The contractor agreed to wait two weeks for the change, but in fact, was not given the new specifications for about ten months, at which time an appropriation had been made by Congress. The change substituted marble for limestone, increased the contract by $210,500, and made an extension of time necessary. During this ten-month period, the contractor had completed excavation, foundation, and the structural steel erection. The government anticipating a major change in the scope of work with Congressional approval of parcel post ordered a delay that shut the job down for six months. The contractor sued for damages because of both delay periods.

The court interpreted the contract provisions that permitted the government to extend all or part of the work "without expense" but with additional day-for-day time extension and also a "no damages for delay" clause. The court refused the contractor's claim on the basis that the contract clauses were plain and comprehensive. The court, however, went on to make a philosophical statement that included a major presumption with regard to the manner in which contractors prepare their bids: "Men who take million dollar contracts for government buildings are neither unsophisticated nor careless. Inexperience and inattention are more likely to be found in other parties to such contracts than the contractors, and the presumption is obvious and strong that the men signing such a contract as we have here protected themselves against such delays . . . by the higher price exacted for the work."

The federal courts continued to find in favor of the government position in the enforcement of the "no fault to the government" interpretation of the change and delay clauses. A 1946 case (*United States* v. *H. P. Foley Co.*; 329 U.S. 64) involved a law suit for damages for delay. The delay occurred at the beginning of the project when the government was unable to make a site available to Foley, an electrical contractor who had bid a fixed fee for the installation of a field lighting system at National Airport. The lighting system involved the runways and taxiways that were under construction. Before the areas could be stabilized enough for the electrical work to go in, hydraulic dredging, and subsequent earth work had to be completed. The dredging required more time than the engineers had anticipated, due to instability of some of the dredged soil. The court found that the government and their engineers had been diligent and stated: "The government cannot be held liable unless the contract can be interpreted to imply an unqualified warranty to make the runways promptly available." Finding that no such warranty was expressed in the contract, the court disallowed the claim. In its opinion, the court relied upon *H.E. Crook Co.* v. *United States* (270 U.S. 4; 1926) and *United States* v. *Rice* (Reference Case 59). The court stated:

> "*The contract reserved a governmental right to make changes in the work which might cause interruption and delay, required (the contractor) to coordinate his work with the other work being done on the site, and clearly contemplated that he would take up his work on the runway sections as they were intermittently completed and paved. . . . The contract . . . set out a procedure to govern both parties in case of [contractor's] delay in completion. . . . If delay were caused by [the contractor], the government could terminate the contract, take over the work, and hold the [contractor] and its sureties liable. Or . . . the government could collect liquidated damages. If, on the other hand, delay were due to 'acts of the government' or other specified events, including 'unforeseen causes' procedure was outlined for extending the time in which respondant was required to complete his contract, and relieving him from the penalties of contract termination or liquidated damages.*
>
> *In the Crook and Rice cases, we held that the government could not be held liable for delay in making its work available to contractors, unless the terms of the contract imposed such liability.*"

A 1955 case signaled a turning point in the federal court interpretations of delay damages. In *Ozark Dam Constructors* v. *United States* (120 Ct. Cl. U.S. 354; 1955), a joint venture contracted for the construction of a dam on the White River in Arkansas for the government. The government was to furnish cement at Cotter, Arkansas, and the contractor would unload and transport it at his expense. The general conditions to the contract included the standard Article 9, damages for delay article, exempting the government for damages due to delay, and also noting that for causes beyond the control of the contractor, including strikes, the contracting officer would extend the contract time on a day-for-day basis.

The contract promised that upon thirty days notice, government would ship cement by railroad to Cotter, Arkansas. The contractor requested 12,000 barrels of cement for September delivery and 41,000 for October. A railroad strike prevented the deliveries, and the suit by the joint venture was for damages for nondelivery. Evidence established that both the contractor and the government had anticipated the possibility of a railroad strike. However, the government did nothing to seek out possible alternate methods of making delivery. Further, evidence indicated that delivery could have been made by truck.

The contract also included a clause that stated that: "The government will not be liable for any expense or delay caused the contractor by delayed deliveries except as provided in Article 9 of the contract." After administrative reviews by the contracting officer and the Secretary of the Army, suit was entered. The opinion of the court stated: "A contract for immunity from the harmful consequences of one's own negligence always presents a serious question of public policy." In regard to the specific failure to deliver the cement, the court stated: "The possible consequences were so serious, and the actions necessary to prevent those consequences were so slight, that the neglect was almost willful. It showed a complete lack of consideration for the interest of the [contractor]. . . . Our conclusion is that the nonliability provision in the contract, when fairly interpreted in the light of public policy, and of the rational intention of the parties, did not provide for immunity from liability in circumstances such as are recited in the [contractor's] petition."

This court, viewing construction in a broader context, felt that such immunity clauses, particularly when poorly administered in the field, could only serve to require all contractors bidding for government work to include a prohibitive contingency in their price. In an earlier finding, the courts held that the government had the responsibility to be reasonable in its adminstration of contracts. In *Severin* v. *United States* (102 Ct. Cl. U.S. 74; 1943) a hospital was to be constructed within 500 calendar days. While the work was in progress, the government stopped all work above the ninth floor pending certain changes. This delay continued for five months. At that time, the contractor was ordered to proceed with changed work. After some of this work had been completed in its new configuration, the government issued an order cancelling the changes and reverting to the original plans. A change order was allowed increasing the price and establishing a three-month extension. However, the court found that the change orders were simply for the actual cost of the actual work and had nothing to do with the delay. Despite the standard federal phrases in the general conditions, the court allowed damages because: the contractor "was delayed by the non-use of his equipment, the idleness of his supervisory employees, rental cost of equipment, and extra costs of operating his sand and gravel pit, and the extra costs of the subcontractors. . . . Due to the [government's] procrastination and its inability to decide definitely what it proposed to do . . . the contractor's extra costs were all in addition to the work which was performed under the change orders."

The finding here did not actually run against findings in cases such as *United States* v. *Rice*, but saw the unwarranted interference with the contractor's operations as being beyond the contract, and therefore not limited by the clauses of the contract.

Authority for Change; Waiver; Breach

The general conditions usually include a statement that changes to the work will not be authorized unless they are approved in writing by the owner. Also, the contract generally includes specific language limiting the authority of the architect or engineer to make such authorized changes. Thus, in *Reid Co.* v. *Fine* (Reference Case 50), deviations from the plans and specifications by the contractor were found to be unauthorized, even though the architect and engineers for the owner had approved them. The court held: "Whatever may have been said or done by the architect or engineer to lead the [contractor] to believe they had approved the changes, their actions were in direct conflict with the provisions of the contract which required that written approval should be had before major changes could be made. . . . These contractual requirements were well known to the (contractor) and equally as binding upon it, as they were to the [owner], architect and engineer."

While there is precedent for ratification of oral approval of changes in the work, the contractor who accepts such an informal direction is in great potential jeopardy. Similarly, the contractor should be alert to promptly notify an owner that he intends to protest or appeal a change order, when that notice is required by the contract.

There are occasions when the owner waives his right to require notice. One such instance was the *Arundel Corp. v. United States* (96 Ct. Cl. U.S. 77; 1942) in a government contract for the construction of a lock and dam on the Savannah River. The contractor had a proper request for claim on a particular change, but had failed to give notice. The contracting officer, however, considered the claim on its merits without reporting or noting that the claim had been filed late. The court rejected a defense on the basis of failure to make due notice of claim, deciding that the contracting officer's action, had shown that he did not rely on the failure to file the protest and thereby waived the prerogatives for that particular notice under the contract.

The general conditions usually include a requirement to the effect that: "Any claim arising from such delay must be made in writing to the engineer immediately upon occurrence of the delay." Or "If the contractor anticipates any claim arising from delay during construction, notice of such claim must be made in writing to the owner or his authorized representative immediately upon occurrence of the delay." While sometimes difficult to implement, since the actual impact of a delay may require some substantial time to evaluate, nevertheless it is relatively easy to notify the owner that delay has occurred and that its impact is being evaluated. In fact, a form letter can be a mutually convenient means of so stating.

In *Roanoke Hospital Association v. Doyle & Russell* (Reference Case 47), the Doyle & Russell general superintendent had testified, in effect, that their organization had not been regularly making written notice of delay because they did not want to irritate the owner. Constant notices of delay and claims for impact from the contractor can create an image of a contractor who is preparing a major claim. Generally, it is the project management representatives of the owner who are annoyed, but any attempt to modify or waive this requirement would be frowned upon by the owner's legal counsel.

The courts have acknowledged that notice provisions are salutory in construction contracts. In *United States* v.

Cunningham (125 F. 2d 28), one of the contract provisions read: "The contractor shall within ten days from the beginning of any such delay notify the contracting officer in writing." There was some delay in commencing work, but the contractor did not give any written notice. He did give oral notice. The court held that the oral notice was not in compliance with the contract stating: "Obviously, the intent of this provision is to inform the government of the cause of delay and afford an opportunity to remove it, and likewise to warn the government of the intention of the contractor to insist upon it as a means of prolonging the stipulated time for completion of the work."

In *Scott Township School District Authority* v. *Branna Construction Corp.* (409 Pa. 136; 1962) the Pennsylvania Supreme Court held that the contractor's claim for extra work was barred because the contractor had not complied with the contract provision that required communications between the parties to the contract to be in writing. The court held: "Where a public contract states the procedure in regard to work changes and extras, claims for extras will not be allowed unless these provisions have been strictly followed."

The filing of appropriate notice of both delay and the probable impact can be of mutual benefit to contractor and owner when the evaluation of the claims is made. Such notice will serve both parties best if it is factual, and to the point. Argumentative, self-serving discourses are inappropriate as part of a notice of delay and an indication of intent to claim for damages.

In *Legal Aspects* (p. 512), Sweet describes material breach as follows: "If one party does not perform in accordance with his obligation, and the non-performance relates to an important matter, or bears upon the likelihood that the non-performing party will be able to perform in the future, such non-performance may terminate the other party's obligation. . . . Not every trivial defect or non-performance is sufficient to release the other party. Courts often look carefully at these matters, and try to determine whether the party claiming he need no longer perform has merely been looking for an excuse to get out of a bad contract."

Clarence Dunham and Robert Young (*Contracts, Specifications and Law for Engineers*, p. 68) describe performance as a condition precedent to recovery: "When the contractual duties of the respective parties to an agreement are supposed to be performed concurrently, neither party can recover [for breach by the other] without a showing that he himself has performed, has a valid excuse for non-performance, or has made an effective tender of performance—that is, has given timely notification to the other party that he is ready, willing, and able to accomplish whatever the agreement may have required of him."

However, they go on to say (p. 81) that when one party repudiates his responsibilities, this can constitute a material breach that will: "clearly justify the others refusal to perform and will entitle the latter party to any provable damages resulting from said breach."

The Rice doctrine, over the years, has given license to the owner and his representatives to impose unfair advantage upon the contractors in the form of delays that are not compensable because of the bar against claims for the damages due to the delay. In the case of *Ross v. United States* (Reference Case 52), the court found that delay was a breach of contract. Although a change order had been given for work involved, the court held that the amount included in the change order did not compensate for the actual cost of the delay, but only for the work, stating: "In this case, [contractor] accepted the $4,000 without prejudice or any claim for increased costs resulting from delays in performance; but, independent of this reservation, we think [contractor] is entitled to recover, because this was a breach of contract."

This approach was reaffirmed in *F. H. McGraw & Co.* v. *United States* (103 F. Supp. 394; 1955) where it took more than 1000 days to construct an addition to a veteran's hospital as compared to the contract time of 400 days. The contracting officer had found that the contractor was not responsible and had issued extensions of time. At least 159 days of the delay was due to an ambiguous partial stop order that was finally rescinded. The court held that the government had delayed the contractor by taking an unreasonably long period of time to issue the change orders stating: "It is settled that the [government] is allowed under the contract only a reasonable time within which to make permitted changes in the specifications, and that the [government] is liable for breach of its contract if it unreasonably delays or disrupts the contractor's work."

In addition to material breach, the courts will find that a prospective breach can be proper cause for discontinuance of activity. Thus, in *J. D. Hedin Construction Co.* v. *United States* (347 F. 2d 235, Ct. Cl.; 1965), when the government sought to require the contractor to do exploratory work on the nature of the subsurface before the government would revise plans for footings, the contractor refused to do so, and ultimately sued for delay damages. The government defended on the grounds that the delay was caused not by its failure to revise the plans, but rather by the contractor's failure to perform the exploratory work that had been ordered (but which was clearly beyond the scope of the contract). The court rejected the government argument summarily: "The short answer to this . . . is that the (government) could not impose on [the contractor] such a duty without first authorizing a change order or a proceed order assuring [the contractor] compensation for this work which was beyond the scope of the contract."

A contractor is protected only in such situations where he has written assurance, in advance of performing the work, that he will be paid. He is not required to risk financial stability on the possibility that he might be paid for extra work. The contractor often waives this protection without recognizing that he is waiving it. In any case, neither the architect nor the owner can insist that the contractor waive the right to documentation of a change order, either in the form of the actual executed change order, or a proceed order by duly authorized representatives of the owner. Further, such proceed order must be binding upon the owner.

The finding of a breach of contract can open the door to recovery on the part of the contractor of all losses or costs (as the case may be) from the point of breach forward. Once the contract has been breached, the method contained in the contract for making adjustments in compensation is inapplicable. This was the finding in *Merritt-Chapman & Scott Corp. v. United States* (429 F. 2d 431, Ct. Cl.; 1971): "A true breach of contract claim which, by definition is outside of the scope of the contract, is subject to neither equitable adjustment under the contract nor to administrative review or resolution. *Jefferson Construction Co. v. United States*, 392 F. 2d 1006, Ct. Cl.; 1968."

In *George A. Fuller Co. v. United States* (108 Ct. Cl. U.S. 70; 1947) the decision discussed breach due to interference by the owner: "One who, while preventing the other party from carrying out the contract, nevertheless hinders or delays him in doing so, breaches the contract, and is liable for the damage which the injured party has sustained thereby. The Supreme Court so held in *United States v. Smith*, 94 U.S. 214. In this case, it was said 'under such circumstances, the law implies that the work should be done within a reasonable time, and that the United States would not unnecessarily interfere to prevent this.' " This case also introduces the concept of implication of performance in a reasonable time, and avoidance of unnecessary interference.

In the nonfederal environment, an earlier case discussed breach of contract as a means of providing an equitable solution to the no damage clause in a contract. The case was *Selden Breck Construction Co.* v. *Regents of University of Michigan* (274 F. 982, Mich.; 1921). The project was started late and finished late because the university was unable to deliver the site at the time intended. Under the no damage clause, the university sought to avoid responsibility for the delay damages. However, the court held that the contractor's willingness to complete the project after the delayed delivery did not preclude his rights to sue for damages under breach of contract. The decision indicated: "The correct rule is that upon breach of a building contract by the failure of the owner to perform his obligations under such contract, which delays the contractor in completing his work thereunder, the latter is not obliged to abandon such work, but may elect to continue therewith after such breach and, upon performance of the contract on his part, is entitled to recover the damages sustained by him as a result of the delay caused by such owner."

Breach and Progress Payments

One of the principal means of control of a contractor during the course of the construction is by refusal to pay all or part of his requisition for progress payments. Generally, however, the contract includes an agreement to pay for work in place, and in some cases, for stored materials.

The failure to pay may cause actual delay in the progress of the work because it impairs the contractor's ability to finance his work. The breach of payment can end the contract, permitting the contractor to seek all costs following the point of breach, rather than being limited to an evaluation in the terms of the contract.

The court's recognition of failure to make payments as an actual material breach has evolved. In *Wharton & Co.* v. *Winch* (140 N.Y. 287; 1893), the court held that: "the mere failure of the defendant to make punctual payment of an installment due to the provisions of the contract was not such a breach of the entire contract as to permit the plaintiff to refuse to proceed further under it."

This base continued in *Ryan* v. *New York* (159 App. Div. 105, N.Y.; 1913), where the contractor was allowed interest, but not general damages when his payments were delayed. Further, the court stated: "There is no legal ground for awarding plaintiff general damages for any loss occasioned by delay on the part of the City in making its payment to him on contract time. For such delays, legal interest is presumptively sufficient compensation."

However, in *Krotts* v. *Clark Construction Co.* (249 F. 181, Ill.; 1918), the owner refused to pay the contractor his monthly progress estimate, and the court found that the contractor was justified in abandoning the contract and in suing to recover for the breach of the contract.

In *Underground Construction Co.* v. *Sanitary District* (11 N.E. 2d 361, Ill.; 1937), a project was interrupted for ten months because of lack of funding. After sale of bonds issued for the purpose, sufficient funds were available and the work completed. The court held that the payment of $33,000 for the work did not include the cost of delay. The court found that the contractor was not limited to a choice of one of the usual three remedies, but had a right to first suspend the work until his back progress payments were paid, then to sue for special damages due to the delay clause.

In *Shine* v. *Hagemeister* (169 Wisc. 343, 172 N.W; 1919), an architect refused a certificate for payment of a regular requisition because the architect held that a slab failure was the responsibility of the contractor in question. The heating contractor sued to recover the value of the work done. The court held: "The architect clearly attempted to pass upon a matter not submitted to him by the contract. . . . His powers were simply to issue certificates for 'work done and materials furnished upon the premises' . . . that does not include the power to determine that the plaintiff's delay caused the cement floor, which had been laid by another contractor, to heave up. A refusal to award a certificate because of matters entirely outside of the submission is necessarily a mistaken and arbitrary refusal and amounts in law to a fraudulent refusal, even though made in entire good faith." In view of this interpretation, the project manager must take care to operate in complete accord with the limitations of his authority.

Summary

The contractor has the prerogative to select his method of construction, within the limitations of the specifications. Where there is no limitation, he can sue for damages, including delay, if the owner imposes a method of construction upon him.

Unless he has expressly contracted to do the impossible, a contractor may claim impossibility as a defense against delay and can also seek damages for the cost of that delay. Further, the courts have interpreted impossibility to be synonymous with impracticability.

The owner has the right in the usual contract to direct additional work to be accomplished. Usually, there are standard clauses that preclude the recovery of any more than an extension of time as the cost of extra work, beyond payment for the basic quantity of work performed. However, if the owner interferes with the contractor in the completion of work, then there is the basis for the finding of breach of contract which allows the contractor to sue for recovery outside of the contract.

The contractor, in the course of a contract, should be cautious in regard to the manner in which extra or additional work is assigned. It is his responsibility to be sure that the party authorizing the work has the authority to do so. Further, the contractor should be careful to document all delays, as well as changes for the mutual protection of the owner and the contractor.

Chapter Eight · Subcontractors

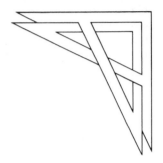

The subcontractor presents a legal paradox. In the aggregate, subcontractors do most of the work on the average construction project. Nevertheless, there is no privity of contract between the owner and the subcontractor; they are legally isolated from one another.

In *Guerini Stone Co.* v. *P. J. Carlin Construction Co.* (240 U.S. 264; 1915), this isolation was noted: "[The] prime contract specifically provided that none of its provisions shall be constituted as creating any contractual relation between the [owner] and any subcontractors . . . and . . . there is no provision in the prime contract which would allow a subcontractor to appear or participate in any way before the [owner] . . . in a dispute which affected it. . . . Indeed, the [owner], as any other owner, may not wish to deal with a subcontractor at all, and we do not criticize this mode of doing business."

Subcontracts range from the very small to the very large. Traditionally, the subcontractor subcontracted to the general contractor. However, in those states in which there must be separate prime contracts under the law, and more recently in the construction management form of contracting, prime contracts for HVAC, plumbing, and electrical can easily exceed the value of the general contract. These larger prime/subcontractors are experienced in working either way, and are experienced in the contractual differences between the two approaches.

Smaller subcontractors, who have traditionally always subcontracted to a prime contractor, may find that the contractual differences in working on a prime contract directly with a construction manager involve substantially different contract administration techniques and requirements. Actually, this type of contract is, in effect, a contract between the owner and the former subcontractor, since the typical construction management contract places the construction manager in the role of "owner's representative."

The Subcontract

In subcontracting, there is a greater opportunity for the prime contractor and subcontractor to have a meeting of the minds, because of the opportunity for negotiation. (In public work, bids are submitted in secret and must be in absolutely proper form to be acceptable; many public corporations follow similar practices as a part of their fiduciary responsibility to their public ownership.) Also, because of the more frequent opportunity to select subcontractors, rather than to have to accept the lowest bidder, prime contractors often have a long-time relationship with their subcontractors. Usually, a prime contractor will accept prices from a limited number of qualified subcontractors with whom he has worked in the past. Thus, reputation and prior working relationships do become factors in the selection process for subcontractors. This tends to limit the risk in the actual working relationship in the field, generating fewer litigation problems. Conversely, there are many more subcontracts than there are prime contracts, so that there is, nevertheless, a substantial number of suits involving subcontracts.

Most prime contractors have developed a standard form of contract that they use as their general conditions, adding any specific or special clauses appropriate to the particular subcontract. These general conditions tend to be carefully drawn, but often the individual subcontract is somewhat loose. Also, subcontracting arrangements can become quite complex.

In *International Erectors* v. *Wilhoit Steel Erectors* (400 F. 2d 465, 5th Cir.; 1968) a prime contractor for the construction of an industrial plant subcontracted the fabrication and erection of the structural steel frame. The subcontractor was Southern Engineering, who fabricated the steel, but sub-subcontracted the erection to Wilhoit. Wilhoit, in turn, sub-sub-subcontracted the erection to International Erectors. Southern did not deliver the steel on time, and International suffered delay damages, and sued Wilhoit. The suit also named Southern as a party.

The court did not find assurances of delivery as part of the contractual obligations that were transferred from party to party. Finding against International, they stated: "Prudence and perhaps foresight might have insisted that a provision creating such an obligation (i.e., guarantee of delivery) be included in the written contract, but the written [contract] expressly and unequivocally negated any such obligation. This was an arms-length transaction between contractors of considerable experience in such matters, and we cannot rewrite the contract just because one of the parties would in retrospection have written it differently."

Incorporation of Prime Contract

It has long been practice to incorporate the construction documents (plans and specifications) into the subcontract, so that the subcontractor is bound by the same scope of work as is the prime contractor. This was the case in the contract between Guerini Stone and P. J. Carlin, in which Guerini was hired to do floor and wall concrete work for a post office on which Carlin was the general contractor. Carlin was slow in supplying materials which delayed Guerini's work. Carlin attempted to avoid liability for a delay damage claim because the prime contract precluded damages for delay. The court refused the defense holding that: "The reference in the subcontract to the drawings and specifications was evidently for the mere purpose of indicating what work was to be done, and in what manner done, by the subcontractor."

However, a more complete incorporation clause is enforceable. Following is a typical subcontract incorporation clause: "Work performed by subcontractor shall be in strict accordance with Contract Documents applicable to the work to be performed and materials, articles and/or equipment to be furnished hereunder. Subcontractors shall be bound by all provisions of these documents and also by applicable provisions of the principal contract to which the Contractor is bound and to the same extent." With this clause, the prime contractor stands in the same position to the subcontractor as the owner does to the prime contractor where applicable.

There are cases, however, where the incorporation cannot completely transpose the roles of the parties. In *Fanderlik-Locke Co.* v. *United States* (Reference Case 22), a general contractor working on an air base construction project attempted to invoke the prime contract dispute clause upon the subcontractor. The court rejected the argument stating: "Language of the subcontract references are to the general conditions of the prime contract, not to the general provisions and they relate generally to performance of the subcontract according to the specifications, not to the settlement of disputes, or the subcontractor's right to sue under the Miller Act."

Further, the court noted that the interpretation of total incorporation would purport to have the general contractor entering into contract on the part of the government, which was beyond his authority. (This would have been an implied contract giving the subcontractor certain rights to have its disputes settled with government administrative procedures in the same manner that the general contractors disputes could be settled; however, in an amiable relationship, the prime contractor often pleads the case of its subcontractor to an owner.)

In *Johnson Inc. v. Basic Construction* (Reference Case 33), general contractor Basic attempted to force subcontractor Johnson to follow the disputes procedure in the prime contract between the owner and Basic. Basic had received a direction to accomplish extra work, and had imposed that same obligation upon Johnson. Johnson brought suit claiming that Basic was obligated to give it a commitment for payment for extra work even though Basic had not received a similar commitment from the owner for the same work. Johnson argued that it was justified in abandoning its work and in being compensated for the work it had performed. Basic argued that it did not have such an obligation because Johnson was bound to the same terms and conditions of the prime contract as was Basic. The court disagreed and found that the disputes clause was incorporated into the contract only insofar as it was applicable to the work performed, and that the clause, by its terms, did not extend to require an adherence by a subcontractor to an administrative remedy designed to be used only by the parties to the prime contract. This limited application is explained by the fact that the incorporation clause made no mention of binding the subcontractors to the general contract provisions containing the disputes clause, to the same extent that the prime contractor was bound. Accordingly, on the basis of a loosely worded clause, the court refused to force the contractor to relinquish a common-law right to abandon the work. However, if the incorporation clause had been more specific, the subcontractor would have been required to respond to the procedures agreed to by the prime contractor. (In the *Johnson Inc. v. Basic Construction* case, the incorporation of the prime contract, however, would not have been presumed to have been a waiver of Johnson's statutory right to sue Basic, unless such right was specifically waived in the contract.)

Coordination

In *Public Construction Contracts and the Law* (p.234) Cohen cites *Norcross* v. *Wills* (198 N.Y. 336; 1910) and states: "A general contractor is obligated to his subcontractor to make good all losses caused by delay in the work not attributable to the subcontractor. The basis of the rule is that the general contractor, in control of the work, might have prevented the delay. As long as he expects the subcontractor to fulfill his obligations, he has corresponding obligation, whether express or implied, to make good any losses of the subcontractor, unless the contract expressly exempts him or permits an intention by inference that the responsibility is not his." An owner who performs as the general contractor (by using the construction management form of contracting) or who is legally constituted to be the general or coordinating owner, as in the case of separate prime contract legislation, has similar responsibilities.

The no damages for delay exculpatory clauses are broad-based attempts to avoid responsibility for coordination by evading responsibility for the natural result of lack of coordination. These clauses, at best, provide limited protection. In *General Building Contractors* v. *County of Oneida* (Reference Case 27), the attempt of the county to transfer its coordinating responsibility to one of the prime contractors was held to be in violation of the state legislation. Similarly, in *Forest Electric Corp.* v. *State* (Reference 24), the responsibility of the state to coordinate work was reaffirmed.

In proving the impact of poor coordination, the subcontractor must clearly demonstrate that any delay for which damage is claimed was due to this specific lack of coordination. Thus, in *Lichter* v. *Mellon-Stuart Co.* (Reference Case 36), a masonry subcontractor was able to demonstrate that a general contractor had caused delays through poor coordination. Testimony clearly demonstrated this poor coordination. The mason's workmen were required to perform an average of thirteen separate operations on each floor of a ten-story structure where normal procedure would have involved not more than two or three operations per floor. Further, the subcontractor had to perform in a piecemeal, haphazard, and disorderly manner, because the building was not ready for the masonry work. The court did not disagree with this contention, but also found that work had been delayed by a number of other factors including delays by other trades, strikes, and change orders. The manner in which the delay claim was prepared did not separate these other causes from the coordination clause, and on this basis, the court refused to award damages.

Similarly, in *United States v. Citizen's & Southern National Bank of Atlanta* (Reference Case 58), a plastering subcontractor alleged that the general contractor failed to coordinate the progress of the work with that of other subcontractors. A lower court awarded damages, but this award was reversed because a substantial amount of the additional costs proved by the contractor, and claimed to be caused by the general contractor, could be attributed to factors for which the general contractor was not responsible.

Interference by Prime Contractor

Just as interference on the part of the owner is the basis for delay claims, so can interference on the part of the prime contractor be the basis for a claim by the subcontractor.

In *Johnson and Lang Bridge Construction Co. v. DeFelite & Son Inc.* (67 Latk. Jur. 96, CP; 1966), Lang was to construct bridges on a highway project for which DeFelite was the general contractor. The contract stated: "The subcontractor shall not be entitled to present any claims . . . for additional compensation for any disputed work unless the subcontractor shall have given to the contractor . . . notice of its intentions to present such . . . claims." Despite subcontractor's failure to give notice, its claim for delay damages was upheld for those delays that were deemed to constitute active interference by the contractor.

In *Manhattan Fireproofing Co. v. Thatcher & Sons* (38 F. Supp. 749; E. D. N. Y.; 1941), the plaintiff was a concrete subcontractor who had been promised by the general contractor that the site would be delivered in such a manner and in such a time so that the subcontractor's work could be done in one continuous operation, to be completed by a specified date. The subcontractor was hindered and delayed and allowed to work only spasmodically. The court imposed the responsibility on the general contractor concluding: "The delay occasioned by the defendant retarded and hindered both the progress of the work and the time within which the plaintiff was able to finish its job. The plaintiff was able to do his work piecemeal at best."

Similarly, in *Mullinax Engineering Co. v. Platte Valley Construction Co.* (Reference Case 43), Mullinax Engineering had been hired by the defendant general contractor to do paving work on a highway. The general contractor had the responsibility for preceding grading and excavation to be completed before the paving company could begin its operation. The subcontractor was directed to begin work as soon as the general contractor had a sufficient amount of work ready so that the operations would not be delayed. After commencing work, upon direction, Mullinax Engineering was delayed eighteen days by suspension of the grading work by the general contractor. The court found for the subcontractor stating: "Where a prime contractor fails to prepare the premises in a state of readiness so that the subcontractor can proceed with the work . . . the prime contractor is liable for the damages caused by the delay."

In *Johnson v. Fenestra Inc.* (Reference Case 34), the subcontractor for erection of curtainwall panels was delayed by late delivery. The court found for the subcontractor on the basis that the contract had given the subcontractor assurance that the prime contractor would perform his obligation to supply panels in a manner consistent with the understanding in the contract that there was to be a prompt beginning and early completion of the installation.

In *Henry Shenk v. Erie Co.* (319 Pa. 100; 1935), the court stated a two-fold test for interference. The court stated that as a general rule to positive acts, they must "materially interfere with the forwardness of the work" or in the case of a negative action, the impact must be upon "something essential."

Even where interference can be proven, however, the language of the subcontract may preclude recovery. In *Carroll Electric v. Irwin & Leighton* (Reference Case 11), a subcontractor in the performance of electrical work on a tunnel construction project was delayed by the performance of the general contractor. The subcontract had indicated "time is and shall be considered as of the essence of the contract on the part of the subcontractor." The subcontractor sued for increased cost of performance due to delays sustained by the general contractor's failure to complete prerequisite work in time. The court held that the "time of essence" clause related only to the subcontractor, and did not have a similar effect upon the general contractor. The court found that with the words added "on the part of the subcontractor" it was evident that the general expression was to be limited to one party.

Unforeseen Circumstances

Delays for unforeseen circumstances are evaluated in the same manner for subcontractors as for prime contractors. It is not unusual, however, for a subcontractor to expect empathy to their problems, since they are subcontractor to a prime who is also in the business, and exposed to similar risks.

In *Moore v. Whitty* (Reference Case 42), Moore was a subcontractor for the installation of bathroom fixtures in two buildings under construction by Whitty. The subcontract had originally required union labor, but after negotiations, Whitty agreed to delete that provision. When the Moore nonunion crews attempted to perform their work there was a labor dispute. Whitty terminated the subcontract on the grounds that this was an unforeseen circumstance. The court disagreed with the defense, since both parties to the contract had been fully informed of the circumstances, and mutually agreed to omit the clause requiring employment of union workmen.

In *Luria Engineering Co. v. Aetna Casualty* (Reference Case 37), a roofing subcontractor for Luria refused to perform after a long delay due to labor difficulties. The subcontractor demanded increased compensation because of escalation during the labor delay period. Luria hired a new roofing subcontractor, and sued the subcontractor's surety (Aetna) for increased cost due to the failure of the original subcontractor to perform. In this case, the court found that it was the subcontractor's duty to perform because "acts of a third party making performance impossible or causing a delay resulting in substantial increase and expense . . . do not excuse failure to perform if such acts were foreseeable." The court decision followed a rationale that a contingency, if foreseeable, must be covered by the contract, or its occurrence will not excuse nonperformance.

Breach of Contract

The principal control that a prime contractor has upon a subcontractor is control of his payments for work accomplished. It is not unusual for the subcontract to contain a clause that states that the subcontractor will get paid after the prime contractor is paid. (A clause of this type would have precluded a suit such as that instituted by *Johnson v. Basic Construction*, Reference Case 33.)

In *Public Construction Contracts and the Law* (p. 239), Cohen states: "It is clear from the following decisions, too, that the party who claims the contract has been breached or broken by the other party has the option to sue for the price of the contract or to claim the reasonable value of his work." (Citations: *Schwasnick v. Blandin*, 65 F. 2d. 354, Vt.; 1933; *United States v. Behan*, 110 U.S. 338, La.; 1884; *Bucholz v. Green Bros. Co.*, 172 N.E. 101, Mass.; 1930).

In a more recent case, *Arc Electric Construction Co. Inc. v. George A. Fuller Co., Inc.* (Reference Case 2), Arc was the electrical subcontractor for the construction of a sugar refinery.

Their prime contractor was George A. Fuller, who terminated Arc at the instruction of the architect. The contract between Arc and Fuller provided for two methods of computing payments for progress. The first method provided for regular monthly progress payments constituting 90 percent of the amount due Arc, conversely with 10 percent to be withheld pending completion of the project. Under this approach, the requisition had to be approved by the architect. A second method of payment was set forth in the article that gave Fuller the right to terminate the contract at any time prior to completion.

Arc had received eight approved requisitions totaling $1.4 million when the architect refused to approve an Arc requisition. This refusal was despite approval by Fuller's project engineer. After this incident, four more requisitions were submitted, all of which lacked an approved requisition by the architect—and none were paid by Fuller. Fuller, apparently under orders by the architect, terminated Arc. They then proceeded to attempt to refuse payment for the work accomplished. Fuller asserted "there is nothing to indicate that the mere passage of time would transform a bad claim into a good one." However, it was clear from evidence submitted that there were no defects in Arc's performance, at least none that could be shown in an evidential process.

The court stated: "It is well established that, where work has, in fact, been substantially performed in accordance with the provisions of a contract, the withholding of approval does not bar recovery." The court agreed that progress payments could be withheld, almost at the architect's whim. However, when Arc was terminated, existing provisions of the contract came into play. These provisions provide that a contractor shall be paid for work accomplished at the time of termination. Failure to approve requisitions by the architect had no impact upon the operation of the contract at the time of termination. The court also noted that failure to issue a certificate would not necessarily have resulted in failure to pay Arc, if the contract had continued. Quoting Nolan v. Whitney, the court stated: "When [the contractor] had substantially performed his contract, the architect was bound to give him the certificate, and his refusal to give it was unreasonable, and it is held that an unreasonable refusal on the part of an architect in such a case to give the certificate dispenses with its necessity."

Summary

The role of the subcontractor is an anomaly. While he has no contract with the owner, he performs most of the work for the owner. His prime contractor, who certainly should be sympathetic to his problems, often acts as though he were an uninformed owner—rather than an experienced fellow contractor. In turn, the subcontractor often demands a level of understanding from the prime contractor that the prime contractor, himself, would be very reluctant to attempt to impose upon an owner. The relationship between prime contractor and subcontractor is often relatively informal—at least until litigation occurs.

Part II·Litigation

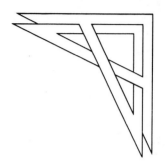

Chapter Nine · Litigation: The Process Pretrial

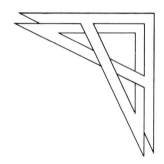

Litigation is not an automatic process. Specific actions must be undertaken by the party desiring to institute suit. During the life of a project, the contractor has limited opportunity to terminate or abandon the work. Although it is the contractor's common law right to abandon the work in the face of certain compelling situations, most construction contracts include a completion bond—which then puts the contractor's surety in the position of completing the work. A construction firm that plans to stay in business cannot afford to deliberately trigger a default, since this would be a negative influence on his ability to get a bond in the future from this surety, or from any other.

If the contractor does default by abandoning the work during the process of the project, the contract is breached, and the owner looks to the surety to finish. If the relationship between the surety and the contractor remains amiable, which is often the case where the contractor had no choice but to default, as in cases of bankruptcy, the surety will often reassign the work to the contractor (or in the case of a joint venture to the most stable member of the team).

Recognizing this proclivity for reassignment of the same contractor, many owners are reluctant to actually default the contractor—even when he is performing poorly. The owner may, in concert with his default action, attempt to preclude the return of the bonded contractor to the job.

In 1975, King County, Washington, owner of Seattle's $40 million dome stadium, terminated the major contract which was with the D. M. Drake Co. of Portland, Oregon. The owner instituted a suit claiming that Drake had "breached and repudiated" its contract by stopping work during a dispute regarding the ability of the workers to lower and reposition a steel truss supporting forms used in casting the large diameter thin shell dome.

The suit, which also named the sureties for Drake as codefendants, for "wrongfully refusing to honor their bonds and accept responsibility for completion of construction," alleged that Drake failed to "cooperate with the County and its design team; . . . to maintain an appropriate rate of progress during construction; . . . to furnish information required by the County and its design team; . . . to properly manage and execute the work; and . . . to follow specified procedures for resolution of contract question." Drake instituted a countersuit for $10 million claiming "multiple changes and interferences" on the part of the county. In this action, King County was then free to proceed with the work, after both the general contractor and his sureties refused to undertake completion.

Default during the construction period is not a common occurrence, since the legal arrangements and remobilization of the job with another contractor involve substantial delays. Most owners would prefer to accept the situation until substantial completion, and then seek damages through litigation.

In New York City's Department of Public Works, under the standard construction contract, Article 45, the commissioner of the Department of Public Works has the right to declare the contractor in default of the whole or any part of the work if:

1. The contractor fails to begin work when notified to do so by the commissioner; or if
2. The contractor abandons the work; or if
3. The contractor refuses to proceed with the work when and as directed by the commissioner; or if
4. The contractor without just cause reduces his working force to a number which, if maintained, would be insufficient, in the opinion of the commissioner, to complete the work in accordance with the approved progress schedule, and fails or refuses sufficiently to increase such working force when ordered to do so by the commissioner; or if
5. The commissioner believes that the contractor is or has been unnecessarily or unreasonably or willfully delaying the performance and completion of the work, or the award of necessary subcontracts, or the placing of necessary material and equipment orders; or if
6. The commissioner believes that the contractor is willfully or in bad faith violating any of the provisions of this contract; or if

7. The commissioner believes that the contractor is not executing the contract in good faith and in accordance with its terms; or if
8. The commissioner believes that the work cannot be completed within the time provided or within the time to which such completion may have been extended, provided that the impossibility of timely completion is, in the commissioner's opinion, attributable to conditions within the contractor's control; or if
9. The work is not completed within the time provided or within the time to which the contractor may be entitled to have such completion extended.

The procedures in New York City for commencing default action involve three specific steps:

1. Field order from resident engineer to contractor (Figure 1).
2. Second warning to contractor from director, building construction (Figure 2).
3. Notice from corporation counsel to contractor to appear at a default hearing.

Contracts by the State of New Jersey include a provision for a three-day notice prior to institution of default proceedings. Figure 3 is a sample letter of the format and type of information that should be in this type of notice. One of the purposes of the notice letter is the opportunity for the surety for the contractor to be advised of an acute problem area, with the hope that they will encourage better performance on the part of their client.

Default notice and default hearings are very serious business. They should not be utilized as a solution to minor problems. Further, the owner should be well prepared with good documentation of the problems and be ready to prove allegations at the default hearing. The owner should also anticipate that the bonding company is very much on the side of its client contractor, and will often assist him with legal specialists in the field. In fact, if the owner and his representatives are poorly prepared, it often becomes difficult to identify the defaulter and the defaultee in this hearing process.

If liquidated damages have been specified in the contract, the owner has a very potent means of capturing the interest of the contractor in projects where there is substantial delay. The owner has the prerogative of assessing the liquidated damages and deducting them from either the retained funds, the final requisition or both. The contractor, if he hopes to regain all or part of the liquidated damages is almost forced into litigation.

The owner, if he anticipates litigation, can retain as a reserve against damages that portion of the retainage on the contract

```
                S A M P L E - (Please copy and fill in blanks)
                           FIELD ORDER
To:                 (Contractor)

From:               (Resident Engineer)

Project No.

Date:

            Re:   Default Proceedings or Liquidated Damages
```

Please be advised that <u>REASON*</u> (copy one of enumerated reasons for being held in default or for which liquidated damages may be assessed).

We call your attention to Article 45 of Chapter X and Article 16 of Chapter III of your contract, which proved that this is one of several clauses for your being held in default or for which liquidated damages may be assessed against you.

If a satisfactory explanation is not received from you within ten (10) calendar days with respect to this item, the necessary steps will be instituted to protect the best interests of the City of New York.

```
                                 _____
                                 Resident Engineer
```

Copy to   Director of Building Construction
            Department of Public Works

Copy of the above should be kept by Resident Engineer and a notation made of date of receipt by Contractor (return receipt of certified mail)

If satisfactory explanation is not received within ten (10) calendar days, Resident Engineer should send copy to Director of Building Construction with comments.

*Example: you have without just cause reduced the working force (finish in full)

Figure 1

S A M P L E --- Director's Notice to Contractor

To: (Contractor)

From: Director, Building Construction

Project No.

Date:

    Re: Default Proceeding
          Second Warning to Contractor

On_____, you received a Field Order
stating grounds that may cause you to be held in default. You
have not responded with a satisfactory explanation to that Field
Order.

Unless a satisfactory explanation is received from you within
ten (10) calendar days, a recommendation will be made to the
Commissioner of Public Works to initiate proceedings to declare
you in default.

                                _____

                                Director, Building Construction
                                Department of Public Works
                                Municipal Service Administration

Figure 2

CERTIFIED MAIL

RETURN RECEIPT REQUESTED

XYZ Contracting Co.

RE: Project 123

Gentlemen:

By letter you were advised of the State's intention of imple-
menting General Conditions clause 20-A regarding Liquidated
Damages if the electrical work is not completed by contract date.
In addition to any liquidated damages, your firm will be assessed
all other costs including overtime, etc. by other trades that are
directly related to your lack of performance.

Job records indicate your reluctance to increase personnel on the
job. The lack of personnel has and is interfering with completion
of the work of other trades, especially in mechanical equipment
areas.

This letter is to be considered as your 3-day notice to increase
job manpower or face addition to liquidated and other damages,
removal from the State's bidding lists.

This project is a critically needed building and further procrastination will not be countenanced.

Very truly yours,

Director

AWW:pas

cc: Architects
    Bonding Co.
    Construction Manager

Figure 3

that would potentially represent payment of damages. (It is quite usual for the owner's suit to specify at least the amount of the retainage, so that the entire figure is held.)

Some owners, as a matter of policy, will not settle requests for time extension until the actual completion of the project. New York City is one with such a policy. A contractor requesting substantial completion payment must have completed on time, or must obtain the city's agreement to an extension of the contract time. (In the absence of a full-time extension for the period of delay, the city may assess liquidated damages for a portion. It is policy for a contractor to have a hearing with the commissioner of DPW or the appropriate department, prior to such assessment.)

The comptroller of New York City, the executive departments involved, and the City Construction Board have agreed upon a series of forms that contractors must submit if they have completed beyond the contract date and are requesting either partial or final payment. The following explanation of the forms is taken from a directive issued by the Office of the Director of Construction of New York City; stating the guidelines to be followed when the contractor requests payment after the time fixed in the contract:

1. The contractor will request a limited extension based on his estimate of time required beyond the time fixed in the contract to complete the job.
2. The request shall be approved in whole or in part by the commissioner or his authorized representative.
3. Where a contract extension is required for a final or substantial completion of payment, the request must be processed through the Board of Extension of Contract Time according to current practice.

The Board of Extension of Contract Time, in the Office of the Comptroller, issued a series of forms to be used by the contractor in submitting such requests:

1. Form A (Figure 4) is to be used by the contractor seeking extension of contract time where the contractor has no claims and makes no reservations.
2. Form B (Figure 5) is to be used where a contractor seeks an extension of time for the purpose of receiving a partial payment and the contractor seeks to reserve certain claims.
3. Form C (Figure 6) is to be used where a contractor seeks an extension of contract time and request is made for a final payment, and the contractor is making claims under the terms of the contract.

```
                            FORM "A"

SUBMIT 4 COPIES ON YOUR LETTERHEAD - ALL COPIES TO BE PROPERLY ACKNOWLEDGED
      AND HAVE CORPORATE SEAL AFFIXED, IF SAME IS REQUIRED.

              (Specimen letter wherein no claims are involved
                and extension of time is 60 days or more)

                                   Date:......................

Hon.

                         Re:  Extension of Contract Time
                              Project
                              Contract
                              Contract Reg. No.

Sir:

We hereby request an extension of contract time on the above contract

from.................................to..........................

a total of ..........................calendar days.

This application for an extension of time is based on the following:
                    (State reasons for the delay)

In consideration of the granting, for the purpose of expediting payment,
by the Board of Extension of Contract Time, of an extension of contract
time fixed in Contract No. ...........for completion of work therein
specified, we agree to and hereby waive and release all claims including,
but not limited to, damages for delay or any other cause whatsoever which
we may have against The City of New York, in connection with the afore-
said contract.

It is understood that the City of New York does not, if the extension of
time is granted, waive or release any claim it may have against the
contractor whether it be for actual or liquidated damages for any
reason whatsoever.

                         Very truly yours,
                         Firm Name

                         (Signature of Contractor)

                                     Title

(Use appropriate form of Acknowledgement: Corporate, Individual or
Partnership)

NOTE:  If a Corporation, Corporate Seal must be affixed.
```

Figure 4

FORM "B"

SUBMIT 4 COPIES ON YOUR LETTERHEAD - ALL COPIES TO BE PROPERLY ACKNOWLEDGED
AND HAVE <u>CORPORATE SEAL AFFIXED</u>, IS SAME IS REQUIRED
(Specimen letter wherein no claims are immediately
involved but are anticipated)

Date...............................

Re: Extension of Contract Time
Project
Contract
Contract Reg. No.

Sir:

We hereby request an extension of contract time on the above contract
from.........................to....................................
a total of ....calendar days.

This application for an extension of time is based on the following:

(State Reason for the delay)

In consideration of the granting, for the purpose of expediting
payment, by the ....of an extension of contract time
fixed in Contract No. ....for completion of the work
therein specified, we agree to and hereby waive and release all claims
which we may have against the City of New York, arising out of the
aforesaid contract, except for the following: delay caused by change of
design; delay caused by failure to give site; or the granting of change
orders, (The contractor may give any other reasons he may have).

I, or we, will at the time of request for an extension of time for
a substantial or final payment, prepare and furnish a verified itemized
statement of claims in accordance with the terms of the contract.

"In connection with the application for extension of contract time
for performance of Contract No. ...., we agree that neither the
fact of the granting of the application for the extension of time, the
papers or records on which it is granted, nor the application itself,
shall be referred to or offered in evidence by the undersigned or their
attorneys in any action or proceeding between them and the City; the
granting of such extension of time shall not be asserted or claimed by us
or our attorneys to be, or to be any evidence of, any admission on the part
of the City that any of the facts stated in said application for extension
of time are true, or as constituting any evidence of their truth."

It is understood that the City of New York does not, if the
application for an extension of time should be granted, waive or release
any claim it may have against the Contractor whether it be for actual or
liquidated damages for any reason whatsoever.

Very truly yours,

(Signature of Contractor)

(Use appropriate form of acknowledgement; Corporate, Individual or
Partnership)

NOTE: IF A CORPORATION, CORPORATE SEAL MUST BE AFFIXED.

Figure 5

```
                         FORM "C"


SUBMIT 5 COPIES ON YOUR LETTERHEAD - ALL COPIES TO BE PROPERLY ACKNOWLEDGED
        AND HAVE CORPORATE SEAL AFFIXED, IS SAME IS REQUIRED.
        (Specimen letter for extension of time wherein
               claims are reserved)
                              Date ......................
                     Re:   Extension of Contract Time
                           Project
                           Contract
                           Contract Registration No.

Sir:

We hereby request an extension of contract time for the above contract
from.....................................to........................,
a total of ....................consecutive calendar days.

This application for an extension of time is based on the following:

                (State reasons for the delay)

Attached hereto is a Bill of Particulars setting forth claims which we
intend to assert under the terms of the Contract.

In consideration of the granting, for the purpose of expediting payment,
by the Board for Extension of Contract Time, of an extension of contract
time fixed in Contract No. ................for the completion of work
therein specified, we sgree to and do hereby waive and release any and
all claims which we may have against the City of New York, in connection
with the aforesaid contract, except the items of claim which are hereby
reserved and are set forth in the annexed Bill of Particulars.

It is understood that the City of New York does not, if the extension of
time is granted, waive or release any claim it may have against the
contractor whether it be for actual or liquidated damages for any
reason whatsoever.
                         Very truly yours,



                         (Name of Firm or Corporation)


          (Signed)       _____
                         (Signature of Contractor)

(Use appropriate form of Acknowledgement:  Corporate, individual or
Partnership)

NOTE:  If a corporation, Corporate Seal must be affixed.
```

Figure 6

The contractors are also required to submit a Bill of Particulars (Figure 7) with the form letters when submitting for partial payment, but Bill of Particulars is not required for substantial completion payment.

Note that the city reserves the right to institute actual or liquidated damages even though the time extension is granted. It was this type of form letter that the contractor signed, and thereby waived his rights to claim in the case of *Egan v. City of New York* (Reference Case 21).

The forms as developed by the city protect the city, and may well prejudice the rights of the contractor. In substituting for the form, however, the contractor must take care that he meets the requirements of the contract. Thus, in *Brandt Corp. v. City of New York* (Reference Case 9), the contractor signed the standard release in his request for final substantial payment. He claimed that he had previously reserved certain claims. The court, however, found against the contractor because he did not assert the claims at the time of request of final payment.

Administrative Review

Many contracts include requirements for review by the owner or his representative. Chapter 5, "The Architect and Engineer in the Field," discusses the role of the design professional as an arbiter and interpreter in the field. While his authority is based on his professional role, as well as the contract, many of the areas upon which he renders decisions are more administrative than related to the physical configuration.

Most contracts, in one form or another, assign a contracting officer. This may be an individual who is part of the owner's staff, one of the professional team, or the construction manager. His limits of authority, particularly in the area of changes to the work, are defined by the contract. Most contracts have some form of a disputes clause similar to Clause 6 in the Standard Federal Construction Contract Form 23 which reads as follows:

Except as otherwise provided in this contract, any dispute concerning a question of fact arising under this contract which is not disposed of by agreement shall be decided by the Contracting Officer, who shall reduce his decision to writing and mail or otherwise furnish a copy thereof to the Contractor. Within 30 days from the date of receipt of such copy, the Contractor may appeal by mailing or otherwise furnishing to the Contracting Officer a written appeal addressed to the head of the Department and the decision of the head of the Department

BILL OF PARTICULARS

1) Complete breakdown of claims.

2) Dates and listing of bills and subs' bills.

3) Separate categories of claims - Extra work, delay, etc.

In connection with the application for extension of contract time for performance of Contract No.   we agree that neither the fact of the granting of the application for the extension of time, the papers or records on which it is granted, nor the application itself, shall be referred to or offered in evidence by the under-signed or their attorneys in any action or proceeding between them and the City; the granting of such extension of time shall not be asserted or claimed by us or our attorneys to be, or to be any evidence of, any admission on the part of the City that any of the facts stated in said application for extension of time are true, or as constituting any evidence of their truth.

We hereby represent and warrant, in consideration of the Board for Extension of Contract Time considering our application for an extension of time, that we have no other claims arising out of the contract; other than those stated in this sworn statement, and we further represent and warrant we will not assert any other claims against the City of New York in connection with this contract.

Very truly yours,

(Name of Firm or Corporation)

(Signed)   _____
                        (Title)

(Proper acknowledgment)

NOTE: If a corporation, use Corporate Seal

Figure 7

or his duly authorized representatives for the hearings of such appeals shall, unless determined by a court of competent jurisdiction to have been fraudulent, arbitrary, capricious, or so grossly erroneous as necessarily to imply bad faith, be final and conclusive: provided, that, if no such appeal to the head of the Department is taken, the decision of the Contracting Officer shall be final and conclusive. In connection with any appeal proceeding under this clause, the Contractor shall be afforded an opportunity to be heard and to offer evidence in support of its appeal. Pending final decision of a dispute hereunder, the Contractor shall proceed diligently with the performance of the contract, and in accordance with the Contracting Officer's decision.

Over the years, many appeals to the courts were attempted. A number of these reached the Supreme Court. One of the most famous is *United States v. Wunderlich* (342 U.S. 98, 1951). The contractor had appealed to the appropriate department head, the Secretary of the Interior. When that appeal was refused, the contractor brought suit against the United States in the federal court of claims. The court of claims agreed with the facts and law as stated by the contractor and reversed the decision of the Secretary of the Interior. On appeal to the United States Supreme Court, the court of claims decision was reversed.

In 1954, Congress passed legislation to permit judicial review of administrative decisions. This legislation is now described in Chapter 5, Title 1 of the United States Code.

Judicial Structure

The judicial systems in the United States are divided basically into the two major areas of sovereignty under the Constitution: federal and the individual states. While the states may delegate certain judicial powers to the local government, these courts handle minor areas and misdemeanors, and would not normally handle delay matters.

In the federal system, most contracts for construction directly involving the federal government include the standard disputes clause, and litigation must be entered in the U. S. Court of Claims, with the review by the Supreme Court if appropriate. However, many cases involving construction are heard in the federal court system, because federal courts have jurisdiction over civil actions between citizens of different states (where the amount in question exceeds $10,000.)

The basic trial court for suits in the federal system is the district court, which is presided over by a district court judge.

A case may be heard in front of the judge alone, or in certain situations, a jury trial can be requested. It is quite usual in involved litigation for the presiding judge to urge that the parties forego the jury trial with a view toward expediting the proceedings.

Decisions by the federal district courts may be appealed to the circuit court of appeals with jurisdiction. There are eleven separate circuit courts of appeal in the United States. The next court of appeal is the U.S. Supreme Court, which usually hears only cases that it feels are significant in terms of national interest, or where a conflict between rules of different federal courts is involved. Appointment to the bench for federal court judges is by the executive branch (the President) with confirmation by the Senate. Appointments are lifetime.

The state judicial systems vary considerably. The basic trial court may be called the district, circuit, or superior court, depending upon the state. The presiding judge may either be elected or appointed by the governor of the state.

There may be a jury for certain categories of suits. Again, the judge will often encourage the parties to forego the layman jury option. In some states, such as the Commonwealth of Virginia, the laws permit the use of a professional jury, often a three-man jury. Each party has the prerogative of appointing one professional member, with the court and the parties agreeing on a neutral third member. The juries are experienced in the specific matter to be covered, and are compensated at appropriate professional fees by the parties. (Reference Case 47 was heard before this type of jury).

There is usually at least one appeal court above the basic court, usually known as the appellate court. In those states not having an appellate court, the decision of the basic trial court can be reviewed by the state supreme court.

Formal Litigation

The first step in the actual litigation is the preparation of a complaint and service of that complaint upon the defendant. The complaint is also filed with the court having appropriate jurisdiction. (In some cases, the plaintiff has an option of courts, and obviously selects the one that provides the best opportunity for presentation of his case in the most favorable circumstance.)

Once served, the defendant has a specified amount of time to respond. His response may assert that the complaint is incorrect in its factual statements, or that the defendant has legal defense, even when the allegations in the complaint are true. Some states permit the defendant to present a claim that the complaint is legally insufficient by filing a demurrer. In addition to responding to the complaint, the defendant may undertake action against a third party or parties. For instance, a general contractor when served a complaint by a subcontractor may file a cross-complaint against the owner. The owner, in turn, if he believes the complaint to have merit, may undertake a complaint against, for instance, his designer.

In deciding which court has jurisdiction, counsel has to anticipate the possibility of interstate situations, not only in the original complaint, but also in the resulting answers and cross-complaints. This can have a relevance to the ability of a court to combine the various actions, so that one trial can hear all of the factors. The problem in combining actions is not only in the jurisdictional aspects, but also must be concerned with the privity of contract between the parties. (For instance, the subcontractor has no direct legal linkage with the owner, and the general contractor has none with the designer —yet these parties may have had interactions that resulted in delays or other problems in the course of the contract.)

Filing of the suit must be undertaken within a specified time period. State law usually specifies a statute of limitations regarding contracts that would apply to the time frame within which litigation would have to be initiated to recover damages for delay. The statute of limitations may start either when an act, such as specific delay, occurs or from the time when the plaintiff became aware that he had suffered a loss. Thus, in a delay claim, the statute of limitations might start running from either the initiation of the delay or from substantial completion, at which time the dimensions of the delay would be known. In construction delay, the statute of limitations would usually start to run when the contract has been substantially completed, or formally completed as evidenced by final payment.

The time frame varies between the states, but is usually in the range of two to five years. Once suit is filed, the litigation is permitted to continue. It is clearly important for a party to a construction contract to undertake a suit promptly, or a valid claim may be forfeited.

The law also recognizes the concept of laches, which is unreasonable delay in seeking damages. In *Halcon International Inc. v. Monsanto Australia Ltd.* (446 F. 2d 156), Monsanto demanded arbitration in accordance with the arbitration clause of the contract between the parties which was written in 1962. The date of the demand was 1969, approximately four years after Monsanto had taken over operations of the facility in question. Halcon filed an answer to the petition to the Federal District Court requesting an order to proceed with arbitration. In that answer, Halcon included an affirmative defense based upon laches. Halcon indicated that a number of factors made it difficult to defend the Monsanto claims because of the time period intervening.

The district court determined that it had jurisdiction and ordered Halcon to proceed with the arbitration. The district court did not adjudicate the laches defense, but stated that the arbitration panel should determine its merits. This finding by the district court was affirmed by the appeals court. However, the chief judge of the court dissented stating: "Laches, like fraud, constitute a defense for the invocation of an agreement to arbitrate. . . ."

One purpose of the complaint (or pleading) is to state the contentions of the plaintiff including the specific remedy sought through the courts.

There are two substantially different schools of thought on the preparation and content of the pleading. The forthright school (probably the minority) attempts to prepare a complete and factual complaint, which is specific. This complaint requires candor on the part of the plaintiff and his counsel. It presents the issues, and is clear to both the court and the opposition. Preparation of this type of complaint requires an investment in time for the development of the case before the pleading.

Another approach to the preparation of a complaint is one in which less preparation time is required. In this complaint, charges, contentions, and statements are made which are claimed to be factual, but which the plaintiff is not necessarily prepared to prove. Further, the complaint pleads a variety of legal approaches sufficient to cover all possibilities. Damages are claimed at the maximum range. This approach permits a maximum of flexibility in pre-trial negotiations toward settlement, and if settlement is not reached—then maximum flexibility in the presentation of the case.

Unfortunately, to the lay parties involved, the broad-based approach to preparation of a complaint can alienate the parties creating polarization in position. This can be counterproductive to settlement. The optimum approach to the preparation of a complaint is, doubtless, somewhere between the two extreme approaches.

Pretrial Preparation

The time period between the initial pleading and the trial varies considerably, dependent principally upon the case load of the court in which the suit has been filed, and the various maneuvers of the parties. The plaintiff, who seeks to recover, is usually the better prepared and the more aggressive in terms of moving the process forward. The defense, unless they happen to have a strong countersuit or counterclaim, are in a position where they can tie or lose—so they are in no great hurry to come to trial.

The process of developing the case includes a specific legal process known as "discovery." It is a mutual process, and each party has a number of processes through which they can request additional information on the other party's case. One such method included in discovery is the "interrogatory." This is usually initiated by the defendant to request specific information in regard to the complaint. The complaint is a concise document, while the interrogatory seeks to expand the information regarding the complaint and if possible, to identify the legal nature of the arguments that the plaintiff intends to undertake, although the interrogatories are intended to disclose fact and not to argue the law. The interrogatory is prepared and forwarded via the court to the other party. It must be answered within a reasonable time, or the offending party will face the displeasure of the court.

The response to the interrogatory is under oath. It is prepared in the privacy of the plaintiff's offices, and with the assistance of his counsel. In fact, usually the party provides information, which is then developed into the answer by legal counsel. The answers to the interrogatories must be careful, truthful, and complete. However, there is considerable latitude in the nature of the response. In areas where the respondant is not certain of an answer, his answer can be general—but it must not be incorrect. Usually, the response to the first interrogatories leads to a second, and even a third, round of interrogatories and responses. The process cannot be prolonged too much, or the court will question the productivity of the time investment.

Following the interrogatories, the parties may request the process of deposition. The witnesses are summoned usually by subpoena or court order requiring appearance at a particular time and place. Attorneys for both parties are in attendance, and if the individual giving the deposition is a third party, he is well advised to have legal counsel available. The deposition process may also include the furnishing of records and documentation related to the case. If this type of information is anticipated by counsel preparing the subpoena, he will request a *subpoena duces tecum* which compels the production of documentation under the witness' normal control.

The deposition is taken with a court reporter in attendance, and is subsequently transcribed and furnished to the parties. The counsel conducting the deposition conducts the direct examination, which is under oath. Counsel for the other party can subsequently ask additional questions for the purpose of amplifying or reorienting the impression given by the initial series of questions on direct examination. The examination is a mini-version of the actual trial testimony procedure, but without judge or jury in attendance. The deposition process provides a means of preserving evidence in a legal suit, in the event of either death or inaccessibility of a witness at the time of trial.

The deposition process serves certain other purposes. It provides both counsel with a direct impression of the value of the individual as a witness, both in terms of the type of performance that can be anticipated by the witness in the trial, as well as defining the actual admissible testimony that the witness has. During the trial, if a witness changes his testimony, away from the specific information given during deposition, the deposition can be used as a means of impeaching the credibility of the trial testimony.

In some states, a pretrial conference is a step in the litigation system. This conference is usually conducted in chambers in the presence of the judge, the counsel, and the parties. The purpose is to review the issues stated now through pleadings, interrogatories, and depositions with a view toward reducing the number of issues through stipulation of situations that are obviously irrefutable. Also, certain portions of the complaint may be settled without prejudice to proceeding with the balance.

The interrogatory and deposition procedures can limit the range of the evidenciary process. For instance, if a particular record or document is requested, either in the interrogatory or during the deposition, and cannot be produced, it will probably be precluded as a possible part of the evidence during the trial, unless the circumstances can be clearly documented—and even then the judge may preclude its admission on the basis of its previous unavailability to the other party.

During the pretrial conference, the judge may request that the counsel for each side state his legal argument to support the pleading, as well as the evidence (as supported by the interrogatories and depositions) that he is intended to submit. The judge has great power of persuasion implicit in his position. Thus, if during the pretrial conference, he suggests that certain weak arguments and/or potential evidence would best be dispensed with, counsel affected is well advised to follow that specific suggestion.

In federal court and some states, it is permitted to the court to assign a master of chancery or commissioner to review the case with a view to sorting out noncontested facts. The result can be a narrowing of the matters to be considered, and often recommendations that certain areas be dismissed. For instance, a U. S. district judge postponed the trial date for more than two months in the case of *R. F. Ball Construction Co.* v. *City of Houston* so that a master of chancery could sort out noncontested facts. The plaintiff, Ball Construction Co., entered suit for $8 million claiming it suffered financial losses in the construction of terminals at the New Houston Airport when the city ordered changes in architectural plans, causing a 760-day delay in construction.

In *Werthheimer Construction Corp.* v. *United States* (Reference Case 62) the federal court assigned a trial commissioner to sort out the many facets of the case. He was able to reduce a number of the claim areas alleged by the plaintiff.

Summary

Pretrial preparation is lengthy and expensive in terms of both manpower and money. It is also complex and worthy of a well-defined game plan and schedule. Failure to perform and prepare well in the pretrial stage will almost guarantee failure in the trial, although no amount of preparation can change a bad set of facts into a good one.

Chapter Ten · Litigation Process: Trial or Arbitration

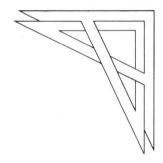

In a jury trial, the judge acts as the enforcer of the courtroom rules of decorum, in accordance with the laws governing the court. He also rules on the law regarding evidence and other legal matters as the trial proceeds. He has the power to cite individuals for contempt of court if they fail to follow his direction. The parties may agree to try the case without a jury, and in many jurisdictions, civil trials do not have a jury. In either case, the judge rules upon both the law and the facts of the case.

In a jury trial, the counsel for the plaintiff usually makes an opening statement in which he states the salient features of the case, including those areas that he is setting out to prove through the development of evidence. In a nonjury trial, the opening statement may be omitted, or will be more brief. The defendant's attorney may be allowed to make an opening statement following that made by the plaintiff's attorney.

Following the opening remarks, the attorney for the plaintiff presents the case. The facts are developed through the questioning of witnesses under oath. Physical evidence and exhibits, including documents, are usually offered in evidence during the questioning of a witness who can validate their authenticity, and correlate them to the case in hand. In civil actions, the other party may be called as a witness by the opposition (since there is no question of incrimination per se).

Immediately following the examination (direct), a counsel for the opposing party (defendant) may cross-examine the witness. This cross-examination is limited to matters that were covered in the direct examination. During cross-examination, the attorney may not open up new areas of evidence. During cross-examination, the attorney will attempt to develop additional information favorable to his view of the case, or may attempt to impeach the credibility of the witness by showing that his statements are contradictory or incorrect.

After the plaintiff's case has been presented, including the cross-examination of witnesses, the defense is given an opportunity to present his view of the case. This is done in a similar manner with the attorney for the defendant calling witnesses and examining them (direct examination) through questioning. Each witness may be cross-examined by the attorney for the plaintiff. Again, questions on cross-examination can relate only to the direct examination immediately preceding. Following cross-examination, the attorney who conducted the direct examination is usually given the opportunity to ask questions in redirect.

After the case for the plaintiff and then the case for the defense have been presented, the plaintiff is given the opportunity to present evidence in rebuttal of the defense case. Following this, the attorney for the plaintiff may make a closing statement, followed by a closing statement by the defense. The plaintiff gets the last opportunity to make concluding remarks in rebuttal to the defense closing statement.

In the jury trial, this is the point at which the judge makes his instructions to the jury. In preparing these instructions, the judge may ask the collaboration of the two counsels with a view towards presenting instructions that will not result in a mistrial or defective verdict. The instructions by the judge are usually quite specific in terms of the questions of fact that the jury should decide upon. He also instructs the jury on the law of the case, and the latitude which they, as finders of fact, have in reaching a verdict.

The jury meets privately to review the cases presented. This review includes discussions until the jurors are ready to attempt ballots. The jury first decides on the findings of fact. Following this, the jury must decide upon the amounts to be awarded to the winning litigant or litigants. (The jury may find for one party on some of the specifications and charges, and for the other on others.)

If the trial is nonjury, then it is usual practice for the judge to request briefs from the opposing counsel. In preparing a brief, the counsel usually prepares a summary of facts as presented in evidence, extracting those that tend to support their view of the case. The brief is a separate document that lists legal arguments for their position, and against the position of the opposition.

The briefs are exchanged at the same time as they are presented to the judge, and both parties have the opportunity to file counterbriefs.

Evidence and Procedures

To the layman, the procedures followed to develop the evidence in a case appear very stilted and time-consuming—and from one point of view, they are. There are proponents of a more narrative form of testimony that, they claim, would permit the facts to be developed more readily, and in a form much more easily understood by the jury, in particular, and even by judges. However, experience indicates that the narrative form permits the introduction of inadmissible evidence or prejudicial information that might not otherwise be allowed into evidence.

In a trial, almost nothing can be assumed. It is a long recognized principle of law that the judge and jury must base their verdict upon evidence that was actually presented, and not on assumptions. Further, if the court recorder misses the information—then, in effect, it doesn't exist. This is particularly a problem if key information is omitted from the record of a case that goes to appeal. In order to expedite the proceedings, the court can take judicial notice of commonly recognized facts. Further, the counsel for the parties can mutually stipulate to any agreed-upon information or facts.

It is the purpose of the court to provide an environment within which the facts of the case can be developed from evidence available. It is an important rule of evidence that hearsay information cannot properly be submitted as evidence. The most common example of hearsay is a witness stating the facts that someone else told him were true, but that he did not personally observe through sight, sound, touch, taste, or smell. The law holds that it should be presented with the best source of information. Therefore, rather than accept hearsay information, it insists that the source of the information be made available to testify as to what had been specifically and personally observed.

There are exceptions to the hearsay rule. One is that of the dying declaration, where the person who made the statement has knowledge that he is mortally sick or injured, and makes the statement knowing that it will be used. Another exception is an admission made by an individual. Hearsay statements may be admitted as evidence to impeach a witness. Thus, the hearsay statement is not admitted for its content, but rather to demonstrate that a witness had spoken differently in a different situation.

Another purpose of the hearsay rule is to permit the party adversely affected by the evidence to cross-examine and question the bearer of that evidence. This cannot be done through a third party, so it is preferred that the witness be made available. A deposition made by a person without giving the other party an opportunity to cross-examine during the deposition has a built-in flaw, and may not be admitted. If admitted, the judge may direct that a lesser weight be given to the evidence.

Documents are actually hearsay testimony in the sense that they are writings made by persons who are not present. Thus, the best approach in introducing documents is to have them introduced by witnesses who either prepared the documents, or observed their preparation. It is important in evaluation of documents to develop evidence showing that they were prepared in the normal course of business—and not as a self-serving document specifically for the case at hand. In civil cases, courts are generally inclined to be flexible in their acceptance of documents, particularly those that are official records or that can be identified as normal business entries.

In jury trials, federal judges often comment on the relative weight of evidence, the state courts generally less so. In a non-jury trial, judges tend to admit information into evidence that might be precluded from a lay jury. This is done on the basis that the judge has experience in the law, and can assign to each piece of information the weight that it deserves.

In the course of testimony, counsel will object at certain points to the admission of evidence or to statements by a witness, or to questions posed by the opposition counsel. These objections have a number of purposes. One is to register the objection, even if it is overruled, so that the objection can be carried into an appeal action if appropriate. If the objection is not made, there is nothing on the record to indicate or provide a foundation for the appeal. Counsel will often, after being overruled on an objection, request that his exception be noted in the record.

If records are being submitted into evidence, the custodian of the records or someone else normally working with them, such as an accountant, is often used as a witness to describe the contents. If a summary of the contents is to be used, the witness is well advised to have the original records at hand for review by the opposition. In the absence of the actual source documents, opposing counsel may successfully object to the presentation of the summary—since it does not represent the best source or best evidence. (If the source material is available—opposing counsel may request time to review the material, but in most cases such a review is perfunctory.)

In directing questions to a witness, counsel is not permitted to utilize leading questions. Leading questions have the answer implicit through the manner in phrasing the question. The answer to a leading question can usually be yes or no.

An exception to the rule on leading questions is the situation of a hostile witness. If, for instance, counsel decides to use the opposite party as a witness, he would normally suggest to the judge that he anticipates that this witness will be hostile and requests the prerogative of using leading questions. A typical response from the judge would be to first see if the witness is hostile, but then to permit leading questions if, in fact, the witness is not cooperative. Again, in nonjury cases, judges will generally permit more latitude in the use of leading questions, since they do expedite proceedings.

While the normal witness can testify only as to actual observation of fact, either or both sides may utilize expert witnesses. This witness will be first qualified by his counsel through questions on his education, professional registration, membership in professional societies, his job experience and present occupation, publications or other signs of his expertise, special honors and other indications of knowledgeability.

The expert witness is permitted to give opinion testimony in the areas of his expertise. The degree of expertise demonstrated by the expert will directly correlate with the weight that is given to his testimony. The expert witness should describe the foundation for his opinions and the rationale by which he arrived at them. An expert witness will often work with the counsel and his party for some time before the trial to ascertain the facts, and to develop an opinion that assists the case. (On occasion, during the pretrial preparation, the expert witness may well point out weaknesses in the case—and may not be included as part of the trial presentation. Though unfortunate, this situation can work to the benefit of the party by encouraging settlement, or by dropping weak portions of the case and concentrating on those parts that have merit.)

Testimony

The true experts in a trial are the judge and the lawyers. Lay witnesses and expert witnesses alike should testify with great care, recognizing that the questioners are specialists in their field. When you are on the witness stand, you are in a battle of wits. Without exception, you should (and you must) tell the truth. However, the manner and demeanor with which you tell the truth, and the way in which the counsel (particularly during cross-examination) phrases the questions may communicate an entirely different view of the truth than you believe it to be. You must be on your guard, and you must think. The following are some items of advice for witnesses based upon prior experience:

1. *Listen to question.* Be careful to listen to the question as it is asked. Do not be in a hurry to respond. Listen for key words that may have special significance. If you do not understand the question, say you do not understand the question—it is proper to request that the question be asked again.

2. *Do not be careless.* Do not answer questions in a hurry. Each question is important, so listen and answer carefully and truthfully. One tactic sometimes used is to ask a series of questions that evoke ready answers, then slip in a more subtle question hoping for a quick and damaging answer.

3. *Do not volunteer.* It is said that the law hates a volunteer. This certainly is the case with witnesses. Answer the question, but do not answer what you think may be the next question—wait and be careful. (Clarence Darrow told the story of the witness who was prompted into volunteering more information than the questioning attorney really wanted to know. The attorney first asked, "How do you know my client bit off the ear of the plaintiff, did you see him do it?" The witness answered, "No." The attorney then continued, "Then how can you state that you know he did it?" The response was "Because I saw him spit it out.")

4. *Take care with semantics.* A proper answer to the question "Did you discuss this case with your attorney?" is yes if you did—and you certainly should have. However, if the question is "Did you rehearse your testimony with your attorney?"—a simple yes would be very harmful.

5. *Control your emotions.* Do not lose your temper or become angry, testify quietly and calmly, do not be flip or jovial— litigation is a serious matter—and show proper respect for all parties, particularly the judge, but the attorneys as well.

6. *Do not guess or speculate.* If you don't know, it is proper to say you don't know. If you can't remember, it is proper to say that you can't remember, and you may receive assistance from your counsel in the form of evidence or documents that will help to refresh your memory.

7. *Advice from your counsel.* During testimony, you cannot request advice. You must be prepared to answer, if you know the answer. However, listen to the objections placed by your counsel. He will usually attempt to preclude improper lines of questioning. Do not continue to answer question after your counsel has objected to it (unless his objection is overruled).

8. *Compensation.* If as a witness, you have been compensated for your travel and possibly for your lost work time, or as an expert witness if you are being paid (as you should be), the proper answer to the question "Are you being paid for this appearance?" is yes.

Arbitration

The following description of arbitration in the construction industry is taken from an American Arbitration Association publication:

Until 1966 construction industry arbitration cases under the existing American Institute of Architects Conditions were either arbitrated informally by each party selecting their own "arbitrator" and these two "arbitrators" selecting a neutral arbitrator, or they were administered by AAA under its Commercial Rules.

The former system resulted in many complaints because there were no rules and no supervision. Moreover, many cases dragged on and created procedural problems.

On the other hand, the AAA procedures, although well-tested, were not specifically designed for the construction industry. And the arbitrators on the National Panel of the AAA were not always suitable for construction cases.

A joint committee of engineers and architects comprehensively studied the use of arbitration in the industry and concluded that, although it provided a generally effective method for resolving contractual disputes, the procedure could be greatly improved by creating a nationwide uniform system specifically for the construction industry.

In 1965 the joint committee was enlarged to include the following organizations: American Institute of Architects; Associated General Contractors; Consulting Engineers Council; Council of Mechanical Specialty Contracting Industries; and National Society of Professional Engineers.

After a year of study, new rules were adopted, known as the Construction Industry Arbitration Rules, to be administered by the American Arbitration Association. These rules are now recommended for use by all the organizations in the industry. An arbitration clause referring to these rules is generally contained in construction contracts.

Since that time, two additional national organizations have provided for the use of this arbitration system in their form documents—the American Society of Civil Engineers and the American Institute of Interior Designers. Thus, there are now seven national construction associations using the Construction Industry Arbitration Rules.

Under the Construction Industry Arbitration Rules, arbitration can be provided for in the original contract. This provision is expressed in a future dispute arbitration clause of a contract. A clause reading:

> Any controversy or claim arising out of or relating to this contract, or the breach thereof, shall be settled in accordance with the Construction Industry Arbitration Rules of the American Arbitration Association, and judgment upon the award may be entered in any court having jurisdiction thereof.

can be used to take advantage of the new procedures.

In the absence of such a clause, parties can bring an existing dispute to arbitration by means of a signed statement in which both parties briefly describe the issue between them and agree to arbitrate under the Construction Rules.

On receiving the Demand for Arbitration or Submission Agreement, the Arbitration Association sends each party a copy of a list of proposed arbitrators technically qualified to resolve the controversy. In a construction dispute, these names may include builders, contractors, engineers, architects, other businessmen familiar with the construction industry, and attorneys who customarily represent such clients. In cases involving lesser sums one arbitrator is generally appointed. But in larger cases, it may be preferable to have three neutral arbitrators.

Parties are allowed seven days to study the list, cross off any name objected to, and number the remaining names in order of their preference. Where parties want more information about a proposed arbitrator, such information is given on request.

When these lists are returned, the American Arbitration Association compares them and appoints the arbitrator whom the parties have approved. Where parties were unable to find a mutual choice on a list, additional lists may be submitted at the request of both parties.

If parties cannot agree upon an arbitrator, the Association will make administrative appointments, but in no case will an arbitrator whose name was crossed out by either party be appointed.

Arbitrators on AAA panels are generally willing to serve without fee. They volunteer an occasional day as a public service. But after spending two days on a case, the arbitrator must be compensated by the parties. The rate of compensation will then be based upon the amount of service involved and on the number of hearings. Any arrangement for the compensation of an arbitrator is made through the AAA, not directly by him with the parties.

After the arbitrator is appointed, the AAA consults with the parties to determine a mutually convenient time and place for the hearing. Arrangements are made through the Association, rather than directly between the arbitrator and the parties. The reason for this is twofold: it relieves the arbitrator of routine burdens and it eliminates the danger that, in the course of conversations outside the hearing room, one party may offer arguments on the merits of the case that the other has not had an opportunity to rebut.

Arbitration hearings are less formal than court trials. Arbitrators are not required to follow legal rules of evidence. Rather, they are empowered to listen to all evidence that is relevant and material. Arbitrators often accept evidence that might not be permitted in court. But this does not mean that all evidence is believed or given equal weight.

Each party has a right to be represented by counsel, and the hearing is conducted in a businesslike manner. It is customary for the complaining party to proceed first with his case, followed by the respondent. This order may be varied, however, when the arbitrator thinks it advisable. Each party must try to convince the arbitrator of the correctness of his position and the hearing is not closed until each has had a full opportunity to present his case.

The purpose of the award is to dispose of the controversy finally and conclusively. It must be handed down within thirty days after the close of the hearing. The power of the arbitrator ends with the making of the award; the decision cannot be changed unless both parties agree to reopen the case, unless the applicable law provides for reopening.

In *Bel Pre Medical Center v. Frederick Contractors Inc.* (320 A. 2d 558), the contractor attempted to refuse arbitration, preferring to take his case to the courts. While agreeing that there was a dispute that normally would be subject to arbitration, the contractor held that the owner had filed too late, since the arbitration agreement also required a request for arbitration within thirty days from the date of a dispute. The circuit court to which the contractor appealed found that the procedural situation precluded arbitration. The owner appealed to the Special Appeals Court in Maryland. In answering, the court reviewed the basis for arbitration. Under common law, an agreement to arbitrate that precludes redress in the courts is against public policy and illegal. Therefore, an agreement to arbitrate in the common law base for the laws in this country is not enforceable and would not constitute or preclude an attempt for legal redress in the courts. The court said,

Thus, while suits to enforce an arbitration award were viewed as 'favored' actions, executory agreements for arbitration were consigned to an 'unfavored' status and suits to compel arbitration or to stay court proceedings pending arbitration could not be bought.

In Maryland, arbitration was governed by the common law rules until 1965, the year in which the Maryland Uniform Arbitration Act . . . was enacted by the General Assembly. . . . The Uniform Arbitration Act constitutes a radical departure from the common law. Executory agreements to arbitrate are to be deemed 'valid, irrevokable, and enforceable,' and suits to compel arbitration or to stay the action of a court pending arbitration may now be bought. The prime purpose of these provisions is to discourage litigation and to foster voluntary resolution of disputes in a form created, controlled and administered according to the parties' agreement to arbitrate.

The court went on to discuss the verdict in the U. S. Supreme Court case of *John Wiley & Sons Inc.* v. *Livingston*. In that case, Wiley claimed that it was not required to arbitrate a dispute because the defendant had failed to comply with certain procedural prerequisites to arbitration. The Supreme Court found in favor of requiring the arbitration stating: "We think that labor disputes of the kind involved here cannot be broken down so easily into their 'substantive' and 'procedural' aspects. Questions concerning the procedural prerequisites to arbitration do not arise in a vacuum; they develop in the context of an actual dispute about the rights of the parties to the contract or those covered by it. . . . Once it is determined, as we have, that the parties are obligated to submit the subject matter of a dispute to arbitration, 'procedural' questions which grow out of the dispute and bear on its final disposition should be left to the arbitrator." The Maryland Court found in favor of the arbitration and reversed the decision of the circuit court.

An interesting, and important, aspect of arbitration is its finality. Not only is substantial time saved through more simple filing procedures, and informal hearing procedures, but there is generally no appeal from an arbitration unless evidence can be presented that there has been a misconstruction or disregard of the law in arriving at the result, or that there has been some form of fraud or misconduct on the part of the arbitrators.

In *Scherrer Construction Co. Inc.* v. *Burlington Memorial Hospital* (221 N.W. 2d 855), an owner appealed a finding in arbitration, claiming that the arbitrators were partial to the contractor and had refused to hear relevant evidence. The owner also contended that the arbitrators had exceeded their powers. After review of the facts, the trial court rejected the owner's contentions and confirmed the award. The owner then appealed to the Wisconsin Supreme Court. The court reviewed three major issues:

1. What is the scope of judicial review of arbitration awards?
2. Did the arbitrators exceed their powers in making the award?
3. Was the award mutual, final, and definite?

The court noted that an arbitrator is not free to ignore the contract between the parties in making an award but found that there was no showing that the contract in the instant case was ignored.

The court reviewed the question of finality of the award. The owner argued that the award was incomplete and indefinite because it did not allocate the damage award between special and general damages. The contractor's claim was made up of two portions, $65,652 for the cost of additional underpinning and $76,140 for delay. The arbitrators awarded $56,830, but offered no explantion. The owner argued that damages due to delay were prohibited by the contract and since the award did not allocate amounts to delay and underpinning, the award should be vacated.

The court stated that the owner's argument misconceived the court's function in the review of arbitration award. The court stated: "such awards are presumptively valid, and invalidity may only be shown by clear and convincing evidence. . . . Arbitration awards need not separately treat each claim and counterclaim where a specific sum is awarded expressly to satisfy all such claims and counterclaims." The court affirmed the award.

While rules of procedure must not be necessarily followed, it is quite common for construction claims for delay, if major, to be handled by a three-man arbitration board. The board usually includes a lawyer, and it is quite common for the legal member to act in the role of judge in reviewing the admissibility of evidence, and the form of presentation. Experience indicates that while the proceedings can be informal, it is advantageous to follow the general rules of procedure and evidence.

A transcript is kept of the arbitration proceedings. However, the arbitrators do not have to write an opinion or explain their award. This serves to make the overturning of an arbitration award considerably more difficult, since errors in the law are not as easily discerned, as they are in a trial opinion.

Chapter Eleven · Damages

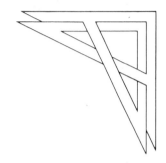

The setting of the amount to be claimed for damages is an important step. Early in a suit, parties tend to set high numbers on their claims and counterclaims. These can later become an embarrassment, if there has not been a reasonable rationale behind the claim.

In *F. H. McGraw & Co.* v. *United States* (130 F. Supp. 394), the court held: "The plaintiff must prove its damages with reasonable certainty, but they do not have to be proved with absolute certainty. It is sufficient that plaintiff furnishes a reasonable basis for its computation, even though the result is only approximate."

In *L. L. Hall Construction Co.* v. *United States* (379 F. 2d 559, Ct. Cl; 1966), the court held: "Although the proof may not be so positive to enable the court to make an absolute determination of the precise excess costs resulting from delays chargeable to one party, an approximate and reasonable determination may be made on the basis of the facts and the circumstances and the best available evidence, in such amount as, in the best judgment of fair men, resulted from the breach."

Damages for delay can be categorized into actual damages and liquidated damages. Liquidated damages is a special means of establishing the cost of delay, which can result in an expeditious means of settlement, often without litigation.

Actual Damages

If liquidated damages are not included in the contract, the owner can attempt to recover the actual damages for delay. In any case, the contractor cannot avail himself of the liquidated damages clause, and must seek recovery of actual damages due to delay.

Actual damages can be either direct damages from delay, or consequential damages. Direct damages include costs such as additional field management due to extended time in the project; additional home office management and overhead tied up by the job; extended use of equipment; escalation of wages during the extended work period; increase in materials costs; continued items such as security, utilities, and other costs directly related to the longer project implementation period.

In *Roanoke Hospital Association* v. *Doyle & Russell* (Reference Case 47), the court discussed the distinction between direct and consequential damages: "Direct damages are those which arise 'naturally' or 'ordinarily' from a breach of contract; there are damages which, in the ordinary course of human experience, can be expected to result from a breach. Consequential damages are those which arise from the intervention of 'special circumstances' not ordinarily predictable. If damages are determined to be direct, they are compensable. If damages are determined to be consequential, they are compensable only if it is determined that the special circumstances were within the 'contemplation' of both contracting parties. Where the damages are direct or consequential is a question of law. Where the special circumstances were within the contemplation of the parties is a question of fact. . . . As a general rule, contemplation must exist at the time the contract was executed."

In that case, the court agreed with the owner and the trial court that extended financing costs are direct damages. Thus, both the cost of interest on the construction loan during the extended delay, as well as the loss of revenue, which could have been anticipated from the facility, are predictable results of the delay on compensable direct damages.

However, the Virginia Supreme Court held that the increases in interest rates that occurred during this particular delay were caused by the pressures of the financial market, and for that reason, the increases in the interest rates were in the category of special circumstance, and therefore a consequential damage. In that case, the reviewing court allowed the finding of additional interest costs, but not the increment of interest which was greater than the anticipated rate. However, the owner's evidence of $690,287 in additional interest costs did not break down into the two areas of "extended interest costs" and "incremental construction interest cost." Therefore, the court held that the jury had no basis upon which to separate the two, and remanded the case for a new trial to fix the quantum of direct damages.

Similarly, in *Lichter* v. *Mellon-Stuart Co.* (Reference Case 36), the masonry subcontractor proved the facts of delay, and the interference by the general contractor. However, in claiming the amount of damage, the subcontractor did not separate the delay costs into those causes due to the general contractor's interference, and those due to causes for which the general contractor would not be responsible. The court found that this provided "no basis . . . for even an educated guess as to the increased costs suffered by plaintiffs due to that particular breach or breaches as distinguished from those causes from which defendant is contractually exempt." Further, the court concluded: "Inability to break down its lump sum proof of extra costs justifies the denial of any recovery if on the record any substantial part of the added cost of the performance was chargeable to non-actionable causes."

The court in *United States* v. *Citizens and Southern National Bank* (Reference Case 58), cited that same case in finding that "It appears that a not insubstantial part of the extra costs for which [subcontractor] sought reimbursement could be attributed to factors for which [general contractor] was not responsible. As the evidence does not provide any reasonable basis for allocating the additional costs among these contributing factors, we conclude that the entire claim should have been rejected."

In *Forest Electric Corp.* v. *State* (Reference Case 24), the contractor plaintiff was fortunate in that the court chose to make broad assumptions regarding the amount of damage, having found that the defendant [State] was responsible, indirectly, for the delays. Testimony indicated that there were various strikes, but the evidence also showed that had the State required the general contractor to perform in keeping with the contract, progress would have been ahead of the several strikes in most instances. The court stated: "Although it is difficult to assess how much could have been thus gained or lost by virtue of the strikes, the Court feels that no more than ¼ of the time lost could or should be assessed in favor of the State in regard to this claim. Likewise, since the claim for time lost waiting for hoists and rehandling of fixtures is an estimate, the Court allows only ½ of the time claimed as a reasonable estimate of that time." Similarly, in *Luria Brothers* v. *United States* (Reference Case 38), the plaintiff claimed $131,117 for loss of productivity during the delay period. The principal cause of the lower productivity was the necessity to work in bad weather. The chief of construction for the plaintiff was the single witness. He claimed that in his opinion, which was deemed to be the equivalent of expert, the production loss was 33 percent. The government did not refute this evidence. Weighing various factors in regard to the credibility of the witness, the court agreed that there was a loss of productivity, saying: "In view of the fact that no comparative data, no standards and no corroboration support his testimony, we are constrained to reduce his estimates based upon the record as a whole, and the court's knowledge and experience in such cases to 20 percent or $11,091 (for one period) . . . to 10 percent or $13,015 (for a second period) . . . and to 10 percent or $926 (for a third period)."

In that same case, the court allowed damages for home office overhead in the amount of $62,948 which had been refused by the trial commissioner. The court also confirmed damages for costs of idle equipment, field supervision, winter protection, maintaining excavations, wage increases, insurance premium, and material increases. These damages were allowed for the fraction of time through the entire 518-day overrun that was attributable to the government—420 days.

Damages must be documented and must actually have been suffered. In *Harper Drake v. Jewett & Sherman* (Reference Case 29), the plaintiff architect was claiming for work accomplished during negotiation of a contract. His claim was for a percentage of the total design effort, based upon his estimate of the level of the design work at the time at which his services were terminated. This contention was refused, but he was paid for all work that could be documented. As a result, he was paid for all of his payroll, but it turned out that his own time was not clearly documented. The court found: "The amount of work Harper performed, and therefore the compensation to which he was entitled must rest upon a foundation of rational and credible evidence, not speculation and guesswork. . . . We conclude . . . the evidence does not support the verdict. Consequently, the amount of the verdict must be reduced."

In *County of Tarrant v. Butcher and Sweeney* (Reference Case 19) the county commissioners filed a claim for $128,722 alleging that the building that resulted was not the facility that was specified in their contract. While not disagreeing, the court found that the county was unrealistic in its demands, and awarded a token figure of $700.

Consequential Damages

Consequential damages result from the delay, but are not a direct cost due to it. Consequential damages are also not necessarily part of the contract considerations and include claims for losses such as: loss of bonding capacity; limitations on work load due to limited working capital; losses due to failure to undertake additional business; and loss of profit or income.

One approach to delay damage claims is to place all loss in the category of a consequence of actions by the other party. Thus, a contractor may base his claim on the amount that he bid for the job versus the amount that it actually cost him to do the job. A foundation for this type of claim must be a validation of the contractor's estimate, indicating that there was no mistake. Further, the contractor has to demonstrate that he worked efficiently, or at least as efficiently as the average contractor in the trade. This is a very hazardous approach, and relatively easy to discredit. (Note that the other party need not disprove, but only show that part of this claim is incorrect—and the baby gets thrown out with the dirty bath water.)

Sometimes the precision with which a damage can be identified may influence its identification as direct or consequential. In *Hammermill Paper Co. v. Rust Engineering* (Reference Case 28), the court allowed a claim due to loss of "use and occupancy" in the amount of $70,393 because the amount was arrived at with a specific rationale. (This rationale was accepted by the insurance company previously.)

In *Clark v. Ferro* (Reference Case 16), the court ruled that evidence in regard to claim for loss of profits due to the inadequacy of new equipment (the subject of the claim) did not establish such loss with a sufficient degree of certainty required. Accordingly, the only damages allowed were those required to put the equipment into proper working condition.

Statement of the Claim

The statement of the claim should be made in clear and rational format. In *Egan v. City of New York* (Reference Case 21), the following list of delay damages was submitted by the plaintiff, and stipulated to by counsel for the city.

Category of supervisors & foreman non-productive labor after March 9, 1955	$39,827
Wage increases, increments not otherwise applicable except for the alleged delay	26,102
Field expenses after March 9, 1955 electrical work & telephone in field office	557
Fire insurance premiums March 9, 1955 to December, 1956	6,004

Interest on retained moneys, 223, 526 for 338 days   9,382
Increase in cost of material   7,500
10% Overhead   8,937
5% Profit   4,915
    $103,224

The list does not include two important items: the rental value of equipment and the costs due to delays through lack of coordination.

Egan had attempted to prove the rental value of the equipment as a cost factor during the period of delay. There was no concession to this by the opposition, but did not preclude recovery through award by the jury.

It is interesting to note the inclusion in the stipulated list of 10 percent overhead and 5 percent profit. While these figures would reasonably be included on cost items that would normally be part of the work—insurance, field expenses, wages, and management—the stipulated figure also allows 10 percent overhead and 5 percent profit on the interest on retained money—which would in no way be part of the normal project cost. The summary of days delay, upon which the $103,224 amount was stipulated, is as follows:

Claimed Delays

Item	Days	Reasons
(1)	88	Egan could not get into building up until April 6, 1953.
(2)	21	Redesign of partitions.
(3)	90	Correction of layouts until March 9, 1955.
(4)	5	Inclement weather (not attributed to the City).
(5)	30	Strikes (not attributed to the City).
(6)	90	Carryover of delays relative to layouts to March 9, 1955, up until March, 1956.
(7)	53	Strikes after March, 1955 (no testimony relating thereto admitted by Trial Court).
	377	

Egan claimed the city responsible for a total of 348 days, but the city pointed out that causes 4, 5, and 7 totaling eighty-eight days were due to factors for which the city could not be held responsible. Therefore, the maximum amount that the city should have been liable for due to delay for the stipulated amount would be 77 percent of the total, or $79,070.

The jury awarded $120,000 for delay. The appellate court stated that the jury's verdict on the delay claim could not be substantiated because the amount was in substantial excess of the supporting figures. In the final appeal, the city concurred with the appellate division finding, but the plaintiff's counsel pointed out that the additional $40,000 was easily supported by the single cause of lack of coordination.

Summary

Proof of the case requires a clear presentation of cause and effect. When the cause of damages has been proven, it should be made easy for the judge and jury to connect the cause to the purported effect. Failure to do this will introduce a fatal flaw in the presentation, and thereby lead to loss either immediately or in appeal.

Chapter Twelve · Preparation of the Case

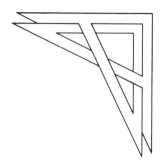

When the decision to litigate, or even to consider litigation, is made, the nature of the case must be considered. Up to that point in time, the situation is viewed from the partisan position of people or organizations (or both) involved in a problem. The dimensions of the problem are generally known, usually in terms of financial loss. Since the matter has not been settled through negotiation, there is usually a substantial degree of polarization. The party or parties are well aware of what "they" (the opposition) did, or didn't do.

All too often, the corporate or house counsel for the party deciding to litigate has not been kept in close touch with the dimensions of the problem as it has evolved. Fortunately, most projects are not managed as though they were going to end up in litigation. Unfortunately for those which do, the various actions and procedures utilized to implement a project are often different than those that might have been utilized if litigation were anticipated.

One prominent construction lawyer has commented that the parties rarely know what their problem (or problems) really were, and it depends upon the experienced attorney to evaluate the facts and define the problem areas. Pompous as it may sound, the proposition has a certain element of truth. During a project, the parties encounter—and solve—many major problems. However, the cumulative effect of these solutions may result in delay and/or other damages, or may cause the parties to take certain actions that result in delays and/or damages.

The preparation of the case requires analysis of the facts,

identification of the damages, correlation of facts and damages, and identification of the legal relief.possible under the contract (or beyond the contract if breach of contract can be established.)

Project Documentation

During the development of the case, project documentation plays an important role establishing the facts, and is an important part of the evidence to be presented. Proper notice of delays and other problems presented in a timely fashion is one of the prime categories to be drawn from the mass of project documentation. Payroll records and purchase orders provide a base for demonstration of escalation, actual overhead staff, and other costs of delay.

There can be a negative factor in the project documentation. Research through the internal memoranda often discloses information critical to the mode of operation of the organization preparing the case. Under the rules of discovery, these records and memoranda may be turned over to the opposition—and are potentially quite embarrassing. For a case in progress, there is no remedy. The documents may not be withheld when subpoenaed, even though they have been labeled confidential or company private. In fact, even the personal diaries and similar records of individuals involved in the design or construction are accessible by means of a subpoena. This leads to some rules for the maintenance of proper project records for future projects:

1. Factual accuracy. Written project documents should be factual and to the point. Speculation or unsupported allegations should be avoided. Irresponsible statements or statements for which inadequate justification exists should be avoided.
2. Precision. Letters, memos, and reports should be written with sufficient precision so that a third party reviewing the document without the benefit of substantial factual background will not misconstrue the intent of the documents.
3. Completeness. Every change, correction of a deficiency, explanation or rebuttal of a problem area should be recorded, particularly where the topic of deficiencies or alleged deficiencies has been raised. For instance, punchlists should have a close-out corrective action list, or a sign-off.
4. Impersonality. Unnecessary or unjustified remarks concerning the competence or motives of others should be

avoided. All reports and records should be as factual as is possible and should avoid the use of unnecessary adjectives that unduly emphasize or exaggerate the gravity of a problem being described.

Establishing the Facts

In developing the case, documentation is invaluable in establishing the facts. The time required to develop the story of what really happened can be reduced if knowledgeable project personnel are still available. Because of the nature of construction, as well as the length of time usually required to bring a suit to trial, it is not unusual for key personnel to be unavailable— beyond the reach of subpoenas for civil suits.

If properly set up, the documentation file will include a section on notices of delay or a delay file. (Because the file can be recovered as part of discovery, contractors would do well not to call this file the claim file.) Another file that should be segregated in the documentation is the file on time extensions. Correspondence in this file (whether owners, designers, or contractor's file) should describe the when, how, why, and how much involved in each time extension.

Time extensions are often withheld by owners, even when justified. This is done, often as not, on the advice of the architect when he is performing as field consultant, with a view toward maintaining control over the contractor. This lack of candor, however well intentioned, often boomerangs. Where the owner could issue a deserved time extension, at no cost, which would usually be accepted by a contractor early in the contract (so that he can avoid the risk of liquidated damages), the time extension is not issued, and the owner ultimately pays twofold.

In New York City, a college had a fixed price contract, with a general contractor for the construction of a high-rise science building costing about $10 million. The contractor delivered more than one year late—and then presented a claim for $2 million indicating that the owner and his architect had caused specific delays that in turn resulted in damages in the amount claimed. The project documents indicated that early in the contract, the general contractor had requested several time extensions (which were deserved) but which were denied on the advice of the architect. These proper extensions, had they been given, would have specifically reduced the scope of the damages claimed. Instead, the owner had to start from scratch in his defense of the claim.

At another academic building in New Jersey, the state accepted periodic reports on recommended no fault time extensions. The effect was to reduce the apparent time overrun, reducing the difference between the parties. This prevented polarization that might otherwise have led into litigation.

Some contract administrators believe they are building a good position for the owner when they negotiate change orders, and offer no time for the impact or effect upon the end date. Most standard change order forms have a space for number of days extension allowed, and in this type of negotiation a zero is filled in that slot. Most contractors who accept this type of unilateral action do so because they are interested principally in being paid for the work, and at that point in time are not concerned about the actual completion date. In *Ross & Co. v. United States* (Reference Case 52), the court found that this type of zero impact negotiation clearly demonstrates that the contractor was negotiating only the change order or extra work, and only in the context of that segment of work. The court allowed Ross to make an additional claim for increased costs for the delay to the balance of the contract imposed by the change order. This, the court held, was not included in the original negotiation. (In fact, in some jurisdictions, such as New York City, the administering agency such as Department of Public Works is not permitted to negotiate for time extensions until the actual completion of the job.)

Another important segment of project documentation is the field report. These are usually prepared on a daily basis, and contain a substantial amount of detail. Unfortunately, they contain details about areas that are not in contention—so that the reports must be screened to produce that information necessary to establish the facts for those areas in contention. One approach to analyzing the daily reports is an identification of those areas of information that are required, so that the information can be extracted as the reports are read. (The daily reports are just too voluminous to permit a meaningful retention visually without some routine for extracting or at least identifying those reports that bear upon the problem areas.)

In *Consumers Construction Co. v. Cook County* (275 N.E. 2d 697; 1971) the admissability of project documentation was an important question. The project had a base value of $531,900 for additions and alterations at Cook County Children's Hospital. The base contract time was 210 calendar days. Evidence presented showed that extras required by the county accounted for an additional 473 days beyond the contract date. However, the entire project required 972 days, so that some 289 days of delay were in contention.

The court refused to allow the contractor to present into evidence the daily progress reports. These reports had been prepared in the normal order of business, and were regularly forwarded to the architect for the county. The appeals court did not rule on the content of the reports, but did find that they should have been considered as evidence by the trial court. Accordingly, the case was remanded back to the trial court for a finding of fact in regard to the responsibility for the 289 days of delay.

Network Systems

Network systems, in particular Critical Path Method (CPM), can be useful in establishing the facts, and also the intentions, of the parties. The most important CPM is the initial approved CPM network. This one describes the manner in which the contractor intended to meet the requirements of the contract at the start. This can be used by the owner to demonstrate areas of failure on the part of the contractor, and can be used by the contractor to demonstrate points at which he was interfered with by the owner or his agents.

A project that had regular (usually monthly) reviews or updatings of the CPM should provide a good base through the CPM report for evaluation of the progress. Unfortunately, many such projects have only a collection of CPM diagrams and computer runs. To the investigator who is not familiar with the project throughout, these exhibits are analogous to artifacts unearthed by archeologists. They require much investigation, interpretation, and explanation. The CPM reports are far more valuable if they are accompanied by a comprehensive narrative with each updating. These narratives, which are normal portions of the project documentation, are prepared in the normal order of business—and can be accepted at face value, with due weight given to the origin of their preparation.

It is usual practice for the CPM scheduling team to periodically readjust the schedule to attempt to maintain the end date, or to accommodate problems and unexpected situations. Figure 8 shows an example of this on a major pollution control plant. The graph was included as part of the narrative report to provide the reader with a measure of what the term "schedule" meant on this project. Thus, during periods of rescheduling, it would appear that the project was either on schedule or did not fall further behind schedule, while in reality, the dates were being revised in terms of overall plan, but not necessarily reflecting true progress.

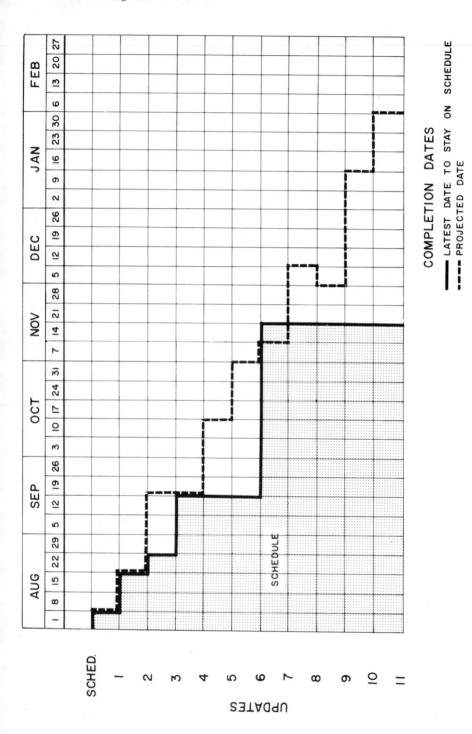

Figure 8

Figures 9 and 10 are similar charts utilized in actual project updatings. In these illustrations, the 45° line represents the track along which the monthly status falls. Relative to this, is plotted the end date projection for the updating. If the track of the end date is vertical, or trends to the left, the project is on schedule or ahead of schedule. If the trend is to the right, then little or no progress has been made.

A graphical version of the CPM can be utilized to demonstrate the impact of external factors upon the project's progress. This approach was used to explain the impact upon the construction schedule of a series of decisions (and lack of decisions) on the part of the owner's architect for a college project. In the course of construction, a number of major discrepancies in design were identified. The contractor happened also to be a very well regarded engineering firm, so that there was a definite validity to the problems identified. There was limited or negative response to many of these queries, and the contractor completed the project under protest—documenting all of the problems. The project finished approximately nine months late, and litigation in the amount of more than $1 million dollars was filed.

Figure 11 shows the series of CPM studies used to summarize the impact of the delays. There were four major segments of the complex, each shown in a horizontal fashion. The initial schedule ran from June 1969 through August 1970, and as illustrated, contained approximately 16 percent time contingency. The initial portion of this was utilized when rock was encountered and the architect refused to initiate a change order that would permit the pool area and other foundations to proceed. This forced the work into the winter season during which time weather sensitive work had to be performed in an inefficient manner. Following these delays, there was a controversy regarding waterproofing of the swimming pool, with an extended delay of some 171 days. In this same period of time, there was a strike of 45 days. The overall impact had the effect of driving the end date out to April 1971 in the swimming pool area. All of the graphic adjustments were done to an exact time scale, so that the charts represented an actual solution. In the graphic solution, it was a great advantage to have the initial network as developed by the contractor. (If that initial network plan is too large, a summary can be prepared, and then the graphical analysis performed.)

Another approach involves the computerization of the work. At a major airport, the airport authority installed a $15 million underground fueling system. The contractor, who was low

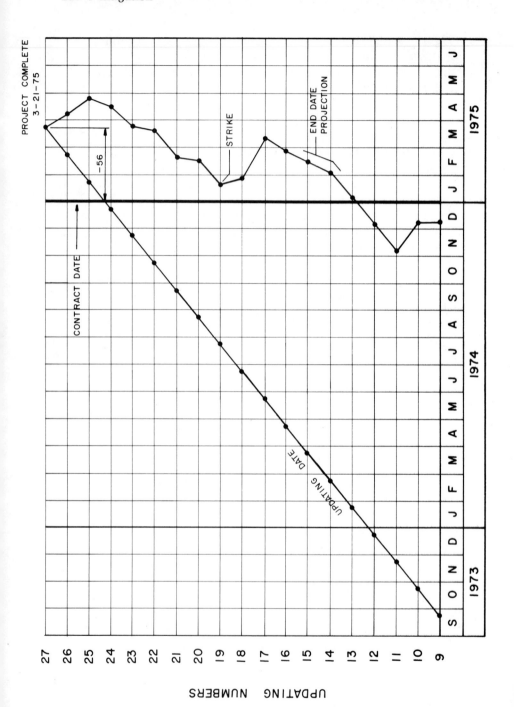

Figure 9

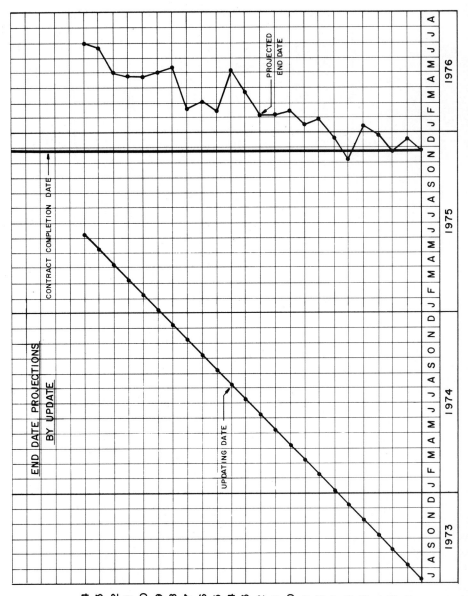

Figure 10

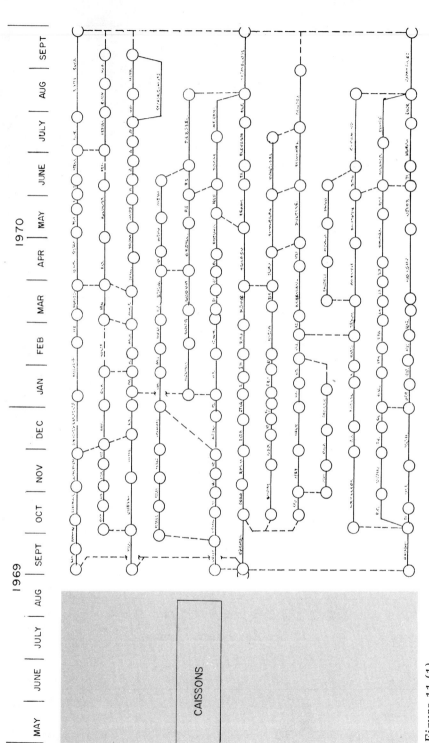

Figure 11 (1)

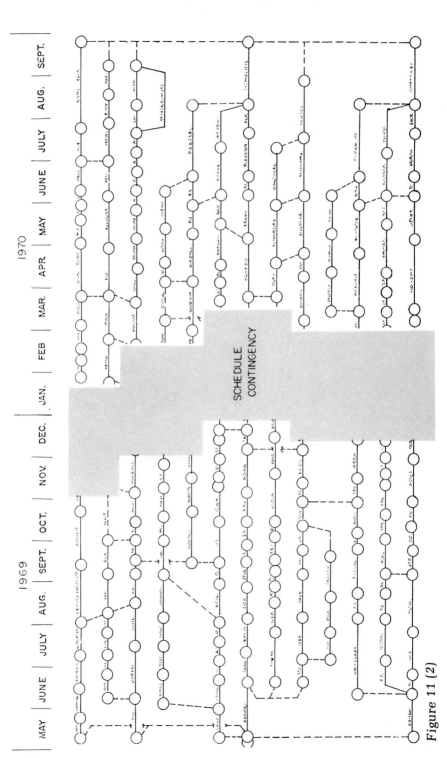

Figure 11 (2)

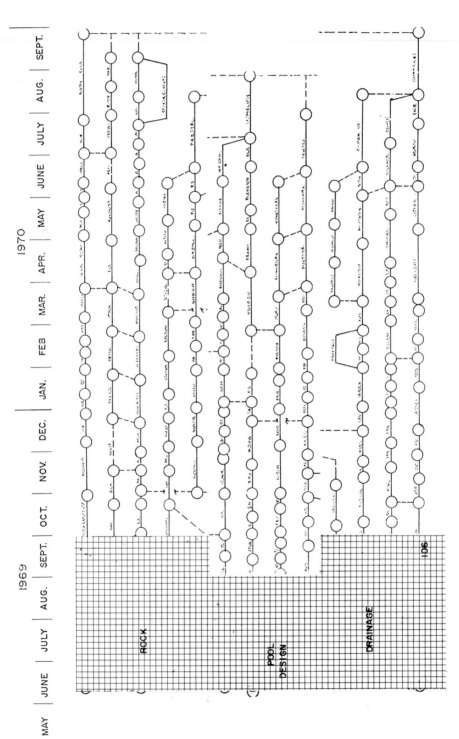

Figure 11 (3)

Figure 11 (4)

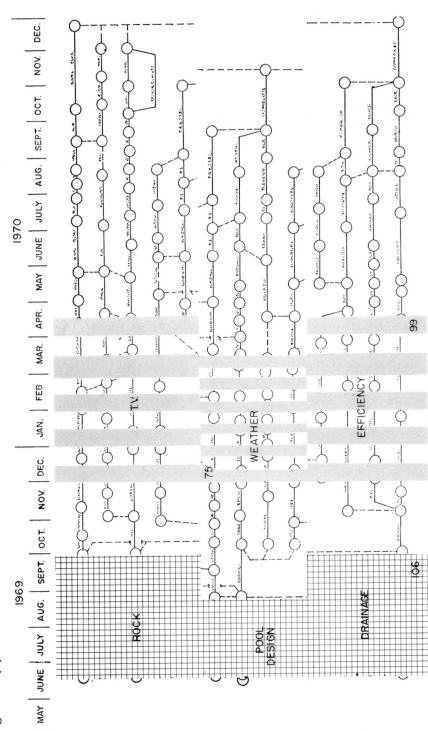

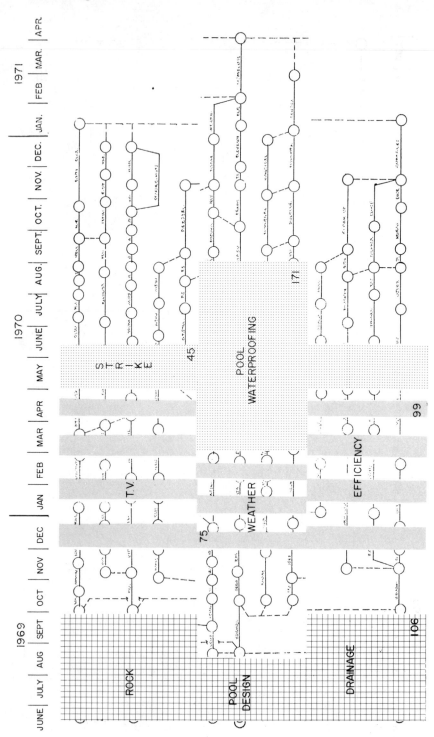

Figure 11 (5)

bidder by several million, prepared a construction CPM that was never accepted by the owner. All milestone dates were completely missed. The authority took under advisement the matter of whether or not to enter suit for delay damages through losses in interest, operating efficiency, and other direct delay damages. In the meanwhile, the contractor filed a $6 million delay suit against the authority. The authority promptly counterclaimed and entered litigation.

In the absence of a viable CPM representing what actually happened, the owner directed that a CPM be prepared to evaluate the real causes of delay. The daily, weekly, and monthly reports, as well as personal observation by the owner's field team and the CPM consultant, were utilized to develop a comprehensive CPM. This CPM had milestone points reflecting actual dates of accomplishment. Between milestone points, the CPM team developed estimates for the time that the work should have taken, and then divided the delay by cause. The causes were either: contractor; owner; combined; or no fault. The first computer evaluation reflected the actual dates for all events. The next computation established the amount of delay due to the contractor alone. The next established the amount of delay due to the owner alone. The fourth identified the amount of delay due to both. The total delay was less than the combined values of the delay due to the owner and to the contractor.

Using this very specific information, the managing engineer for the owner was able to direct efforts toward an out-of-court settlement that took more than one year to negotiate. (Part of the willingness to negotiate on the part of the owner's management structure was the identification of the very real delays caused by slow shop drawing review. Many of these delays were due to the high work load that the owner's engineering department was carrying, but many were also identified as delays while the owner's engineers attempted to redesign the shop drawing submissions, a common mistake.)

In a similar computerized evaluation, a major bridge-tunnel project valued at more than $200 million was completed more than six months late. The bridge authority incurred an additional interest cost of $5 million plus a loss of more than $5 million in anticipated revenues. Anticipating litigation, the contracting joint venture set up a CPM evaluation to examine three major causes of delay that included a dredge fire, cave-in of a coffer dam, and a series of strikes. The CPM study showed that the contractors would have completed on time without these unusual interruptions. The report was then submitted to the bridge authority which decided that it was not in the public interest to sue—and an expensive litigation was avoided.

Rate Analysis

One approach to the establishment of the actual progress of the project is the plotting of the actual rates of progress for various components of the project throughout its life. Figure 12 shows a plot for various stages of the work including foundations, structural steel, metal roof deck, slabs on deck, slabs on grade, panels, and windows. The project involved was the installation of several long passenger terminal gate position structures. The plot on the vertical axis is percentage complete, and the horizontal calendar months.

In the example case, a general contractor had an $8 million contract for renovations and alterations at the airport. The specification required a proprietary external skin that represented approximately 25 percent of the construction value. For a variety of reasons during construction, the project was completed one year late. Initially, the general contractor blamed all of the delay on his major subcontractor—but after evaluation recognized that about 50 percent or six months of the delay was the fault of this subcontractor, while the balance was involved in delays imposed by the owner and the users in change orders. Litigation started, and the subcontractor promptly filed a $2 million countersuit.

The project had an approved CPM schedule, which the general contractor and subcontractor had coordinated in preparing. Figure 13 shows the CPM start and completion dates for two major areas involving the subcontractor: metal deck and window wall. The CPM rate of progress lines are shown as straight lines with the metal deck to have started on January 27 and the window wall to have started March 3.

There were various reasons why the start dates could not be met, which were the fault of neither contractor. However, by moving the rate of progress from the CPM to coincide with the actual starting dates for the two categories, Figure 14 illustrates that the major subcontractor initially fell behind in his work, and then gradually met the rate of construction for metal deck and approached it for window wall. The fact that the rates of progress were either met or approached confirms the validity of the original CPM as to time estimates. The evidence then went on to show that actual and specific delays had occurred. Further, no other areas could progress until the building was closed in, so these delays were not concurrent with other de-

Figure 12

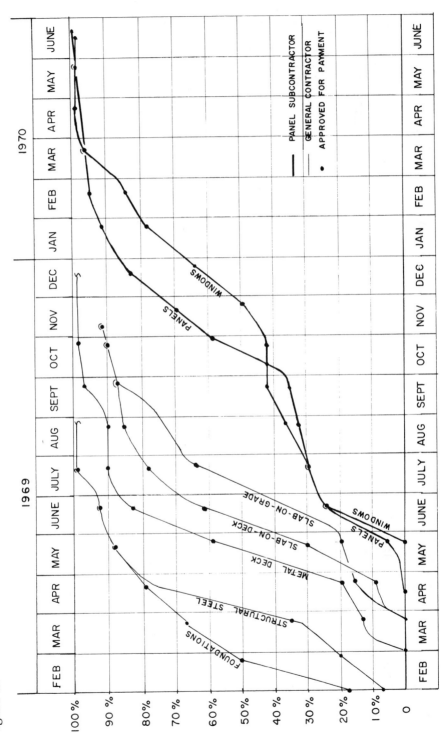

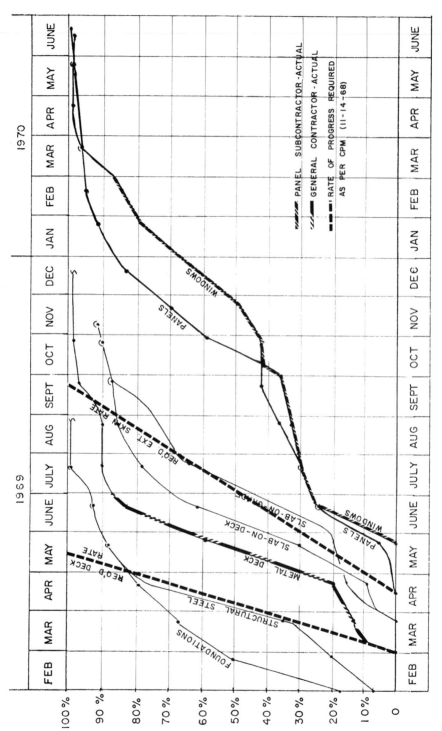

Figure 13

Figure 14

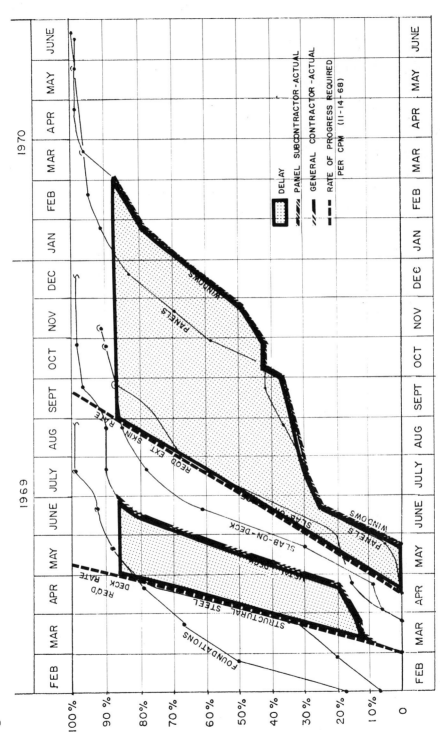

lays, and therefore, directly impacted the general contractor. This analysis was a key to a $250,000 award by an arbitration panel specifically for delay as part of an overall award in favor of the general contractor.

If cost is tied directly to the CPM, a cost versus time curve can be generated which correlates to the CPM. This will follow some form of an S-curve. If that curve can be generated, then similarly a manpower curve can be generated to reflect the manning level which would have been required for the project.

Figure 15 combines the rate of progress curves and an actual manpower curve on the airport project. This demonstrated to the panel the level of manpower required to produce the projected rate of progress (about seventy ironworkers), rather than the twenty man rate which was the average manning over the first five months of the skin installation.

High-Rise Construction

In high-rise construction, the scheduling problem is a hybird. Standard CPM scheduling techniques are excellent for coordination and control of the work up to the first typical floor. At that point, the high-rise construction becomes a production. No trade can progress faster than the various controlling trades, such as structure. Any following trade that produces more rapidly will catch up, and therefore, must stop the rhythm of its work which is a very expensive practice.

Figure 16 is the CPM version of a structural plan for a high-rise and Figure 17 is the computer printout for this approach. Figure 18 shows basically the same material for the same project (a 32-story high-rise condominium). The first line to the left is the rate of progress required according to the schedule for start and completion of concrete on each floor, with the line to the right the rate of removing major shoring.

In Figure 19, the placing of outriggers at the third points of the building (eleven, twenty-second, and roof levels) is superimposed on the concrete. This is the earliest point at which the outriggers can be placed, and it had been agreed with the bricklaying subcontractor that the third points were the optimum points on that building for placement of outriggers. The brick mason indicated that he planned to complete two floors per week, and Figure 20 shows his proposed rate of progress, which would outrun the outriggers at the eleventh and twenty-second floors. While, in this project, the VPM (Vertical Production Method) was utilized to prepare and project the schedule, a similar approach can be used to demonstrate actual progress, or failure to progress.

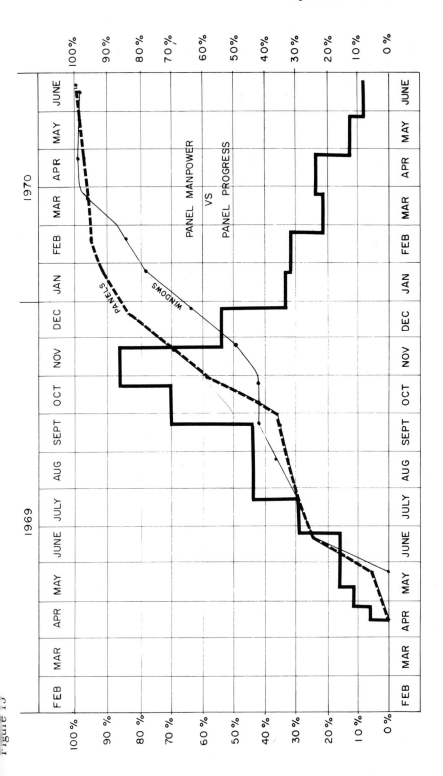

PANEL MANPOWER
VS
PANEL PROGRESS

Figure 13

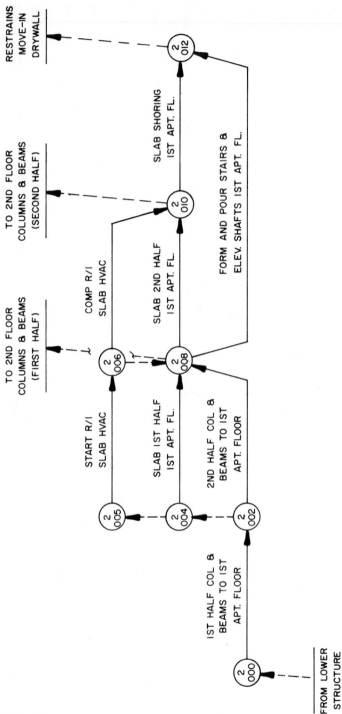

Fig. 16

APARTMENT HOUSE CONDOMINIUM

CPM: JAMES J O'BRIEN

I - J	ACTIVITY DESCRIPTION	ORIG DUR	REM DUR	EARLY START	EARLY FINISH	LATE START	LATE FINISH	TOTAL FLOAT
2000-2002	1st Hlf Col-Beams 1st Flr	2.0	2.0	14MAY74	24MAY74	24MAY74	29MAY74	8.0
2002-2008	2nd Hlf Col-Beams 1st Flr	2.0	2.0	29MAY74	31MAY74	30MAY74	03JUN74	1.0
2004-2006	Start R/I Slab HVAC	2.0	2.0	29MAY74	31MAY74	30MAY74	03JUN74	1.0
2004-2008	Slab 1st Half 1st Flr	3.0	3.0	29MAY74	03JUN74	29MAY74	03JUN74	0.0
2006-2010	Comp R/I Slab HVAC	2.0	2.0	31MAY74	04JUN74	04JUN74	06JUN74	2.0
2080-2010	Slab 2nd Half 1st Flr	3.0	3.0	03JUN74	06JUN74	03JUN74	06JUN74	0.0
2008-2012	Form & Pour Strs 1st Flr	4.0	4.0	03JUN74	07JUN74	01NOV74	07NOV74	107.0
2010-2012	Slab Shoring 1st Flr	10.0	10.0	06JUN74	20JUN74	24OCT74	07NOV74	98.0
2020-2022	1st Hlf Col-Beams 2nd Flr	2.0	2.0	06JUN74	10JUN74	06JUN74	10JUN74	0.0
2022-2028	2nd Hlf Col-Beams 2nd Flr	2.0	2.0	10JUN74	12JUN74	11JUN74	13JUN74	1.0
2024-2026	Start R/I Slab HVAC	2.0	2.0	10JUN74	12JUN74	11JUN74	13JUN74	1.0
2024-2028	Slab 1st Half 2nd Flr	3.0	3.0	10JUN74	13JUN74	10JUN74	13JUN74	0.0
2026-2030	Comp R/I Slab HVAC	2.0	2.0	12JUN74	14JUN74	14JUN74	18JUN74	2.0
2028-2030	Slab 2nd Half 2nd Flr	3.0	3.0	13JUN74	16JUN74	13JUN74	18JUN74	0.0
2028-2032	Form & Pour Strs 2nd Flr	4.0	4.0	13JUN74	19JUN74	07NOV74	13NOV74	103.0
2030-2032	Slab Shoring 2nd Flr	10.0	10.0	18JUN74	02JUL74	30OCT74	13NOV74	94.0
2040-2042	1st Half Col-Beams 3rd Flr	2.0	2.0	18JUN74	20JUN74	18JUN74	20JUN74	0.0
2042-2048	2nd Hlf Col-Beams 3rd Flr	2.0	2.0	20JUN74	24JUN74	21JUN74	25JUN74	1.0
2044-2046	Start R/I Slab HVAC	2.0	2.0	20JUN74	24JUN74	24JUN74	25JUN74	1.0
2044-2048	Slab 1st Half 3rd Flr	3.0	3.0	20JUN74	25JUN74	20JUN74	25JUN74	0.0
2046-2050	Comp R/I Slab HVAC	2.0	2.0	24JUN74	26JUN74	26JUN74	28JUN74	2.0
2048-2050	Comp R/I Slab HVAC	2.0	2.0	24JUN74	26JUN74	26JUN74	28JUN74	2.0
2048-2052	Form & Pour Strs 3rd Flr	4.0	4.0	25JUN74	01JUL74	13NOV74	19NOV74	99.0
2050-2052	Slab Shoring 3rd Flr	10.0	10.0	26JUN74	15JUL74	05NOV74	19NOV74	90.0

Figure 17   Portion of computer printout

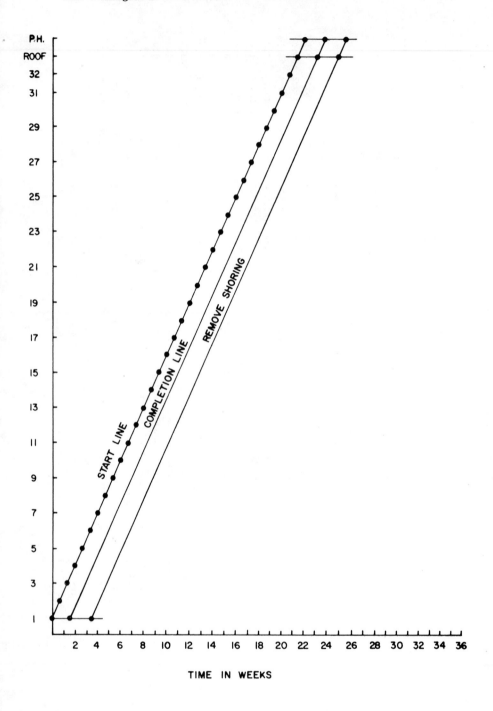

Fig. 18   Structural frame   Rate: 3 floors every two weeks

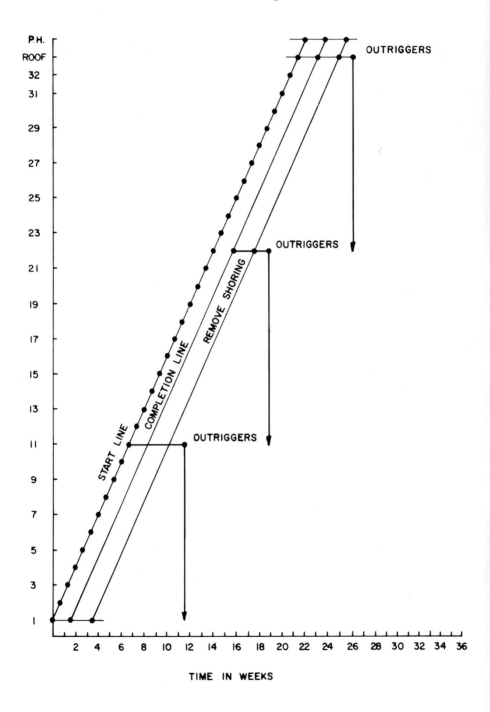

Fig. 19   Structural frame & outriggers

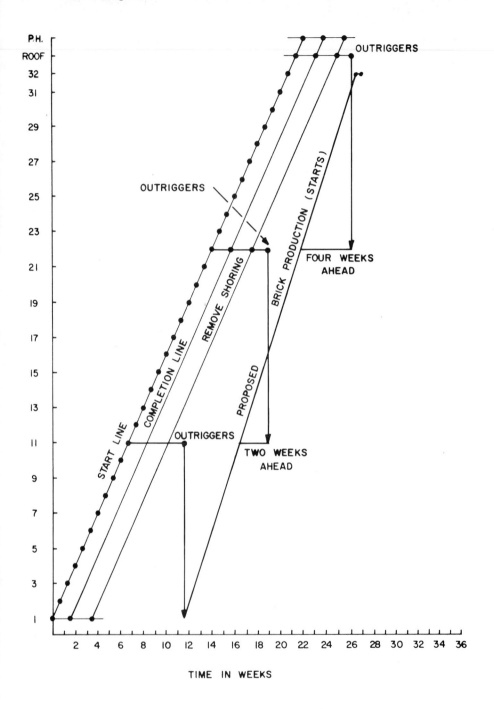

Fig. 20 Proposed brick progress vs. outriggers

Figure 21 shows the overall VPM for this project. Although complex, it is built up by adding one production line at a time. The slower rate curve of the later production lines indicates a typical situation in a high-rise, which is that the mechanical, electrical, and finishing trades usually do not move at as fast a rate as the structure can. Conversely, these slower trades cannot begin until the structure has actually been erected.

Summary

Preparation of the case goes through a series of steps. The primary phase is an information collecting one. If the team preparing a case, whether in defense or as a claim, has direct project experience—then this phase can proceed much more rapidly. The attorneys need the information from this basic phase to orient their activities to the specifics of the case, and to decide which legal approach or approaches to take.

The first phase is one of overview and strategy. Overinvolvement in details is probably nonproductive. In the second phase, after the basic legal scenario has been established, then evidence can be collected and developed into a presentation through summarizing, development of illustrations, cataloging and reviewing potential witnesses who can best bring out the material.

In a dispute, the best solution is settlement. Once litigation has been started, settlement is more probable when the parties have completed their first phase and have evaluated their weaknesses as well as their strengths. If settlement does not occur, a third phase of the case preparation would be finalization of the presentation, and tightening up of the loose ends and trimming down the material as much as practical.

In preparing a case, it is wise to keep in mind that the jury and/or judge are people. They can be bored or even angered by a presumptuous use of their time. A case should be trim, interesting, while still being legally complete. When in doubt, it is prudent to present more evidence rather than less, but in the total view, this is an approach that can win battles and lose the legal war.

Conclusion

When in doubt—Settle. When uncertain—Settle. When in the right—Settle.

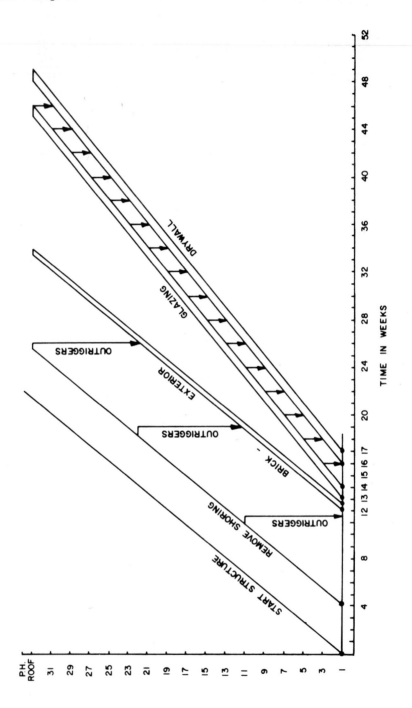

Fig. 21   VPM — Drywall — Glazing interface — initial plan

Part III·Reference Cases

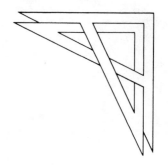

List of Cases

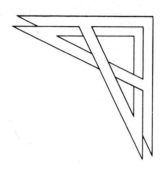

Reference Case 1

Aetna Insurance Co. v. Hellmuth, Obata and Kassabaum, Inc.

392 F. 2d 472

The United States Court of Appeals, Eighth Circuit, examined the responsibility of the architect or engineer in his construction supervisory duties.

A key decision on the part of the appellate court related to the responsibility of the supervising professional to parties which he was not in direct contract with. Following are the appellate court's opinions of the facts:

Westerhold Construction Inc. entered into a contract with the City of St. Louis, Missouri, for the construction of a Plaza at Lambert-St. Louis Municipal Airport. Aetna [the plaintiff surety company] signed this contract as surety for Westerhold guranteeing Westerhold's performance. The Architect, in addition to designing the plans and providing the specifications, agreed to supervise the construction and as listed in the written contract with the City, undertook "to perform professional services in the preparation of drawings and specifications and supervision of construction" and "general supervisory services and advice during the construction period." Aetna knew in undertaking to guarantee the performance of Westerhold that the Architect was the "engineer or architect in charge of work." The contract of employment of the Architect, however, does not define the terms "supervision of construction" or "general supervisory" services.

The construction project met with many difficulties and delays. The Westerhold firm was in financial difficulties from the start and was unable to complete the project without financial assistance from Aetna. Apparently Westerhold used funds from this project to pay judgments resulting from the operation of other projects. Bills on this project, therefore, were left unpaid, though that phase of the work had been completed and Westerhold paid on the Architect's certification. Aetna asserts that the architect was negligent in not making any effort at any time to ascertain to what use funds were put, even after receiving reports that subcontractors were not being paid.

Aetna also alleges substandard performance by Westerhold in carrying out the construction project which necessitated increased costs and some supplication of the work. In partic-

ular: (1) A concrete retaining wall bulged noticeably, apparently due to deficiencies in the forms used and the failure to properly tie in the forms; part of the work had to be redone. An employee of the Architect noticed the misaligned forms and testified he spoke to Westerhold about it, but neither he nor anyone else with the Architect went back to check to see whether this condition was corrected before the concrete was poured; (2) the project included a sewer ditch that was 15 to 20 feet deep at its deepest point. The contractor excavated the ditch with mechanical equipment but left it open and unfilled for a period from two to three weeks, in which time the ditch eroded or sloughed (became V-shaped). The single-strength vitrified clay pipe, called for by the specifications, was unable to withstand the added pressure caused by the increased weight, due to the widening of the ditch (by erosion and sloughing), and the matter had to be corrected by redigging the ditch and replacing the sewer with double-strength pipe. There were also deficiencies alleged in the collapse of the vertical inlets to the sewer pipe; in the actual laying of the pipe, and the failure to backfill the ditch in accordance with good construction practice. The specifications provided for the contractor Westerhold to make tests of the backfilling in the presence of the Architect. However, no such tests were required or performed, nor had the Architect given the contractor any instructions with reference to the procedure to be followed on account of the sloughing condition. Because of this, some pavement had to be replaced on account of settlement condition; (3) in addition to the repaving necessary by reason of the settlement condition of the sewer, some pavement had to be replaced because its appearance was not in accordance with specifications. Also, as an alleged result of the Architect's failure to properly supervise, the project was delayed beyond its completion date, causing additional expense in the performance of the contract.

After this recital of the facts, the circuit court of appeals quoted the trial court's opinion: "Plaintiff failed to demonstrate by substantial evidence that defendant breached any duty owed to plaintiff which would create liability on defendant. The appellee Architect contends that its duty under the contract ran only to the owner [City] and since there was no privity between Aetna and it, no cause of action was stated; and further points out that the construction job was completed in accordance with the plans and specifications." Basically, the trial court had found that there was no privity of contract between the Architect and either the Contractor or its bonding company,

Aetna. The contractual connection was between the owner and the Architect, and it is clear that there might have been an action by the City if any direct damages had been incurred by the City as a result of the Architect's actions in supervising the contract.

The appellate court depended upon an extensive discussion of the law of privity by the Missouri Supreme Court, which in a discussion of the relaxation of the rule requiring privity said: "[Relaxation of the rule] should be done on a case-to-case basis, with a careful definition of the limits of liability, depending upon the differing conditions and circumstances to be found in individual cases." Holding that the lack of privity of contract was not necessarily a bar to the recovery of loss to the surety occasioned by the architect's negligence, the appellate court discussed professional responsibilities as follows:

We think an architect whose contractual duties include supervision of a construction project has the duty to supervise the project with reasonable diligence and care. An architect is not a guarantor or insurer but as a member of a learned and skilled profession he is under the duty to exercise the ordinary, reasonable technical skill, ability and competence that is required of an architect in a similar situation; and if by reason of a failure to use due care under the circumstances, a foreseeable injury results, liability accrues. Whether the required standard of care was exercised presents a jury question. [Citations]

This question was also considered by Judge Donovan in the Minnesota case of Peerless, who aptly noted at pp. 53-954 of 199 F. Supp.:

" . . . the standards of reasonable care which apply to the conduct of architects, are the same as those applying to lawyers,
doctors, engineers and like professional men engaged in furnishing skilled services for compensation. . . . " and that general
negligence principles imply that " . . . reasonable care, which is
such care as a person of ordinary prudence would have exercised under the same or similar circumstances . . . " is imposed
on an architect as related to the skill, ability and professional
competence ordinarily required of a person licensed to practice
that profession. [Citations]

Appellee Architect also contends that Aetna failed to establish the standard of care owned by a supervising architect,
failed to show a breach of any standard, failed to show any
damages proximately resulting from the alleged negligence,
and therefore, failed to make a submissible case. Since this
case will be re-tried no purpose would be served in elaborating

on the evidence. The standard of care applicable is that of
ordinary reasonable care required of a professional skilled architect under the same or similar circumstances in carrying out
his technical duties in relation to the services undertaken by
his agreement. This includes the knowledge and experience
ordinarily required of a member of that profession and includes the performance of skills necessary in adequately cop-
ing with engineering and construction problems, which skills
are ordinarily not possessed by laymen. The words in the architect's contract requiring "supervision of construction" or
words of similar import are not words of art and should be
accorded their ordinary and usual denotation. This should be
true in the absence of evidence showing a different or more
restrictive connotation. There is, however, evidence in the record of what an architect would ordinarily be required to do
under the circumstances presented. While this evidence is not
as extensive as might be desirable, it was sufficient to make a
submissible case on negligence and damages.

The court reviewed the architect's assertion that:

. . . the word "supervision" is a word of art and that evidence
must be presented of what constituted due care in the exercise
of professional supervision. We do not think the common term
"supervision" is used as, or understood to be, a word of art in
the construction contract. If it is a word of art, the general rule
requiring expert testimony to establish the standard of care
applied to professions requiring knowledge, competency and
technical skill would be applicable. Morgan vs. Rosenburg, 370
S.W. 2d 685 (St. L. Ct. App.; 1963) clearly held expert medical
testimony is essential to establish the standard of proper skill
and care required of a physician, as laymen have insufficient
knowledge to pass upon that issue. [Citations]
  Most of the cases stating the general rule on expert testimony
to establish the standard of professional care [are] required [to]
deal with physicians and surgeons, but the same principle is
applicable to attorneys, architects and engineers and other professional men. As Prosser, Law of Torts (3rd Ed.) points out at
164: "Professional men in general, and those who undertake
any work calling for special skill, are required not only to exercise reasonable care in what they do, but also to possess a
standard minimum of special knowledge and ability."
  Prosser notes that expert testimony is necessary to establish
the standard of care required of those engaged in practicing
medicine, as laymen are normally incompetent to pass judg-

ment on questions of medical science or technique, but that: "Where the matter is regarded as within the common knowledge of laymen, as where the surgeon saws off the wrong leg, or there is injury to a part of the body not within the operative field, it has been held that the jury may infer negligence without the aid of any expert."

It is a matter of common knowledge that it is often difficult to secure the services of a professional man to testify in a case involving a claim of dereliction of duty by a fellow member in the profession. This undoubtedly holds true in architectural circles as well as others. There is some evidence in the case at bar regarding the duties of an architect in supervising a construction project and in carrying out his contract duties. This evidence is not as extensive as desired but was sufficient to make a submissible case. It does appear that there are certain duties patently required of the architect that are within the common knowledge and experience of laymen serving as jurors. It requires no particular technical knowledge on the part of the jury to pass upon the failure to supervise the back-filling of the sewer ditch when specifically required under the contract, the failure to correct misaligned forms utilized in retaining and supporting a poured concrete wall, or the significance of a sewer pipe that is misaligned and crooked. The jury is competent to pass on these issues without knowledge of the professional skills and competency required of architects in the ordinary performance of their skilled duties. Questions relating to stress and strain and weight-bearing capacities of structural elements are beyond the ordinary comprehension of most laymen and the court and jury require expert enlightenment on issues of this type. It, therefore, appears that the general rule requiring expert testimony to establish a reasonable standard of professional care is necessary when issues are presented that are beyond the competency of laymen jurors, but is not necessary in passing on factual situations that the ordinary laymen can readily grasp and understand.

Reference Case 2

Arc Electrical Construction Co., Inc. v. George A. Fuller Co. Inc.

24 N.Y. 99, 247 N.E. 2d 111; 299 N.Y.S. 2d 129, N.Y.; 1969

The plaintiff, Arc Electrical Construction Company, was the electrical subcontractor for the construction of a sugar refinery in Cayuga County. It brought the present action against the George A. Fuller Company, an intermediate contractor, alleging that the latter had failed to pay for work performed. After a trial without a jury, the supreme court awarded the plaintiff the full amount of its claim and, on appeal, the appellate division unanimously affirmed.

The contract—a standard printed agreement prepared by the defendant Fuller—provided for two different methods of computing the payments due to Arc. The first method, contained in article XXXI, was intended to apply while the contract was in effect. It provided for regular monthly progress payments constituting 90 percent of the amount due Arc for work performed during the preceding month, with the remaining 10 percent to be withheld pending completion of the project. In order to receive these monthly payments, Arc was required to submit a requisition, "subject to the approval by the Contractor [Fuller] and the Architect." The second method of payment was set forth in article XXXIII, which gave Fuller the right to terminate the contract at any time prior to completion. Unlike the progress payments under article XXXI—which had 10 percent withheld pending completion of the job—Fuller was required, if it terminated the contract prior to completion, to pay Arc the entire amount due at that time. There is no mention, in article XXXIII, of any requirement for the architect's approval.

Arc commenced work on the project in March 1965, and the first eight requisitions submitted, totaling about $1.4 million received the necessary approval and were paid in due course. In December 1965, however, the architect failed to approve Arc's requisition for the preceding month and, even though the work had been approved by Fuller's own project manager, no payment was made. Following this, four more requisitions were submitted, all of which lacked the signature of the architect's representative and none of which were paid by Fuller. Meanwhile, on February 18, 1966, Fuller's representative instructed Arc that it was exercising its option to terminate the contract and told it to cease all further work. The following May, Arc instituted the present suit for the amount due on all work it had performed since November 1965, plus the 10 percent reserve that had been withheld from its previous payments.

In awarding judgment to the plaintiff, the trial judge indicated that recovery was not based upon article XXXI, which provided for progress payments of only 90 percent subject to the approval of the architect, but upon article XXXIII, which contained no such limitations. He rejected the argument that the requirement for the architect's approval should be read into the provisions of article XXXIII, stating that such a construction of the statute "would require the rewriting of Article XXXIII" and that, in any event, the enforcement of such a condition after the contract had terminated would constitute an unenforceable "forfeiture." We agree with this conclusion.

Although the provisions for computing payments under articles XXXI and XXXIII are quite separate and distinct, Fuller contended that, at least where payment is being sought for the same work, the requirement for the architect's approval must, by necessary implication, be applied to both provisions. Otherwise, it said, Arc would be able to obtain payment under the termination provision for work that had already been found to be defective and had been properly rejected. "There is nothing to indicate," Fuller asserted in its brief, "that the mere passage of time would transform a bad claim into a good one."

There is considerable difference between the rejection of a claim for a progress payment and the refusal of payment after the contract has been terminated and all work has ceased. When the architect failed to approve Arc's requisition for a progress payment, this did not mean that its efforts would go permanently uncompensated. Arc was still on the job and could make whatever changes or corrections were necessary to satisfy the architect and qualify for more payment. The withholding of approval, though it may have been postponed, did not eliminate Arc's right to compensation for the work it had performed. However, once the contract was terminated, preventing the subcontractor from curing any defects, it is reasonable to construe the contract as providing for payment for all work actually performed, even though it may not have been entirely completed. If there were any deficiencies in performance, they would merely diminish the amount to which Arc would be entitled but would not result in the forfeiture of its entire right to be compensated. Such a construction of the contract, which adequately protects the interests of both parties, comports best with its language and we see no reason to rewrite article XXXIII of the contract—drafted, as we have noted, by

Fuller—to eliminate any obligation to pay for work performed in the absence of approval from the architect. In fact, Fuller was unable to show any defects in Arc's performance and the trial court awarded the full amount claimed.

It is also significant that there was no showing in this record of any defects in performance that could have justified the architect's failure to approve Arc's requisition. Although such approval, if given, would have been conclusive on the question of satisfactory completion of the work (see *20 East 74th St. v. Minskoff*, 308 N.Y. 407, 412-415, 126 N.E. 2d 532, 534-536), it is well established that, where work has, in fact, been substantially performed in accordance with the provisions of a contract, the withholding of approval does not bar recovery.

The rule is based upon the fact that the architect, in contracts of this sort, rarely a disinterested arbiter, is usually the representative of the party, often the owner, who must ultimately bear the cost of the work. In the case before us, the architect was the Vitro Corporation of America, the prime contractor from which Fuller was to receive its compensation. Since approval, when given, constitutes an admission that the work is acceptable, it may be relied upon as a good indication that the contract was, in fact, properly performed. On the other hand, there is no denying that the architect has some incentive to delay approval or even withhold it entirely, and the fact that, in this case, Vitro may have been reluctant to pay Fuller for Arc's work does not necessarily mean that Arc failed in any way to perform properly under its contract with Fuller.

The leading case of *Nolan v. Whitney* (88 N.Y. 648,) applied this principle in circumstances not too unlike those in the present case. There, as here, a contractor had brought suit to recover for work performed under a construction contract, and the defendant asserted the failure to obtain the architect's approval. A trial was held before a referee, who decided that, except for a trivial defect valued at $200, the work had been substantially performed and awarded judgment despite the lack of an architect's certificate. The court affirmed the award, stating that, "When [the plaintiff] had substantially performed his contract, the architect was bound to give him the certificate, and his refusal to give it was unreasonable, and it is held that an unreasonable refusal on the part of an architect in such a case to give the certificate dispenses with its necessity."

In sum, then, the trial court was entirely correct in applying the contract as it was written, without reading into it a requirement for the approval of the architect after the contract had been terminated. It is undisputed that the work had, in fact, been substantially performed by Arc and the fact that an architect, for some undisclosed reason, had failed to approve the work should not prevent the plaintiff from receiving compensation for its labors.

Reference Case 3
Benjamin v. Toledo Plate & Window Glass Company
8 Oh. L. Abs. 264; 1929

After a fire, the owner contracted with a glass company for the replacement of a number of large plate glass windows. Included in the replacement contract was a requirement that the windows be washed. The cost of the washing was to be shared by the owner and the contractor. Between installation of the windows and the washing, it was discovered that acid used by another contractor cleaning soot and smoke from the walls had etched the glass.

The owner refused to pay the glass contractor on the basis that the installation contract had not been fully completed. The court found that the glass contractor had, indeed, substantially completed, stating as follows: "If there was not a full and final performance as to the installation of the glass, then it might be said that the contract was not complete, and the glass was not delivered . . . in the condition that under the contract it was to be, but the glass windows were installed, the installation was complete, and there was nothing else to do concerning the windows excepting to wash the same and this operation was the joint enterprise . . . of the parties to this litigation, and this circumstance in our judgment, destroys the claim that the contract was not completed in the substantial and legal sense from which the glass company would retain responsibility for the delivery and installation of the glass itself."

Reference Case 4
Bentley v. State
41 N.W. 338, Wisc.; (1899)

The state hired an architect employed by a state commission to prepare plans and specifications for an addition to the state capitol building. The architect was also to superintend the work as the representative of the state. The work was well advanced when part of the structure collapsed. The contractor was required to restore the damaged section of the walls. He did so, and then undertook suit against the state for the additional cost involved in the restoration. The court found in favor of the contractor, ruling that the state was responsible for the specifications as furnished by their architect. From the decision:

According to such facts, the state undertook to furnish suitable plans and specifications, and required the plaintiffs to conform thereto, and assumed control and supervision of the execution thereof, and thereby took the risk of their efficiency. What was thus done, or omitted to be done, by the architect, must be deemed to have been done or omitted by the state. Moreover, we must hold, notwithstanding the English case cited—Thorn v. London, L. R. 1 App. Cas. D.C. 120—that the language of the contract is such as to fairly imply an undertaking on the part of the state that such architect had sufficient learning, experience, skill and judgment to properly perform the work thus required of him, and that such plans, drawings and specifications were suitable and efficient for the purpose designed. There seems to be no lack of able adjudications in support of such conclusions. Clark v. Pope, 70 Ill. 128; Daegling v. Gilmore, 49 Ill. 248; Schwartz v. Saunders, 46 Ill. 18; Seymour v. Long Dock Co., 20 N.J. Eq. 396; Sinnott v. Mullin, 82 Pa. 333; Smith v. Railroad Co., 36 N.H. 459; Railroad Co. v. Van Dusen, 29 Mich. 431; Burke v. Dunbar, 128 Mass. 499; Bridge Co. v. Hamilton, 110 U.S. 108.

Reference Case 5

Bethlehem Steel Corporation v. City of Chicago

U.S. Court of Appeals, 7th Cir.; 1965; 350 F. 2d 649

From the court records:

Plaintiff-Appellant [Bethlehem] brought this action to re-
cover an item of $52,000, together with certain items of interest,
withheld by the Defendant [City], as liquidated damages for
delay in furnishing, erecting, and painting of the structural
steel for a portion of the South Route Superhighway in the City
of Chicago. . . . The District Court concluded that plaintiff's
claims on the items in controversy should be denied and en-
tered judgment accordingly. We agree and we affirm.

The work which Bethlehem undertook was the erection in
Chicago of structural steel for a 22-span steel stringer elevated
highway structure, approximately 1,815 feet long, to carry the
South Route Superhighway from South Canal Street to the
South Branch of the Chicago River. Bethlehem's work was pre-
ceded and followed by the work of other contractors on the
same section.

The all important provision specifying $1,000 a day liquid-
ated damages for delay is as follows:

> *The work under this contract covers a very important section of*
> *the South Route Superhighway, and any delay in the comple-*
> *tion of this work will materially delay the completion of and*
> *opening of the South Route Superhighway thereby causing great*
> *inconvenience to the public, added cost of engineering and*
> *supervision, maintenance of detours, and other tangible and*
> *intangible losses. Therefore, if any work shall remain uncom-*
> *pleted after the time specified in the Contract Documents for the*
> *completion of the work or after any authorized extension of such*
> *stipulated time, the Contractor shall pay to the City the sum*
> *listed in the following schedule for each and every day that such*
> *work remains uncompleted, and such monies shall be paid as*
> *liquidated damages, not a penalty, to partially cover losses and*
> *expenses to the City.*
>
> *Amount of Liquidated Damages per day: $1,000.*
>
> *The City shall recover said liquidated damages by deducting*
> *the amount thereof out of any monies due or that may become*
> *due the contractor.*

Provision was made to cover delay in a contractor's start-
ing due to preceding contractor's delay. Unavoidable delays by

the contractor were also covered, and extensions thereof accordingly granted.

Bethlehem's work on this project followed by the construction of the foundation and piers of the superhighway by another contractor. Bethlehem, in turn, was followed by still another contractor who constructed the deck and the roadway.

Following successive requests for extensions of its own agreed completion date, Bethlehem was granted a total of 63 days' additional time within which to perform its contract. Actual completion by Bethlehem, however, was 52 days after the extended date, which delay the City assessed at $1,000 per day, or a total of $52,000 as liquidated damages.

Bethlehem contends it is entitled to the $52,000 on the ground that the City actually sustained no damages. Bethlehem contends that the above-quoted provision for liquidated damages is, in fact, an invalid penalty provision. It points out that notwithstanding the fact that it admittedly was responsible for 52 days of unexcused delay in the completion of its contract, the superhighway was actually opened to the public on the date scheduled.

In other words, Bethlehem now seeks to re-write the contract and to relieve itself from the stipulated delivery dates for the purposes of liquidated damages, and to substitute therefor the City's target date for the scheduled opening of the superhighway. This the plaintiff cannot do.

Reference Case 6

Bloomfield Reorganized School District R-6 v. E. M. Stites
336 S.W. 2d 95, Mo.; 1960

In 1955 the appellant, E. M. Stites, and the respondent, Reorganized School District R-6 of Stoddard County, entered into a contract in which Stites agreed to construct a combination gymnasium-music building in Bloomfield for the price of $276,247.

In substance the trial court found that the district was entitled to the possession of the building as of July 24, 1957, that Stites had breached the contract in that he had failed to complete the building within the time provided in the contract and therefore the district was entitled to $7,000 liquidated damages.

One of the substantial, controverted issues upon this appeal is liquidated damages. Article 2, after providing that the work was to be commenced immediately and substantially completed in 395 days, that the date of beginning, rate of progress, and time for completion were essential conditions, also contained this provision that was typed into the printed form: "If the said Contractor shall neglect, fail or refuse to complete the work within the time herein specified, then the said Contractor does hereby agree, as a part consideration of the awarding of this contract, to pay to the Owner the sum of $50, not as a penalty but as liquidated damages for such breach of contract as hereinafter set forth for each and every calendar day that the Contractor shall be in default after the time stipulated in the Contract for completing the work, not including Sundays." As indicated, the effective date of the contract was August 8, 1955, and its completion date September 8, 1956. On June 24, 1957, the work was not complete although it was 290 days beyond the promised completion date. Pursuant to the quoted provision of the contract and beginning with the contractor's estimates submitted after September 8, 1956, the school board deducted $50 a day from its payments to Stites, withholding as liquidated damages, according to the court, the sum of $10,300. In this connection the court found, without explanation, that the contractor was liable to the district for liquidated damages in the sum of $7,000 although the contract according to these figures was 290 days in default. But the district has not appealed and unless for some reason the contractor is entitled to a reduction in that item, or unless the contract provision is invalid, the sum found due by the court has finally determined the matter.

The contractor contended that the contract provision is not one for liquidated damages but instead is a penalty provision and therefore valid. If the provision is valid the contractor contended that the school district finally elected to terminate the contract and therefore could not also pursue the remedy of collecting liquidated damages. It was his position, furthermore, that any delays in completion of the work were excusable delays under the contract or were delays caused and brought about by the district or its architect, and therefore he was entitled to credit on the liquidated damages claim for the excusable delays, which, according to him, was the entire period.

The court ruled that: "In this particular contract between these particular parties and in the circumstances of this case, the liquidated damage provision is valid and enforceable and the amount provided is not unreasonably disproportionate to the 'actual injury suffered.' . . . And also in this connection, the district's claim and assertion of liquidated damages as of September 8, 1956, under Article 2 of the contract did not constitute an election of remedies and prevent the district's termination of the contract 290 days later. . . . Upon this subject Article 18 of the specifications provides that 'This article does not exclude the recovery of damages for delay by either party under other provisions in the contract documents.' "

Stites testified that there were delays due to a cement and steel shortage and to the weather, over which neither party had any control. He claimed that there were numerous delays attributable to the misconduct of the architect: denial of permission to fabricate his own steel, delay in supplying information as to light fixtures, refusal to answer inquiries as to two stairways and, in short, just about every item in the plans and specifications. Some of these matters for which Stites claimed credit were not specifically covered by the contract—the architect was not obligated under the contract to furnish some of the information, as to some of the items the architect was inexcusably dilatory, and some of the matters were not a substantial cause of failure to complete within the specified time. On the other hand, Stites was often exasperatingly dilatory and his testimony as to several matters was not too convincing. One item over which there was the greatest controversy was whether Stites could fabricate his own steel, particularly for the most important structural part of the building, the steel trusses. The matter was not specifically covered in the contract. Lorenz first denied and then granted permission subject to certain conditions. Stites was most uncooperative as to the conditions but in the end the fabrication in process was inspected by professional testers, the trusses were likewise inspected and their installation was entirely satisfactory and so this one item illustrates the useless bickering and waste of time.

Reference Case 7
Blount Brothers Corp. v. Reliance Insurance Company
370 F. 2d 733

The case in point involves the plight of a contractor who undertook a job, and then found the specifications to be much more difficult than he had anticipated. The owner required strict performance. The decision by the United States Court of Appeals for the 5th Circuit decided that a contractor who has had a reasonable opportunity to examine and study the work specified, and then overestimates his own ability to accomplish the work in the manner prescribed must suffer the consequences of his decision.

The contractor involved was the painting subcontractor, William Dunbar Company Inc., which was working for the prime contractor, Blount Brothers Corp., in the construction of a nuclear reactor facility in Montgomery County, Maryland. (Reliance Insurance Company was the surety for the performance of the work for the subcontractor.) The following statement of the situation is taken from the opinion of the court of appeals:

On April 25, 1963, Appellant Blount Brothers Corp., entered into a contract . . . for the construction of a nuclear reactor facility. . . . Blount entered into a subcontract with the William Dunbar Company . . . to perform certain portions of the prime contract, specifically the application of the special coatings in the nuclear reactor building and the painting in the laboratory and administration buildings.

By November 23, 1964, Blount, purporting to act pursuant to the authority of . . . the general terms of the contract, notified Dunbar of a termination of the subcontract. Thereupon, Blount found another subcontractor who was engaged to complete the work (a substantial part) not already finished by Dunbar, and filed this suit against the bonding company to recover damages by reason of the fact that the subsequent contract cost substantially more than the unpaid balance due on the original contract with Dunbar. . . .

As might be expected from the fact that the work related to rooms to be used in connection with the housing of a nuclear reactor, the wall, floor and ceiling coverings, the subject of this contract, were of unusual (called by some "sophisticated") coverings, quite different from the ordinary interior house paint. . . . GSA desired to have this building completed exactly as prescribed in the specifications.

. . . The subcontract required something unusual in the way of performance. It went much further than requiring that Dunbar cover the walls with a certain specified quality of wall covering. It required among other things, that, as to some of the work, the material to be used would have to be approved before application and it required further, that Dunbar be approved by the manufacturer of the material as a qualified applicator, and that Dunbar also be approved by the GSA as an approved applicator.

These requirements applied to four of the thirteen types of materials that were to be used in satisfaction of the painting and covering subcontractor. The types were numbered 1 to 13, but the materials required under categories 1 through 9 were promptly approved. The difficulty arose from the ultimate failure by Dunbar, at the time of termination, to commence applying Item 10 and to obtain approval of the unusual, but somewhat less sophisticated materials required for Items 11, 12 and 13, and the approval of the particular materials to be used to satisfy these requirements.

. . . It required several pages of the specifications adequately to set forth specifications for Type 10. It required 4 other pages to specify the items which Dunbar was required to submit to the government in connection with obtaining approval of a proposed manufacturer of special coating Type 10. . . . Types 11, 12, and 13 are non-elastomeric decontaminable coating intended for walls, ceilings and metal surfaces in the reactor area. It required four pages of the specifications to set forth the requirements as to these types, and six additional pages to specify the items which Dunbar was required to submit to the government in connection with obtaining approval of a proposed manufacturer of special coatings of Types 11, 12 and 13.

. . . Appellee defends largely on the concept that its bonded contractor had undertaken a very difficult subcontract which it was attempting, to the best of its ability, to carry out at the time of termination. A second defense is that at the time of termination others were at fault for the failure of Dunbar Company to satisfy the requirements imposed upon them by the subcontract.

. . . Appellee's brief says: "The fact is, and the record shows, it was Dunbar's contention throughout the proceedings . . . that he did everything possible to obtain approval, exercised due dilligence in doing so, and that the fault and the force of the difficulty encountered in securing the approval of certain coatings, lay in the specifications designed by the government."

It is difficult to see how the fact that Dunbar's difficulties arose from the specifications designed by the government could be in defense to Dunbar's failures. These were the specifications which the subcontractor agreed to be bound to. Moreover, the record is absolutely without dispute that it would be extremely simple for Dunbar to obtain approval of Types 11, 12 and 13, if this subcontractor had been willing to approach sources of supply, the names of which were furnished to Dunbar by Blount early in the period of the contract. Instead of this, Dunbar, entirely possibly because it had an interest in selling Vortex paint and coverings, twice submitted this product after it had been rejected by the General Services Administration. . . .

The absolute failure of Dunbar to furnish any of the schedules or any of the lists of materials and names of suppliers of Types 10, 11, 12 and 13 "before November 23" as required in Blount's letter cannot be excused by any testimony given in the trial.

Reference Case 8

Blount Brothers Construction Co. v. United States
346 F. 2d 962

The United States Court of Claims made the following comments:

Where specifications can and should but do not expressly provide for a desired condition in an end product such omission increases the duty of the drawings to be clear and free from ambiguity in portraying the condition.

Contractors are business men, in the business of bidding on Government contracts. They are usually pressed for time and are consciously seeking to underbid a number of competitors. Consequently, they estimate only on those costs which they feel the contract terms will permit the Government to insist upon in the way of performance. They are obligated to bring to the Government's attention major discrepancies or errors which they detect in the specifications or drawings, or else fail to do so at their peril. But they are not expected to exercise clairvoyance in spotting hidden ambiguities in the bid documents, and they are protected if they innocently construe in their own favor an ambiguity equally susceptible to another construction, for as in Peter Kewit Sons Co. v. United States, 109 Ct. Cls. 390, 419 (1947), the basic precept is that ambiguities in contracts drawn by the Government are construed against the drafter.

Brandt Corp. v. City of New York
14 N.Y. 2d 217; 199 N.E. 2d 493; 1964

In an HVAC contract valued at $350,000 for a municipal power plant, the contractor sued for a $20,000 extra work item that the city had required him to perform. The contract had the following statement in regard to the final payment by the city: "The acceptance by the Contractor or any person claiming under the Contractor of the final payment aforesaid, as audited by the Comptroller, whether such payment be made pursuant to any judgment or order of any Court or otherwise, shall be and shall operate as a release to the City from all claim and liability to the Contractor for anything theretofore done or furnished for, or relating to, the Works, or for any prior act, neglect, fault or default of the Board, the City or of any person relating to, or affecting the Works."

The plaintiff contractor claimed that acceptance of the final payment did not release the city from his claims, because six months earlier, he had reserved the claims in question. However, the court found for the city indicating: "When the plaintiff contracting company accepted the final payment under the contract, it could not thereafter assert claims for additional sums which it had attempted to reserve by a wholly unnecessary and ineffective general release which was not provided for or required by the contract."

Reference Case 10
Burke v. Ireland
166 N.Y. 305; 59 N.E. 914; 1901

In this case, the owner was sued because of the collapse of a building under construction. In the collapse fifteen people lost their lives. During construction, the contractor placed a central support column on an unstable foundation, consisting of backfill rather than solid ground. The suit was brought against the owner, and the court relieved the owner from any liability describing its reasons as follows:

> In this case the owner was not competent himself to plan the building which he desired to erect. He was not competent to construct or superintend the construction. . . . It was his duty to devolve these things upon persons possessing sufficient knowledge and skill to accomplish the result intended, with safety to the workmen and the public. . . . In other words, he committed the whole matter to a competent expert. . . . If the architect, who had general supervision, had insisted upon a careful inspection of every detail of the work and had been present when the concrete was about to be laid upon the disturbed ground outside the old cistern wall, he might have discovered a departure from the terms of the contract in that respect and prevented it. . . . He [the owner] omitted nothing that can be made the basis of a charge of personal negligence in going about the undertaking. He took all such measures to construct the building that any reasonably prudent man would under the same circumstances. . . .
>
> No one could reasonably anticipate or guard against the unfortunate result, except the experts employed to plan and erect the building.

Reference Case 11
Carroll Electric Co. v. Irwin and Leighton
80 Pa. Super. 438; 1923

Defendant general contractor had hired plaintiff to do certain electrical work on a tunnel construction project, the contract specifying completion dates and indicating that, "time is and shall be considered as of the essence of the contract on the part of the subcontractor." Plaintiff sued for increased costs of performance allegedly sustained by reason of defendant's failure to complete necessary prerequisite work in time. The superior court properly held that the time of essence clause related only to the subcontractor and imposed no liability on the general contractor for any of its delays. However, of greatest significance here, is what the court went on to say in reference to the proper construction of such clauses:

Referring to the paragraph first quoted above in regard to time being of the essence of the contract, it will be seen, this covenant relates only to the subcontractor. Had the parties wished to have it apply to both parties, the sentence would merely have stated that time was of the essence of the contract, but with the words added, 'on the part of the subcontractor' it was evident that the general expression was to be limited. As declared by the lower court, the particular mention of the one party excluded the other.

In Carroll, the court established a rule governing the construction of time of essence clauses, i.e., that unless specifically limited in its application, such a clause must be construed as applicable to both parties.

Reference Case 12
Cauldwell-Wingate Company v. State of New York
276 N.Y. 365; 12 N.E. 443; 1938

The plaintiff (Cauldwell-Wingate Company) was the super-structure contractor for a building project. The work was put out in separate phases. The foundation plans were furnished to the superstructure contractor, and indicated a relatively straightforward scope of work. He foresaw no problem in relying on the date specified for completion of the foundation work, and set about preparing to perform his contract.

In the meanwhile, the foundation contractor, who had anticipated demolition of two small brick buildings on the building site, found that the subsurface contained many old walls and masonry footings, as well as a number of wood piles. After this discovery, the state directed a subsurface study which confirmed the situation. Appropriate change orders were issued to the foundation contractor which extended his work for nine months beyond the date that had been utilized in the superstructure contractor's contract. The superstructure contractor sued for the cost of the delay which included escalation in salaries, an increase in the cost of workmen's compensation, and an escalation in the cost of materials. The plaintiff also sued for the imposition of a two-stage sequence where he had planned to develop the superstructure in one stage. Erection of the structure which had originally been scheduled for good weather was now deferred into a winter season, and the plaintiff sued to recover the additional costs of winter work. Another factor in the establishment of the damages was the cost of storage of materials that had been delivered to the site on the basis of the original schedule.

The court in finding for the plaintiff held that he had a contract to erect the superstructure as soon as the foundations were completed, and had entered into the contract on the representation of the state that the foundation work could be done within the date specified in the contract. The court found that the plaintiff had a right to rely on the plans and specifications for bidding purposes. Although these plans and specifications had a requirement for a site visit, the court ruled that the contractor was not obliged to make soundings or borings to validate the plans and specifications.

Reference Case 13
Citizen's National Bank of Meridian v. L. L. Glasscock Inc.
243 So. 2d 67

In this case, a contractor had sued its client, a bank, for extra work that he claimed was beyond the scope of his contract. The work had been ordered by the structural engineer employed by the owner's architect. The trial court awarded the contractor $8,902 on a quantum meruit basis for the extra work. (Quantum meruit operates when a party performs work either without a contract or beyond the scope of a contract. Basically, the law does not permit the individual to receive benefit without paying for it.)

The case involved demolition of an existing bank building and construction of a new bank on the same site in Meridian, Mississippi in 1964. After demolition, the contractor found a conflict between the existing foundations of the old building and the site for new concrete piling. The foundations had not been part of the demolition contract. Their presence was generally anticipated, but the specifics of their location and size was not known. The specification, anticipating the old foundations, had required that they either be bored through or removed. The contractor, with the permission of the structural engineer, chose to remove the foundations rather than bore through them. The removal required substantial expense, but according to his calculations, cost less than boring through them.

There was a conflict in the testimony between the engineer and contractor regarding the scope of the removal. The contractor felt that he was required to remove all of the old foundations, while the engineer testified that he had required removal of only that part which would make room for the new piling. After removal of the foundations, the contractor advised the architect that he considered the work beyond scope and that he required an extra work order. After some discussion, the architect agreed to forward the bill to the owner, but after some review decided that the work really was not beyond scope and therefore, would not certify the work to the owner as extra work. The key specification relating to this work was as follows:

2F - CONCRETE PILING

(a) Scope: Furnish labor and materials to complete bored, cast in place concrete pilings as indicated, specified herein or both . . .

*(4) Equipment: Use drilling equipment generally used in stan-
dard pile boring practice as approved.
(5) If obstructions such as masonry [sic] old foundations, etc.
are encountered, bore them as directed.
(6) Payment:*

> *a. Except as herein provided, no separate payment will be
> made for specified work; include all costs in connection
> therewith in Stipulated Sum for entire work under con-
> tract.*

The court found:

*We are of the opinion that the written contract expresses the
agreement of the parties and that it prevails over custom.
Courts do not have the power to make contracts where none
exist, nor to modify, add to, or subtract from the terms of one in
existence. . . .*

*With the above premise in mind and the contract before us,
there remains the question of whether the terms of the contract
between the parties permit an award on a quantum meruit
basis. We note immediately that such an award, if proper,
would require a finding by the court that the labor was not
anticipated by the contract, and also that there was no provisions of the contract by which payment could be made for
unanticipated labor. In the recent case of* Delta Construction
Co. of Jackson *vs.* City of Jackson, *198 So. 2d 592,600 (Miss.
1967), though relating to a public contract, nevertheless, expresses a principle of law we think equally applicable to private contracts. We there stated:*

> *The contract in the instant case requiring a supplemental
> agreement for extra work over minor changes is essential, be-
> cause municipalities and other governmental agencies obtain
> funds with which to build public improvements from bond is-
> sues based upon estimates furnished to them, and munic-
> ipalities must reserve the right to stop a project if they
> determine the extra work will exceed the amount of money allo-
> cated to any given phase of a project. . . . Furthermore, it has
> been generally held that no recovery can be had on an implied
> contract, or quasi-contract, or upon quantum meruit for extra
> work where the claim is based on an expressed contract.*

*The old foundations were anticipated since Section 2-F of
the contract refers to them with provision of method of procedure upon their being encountered and with the further provision that no separate payment would be made for this labor.
Article 15 sets forth the method of payment for extra work,
notable of which is that, "no extra work or change shall be*

made unless in pursuance of a written order from the owner," and Article 16 provides that in any event no claim for extra work shall be valid unless the contractor gives the architect written notice of his claim "before proceeding to execute the work." Finally Article 38 limits the architect's authority on behalf of the owner to the express terms of the contract or otherwise in writing.

We can only conclude in comparing these plain terms to the vague assumption of the contractor that custom of the trade would implement the written document in his behalf, that the former prevails. The written contract anticipated every contingency upon which this suit is based. Its very purpose was to forestall imposition of vague claims derivative of custom within the trade with which laymen are often unfamiliar. The owner, being desirous of limiting its financial obligation, should not have its pocketbook exposed to the custom of architects and contractors unless it agrees thereto. In this instance, the owner agreed to pay for extra work only if it was authorized in writing prior to its execution. Having contracted directly upon the point, there was no leeway for an award on a quantum meruit basis.

Reference Case 14

City of Lawton v. Sherman Machine & Iron Works

182 Okla. 254, 77 P. 2d 567

This case heard by the Oklahoma Supreme Court in 1938 involved an attempt by a contractor to recover balances he claimed were due according to the final certification of the city engineer. The contract contained the following provision: "To prevent all disputes and litigations, it is further agreed by the parties hereto that the City Engineer shall, in all cases, determine the amount and quality of the work of the several kinds of work which is to be paid for under the terms of this contract; and he shall decide all questions which may arise relative to the execution of the contract on the part of the contractor; and his estimates and conclusions shall be final and conclusive."

The city claimed that their city engineer had prepared a fraudulent certificate, and accordingly, the payment was not due. In regard to the question of actual or constructive fraud, the supreme court found: "Generally where an engineer is designated in a building or construction contract as the person who shall be the arbiter of the amount and character of the work done, and the amount due the contractor under the contract, the final certificate of approval of such engineer is binding upon the parties. The approval or certificate, however, may be avoided upon a showing of *actual* fraud or of such gross errors or mistakes as to constitute *constructive* fraud."

Reference Case 15
City of Littleton v. Employers Fire Insurance Company
653 P. 2d 810

The question considered in this case was that of an impossible specification requirement. As its first step, the court had to adopt a workable definition of impossible. Following this, it had to determine whether the defendant contractor had proved that the job could not be done according to the specifications. The case was heard in the Colorado Supreme Court.

The subject contract called for building two five–million gallon water tanks for the city of Littleton. Ultimately, the contractor (Latimer & Gaunt) defaulted, contending that performance of the specifications was impossible. The city brought an action for breach of contract. The trial court rendered judgment in favor of the contractor, and the city appealed to the state supreme court.

The facts, according to the court records, were: On May 8, 1961, Littleton hired the contractor to build two precast and prestressed concrete water tanks. The city's plans for each tank called for a poured concrete base of 175 feet in diameter. Around the edge, ninety-two precast wall panels 6 ft. by 29 ft. were to be set in slots in the base and joined. Once in place, the panels were to be prestressed by wrapping wire cable around the circumference of each tank. Following this plan, the tanks collapsed. After the collapse, the city and the contractor entered into a supplemental agreement that required reconstruction of the tanks in accordance with the plans and specifications already in existence. However, supplementary instructions were to be supplied by the city's consulting engineer. No work was done pursuant to the supplemental agreement. After the supplemental agreement was executed, the contractor made numerous requests for details regarding reconstruction without receiving the requested additional details in writing. On April 15, 1962, the contractor ended the agreement by telegram explaining that the design was faulty. The city then brought suit charging breach of contract under the supplemental agreement.

The trial court found that performance was impossible as a practical matter. Citing the Restatement of the Law of Contracts, Section 451, the trial court ruled that the impossibility constituted a complete defense to the city's claims. The city contended that the contractor either knew or should have known the facts that supported his defense when he signed the agreement. Further, the city and the contractor in that agreement indicated an intention that impossibility should not be a defense, and therefore that defense was now not applicable.

In reviewing the case, the supreme court first took up the question of what is a legal definition of impossibility:

The law recognizes impossibility of performance as a defense to an action for breach of contract. In his brief, the contractor suggests that we adopt the Restatement Section 454 definition of impossibility. According to Restatement, impossibility means not only a strict impossibility but impracticability because of extreme and unreasonable difficulty, expense, injury or loss involved. . . . "Impossible" must be given a practical rather than a scientifically exact meaning. Impracticability rather than absolute impossibility is enough.

Williston has stated that: "The true distinction is not between difficulty and impossibility. A man may contract to do that which is impossible. . . . The important question is whether any unanticipated circumstance has made performance of the promise vitally different from what should reasonably have been within the contemplation of both parties when they entered into the contract. If so, the risk should not fairly be thrown upon the promisor." [6 Williston, Contract Section, 1931, Rev. Ed.]

In testimony, the trial judge heard fifteen days of testimony including the expert testimony of several consulting engineers. One of the engineers said the construction as originally specified or as modified by the supplemental agreement was not possible either as a structure or as a water containing tank. Another engineer testified that he would not try to reconstruct the tanks on the information supplied. On crossexamination, the city's engineer admitted that the specifications would have had to have been changed to facilitate reconstruction.

The supreme court then considered the city's contention that the contractor made the agreement with the knowledge of the situation and that it precluded the defense of impossibility of performance. In this regard the court said:

According to the Littleton argument, when the contractor entered into the supplemental agreement, it knew or had reason to know of the facts which later furnished the basis for the trial court's finding of impossibility of performance. If the evidence supports this assertion, the impossibility of performance would be no defense to Littleton's case.

The supplemental agreement which had been submitted to the contractor by Littleton was signed by the contractor on November 11, 1961 and by Littleton on December 5, 1961. Since Littleton's argument bears directly on the knowledge which the contractor had when it executed the agreement, we will treat November 11, 1961 as a significant date.

The court noted that the agreement outlined the scope of work subject to modifications as the work progressed and promised additional information from the city's consulting engineer. Noting the evidence, the supreme court said:

The record is complete with evidence to support the proposition that conclusions as to the cause of collapse were not reached until well after the supplemental agreement was signed. For instance, Latimer testified that after signing the agreement he talked to other engineers and then came to the conclusion that the tanks could not be built according to any plans that had been furnished to that date.

The consulting engineer for Littleton theorized that the basic cause for collapse was an absence of grout in the joints and misalignment of the panels. But he testified that he had not reached a conclusion as to the cause of the collapse until March 1962, over a year after the supplemental agreement was signed.

Twice in April 1962 . . . the contractor requested additional instructions, and was told that the instructions given were sufficient. Only after Littleton once more demanded that reconstruction begin, without supplying additional instruction, did the contractor terminate the agreement.

Judgment of the trial court in favor of the defendant contractor was affirmed.

Reference Case 16

Clark v. Ferro Corp.

273 F. Supp. 230

This case involves the question of substantial completion in a performance contract. The case is by the United States District Court, Eastern District of Tennessee, in a dispute between a tile manufacturing company and a design-build company. The construction company had designed and built a new kiln for the tile company. The suit was brought to federal court because the failure of the new kiln had been a key factor in driving the tile manufacturing company into bankruptcy. The trustee in the bankruptcy appointed by the federal court brought action on behalf of the plaintiff.

The plaintiff, Hood Ceramic Corporation, was engaged in the production and sale of quarry tile with a plant located in Daisy, Tennessee. Hood was, at one time, the largest producer of the red and buff colored floor tile known for its durability. The Hood production facilities were beehive kilns of the traditional style.

By 1949, Hood was in competitive trouble because of the development of tunnel type kilns that permitted much greater production at lower cost by their competitors. Hood did not decide to make the move to tunnel kilns until 1957, as events proved too late to rescue its weak position. At that time they made a contract with Ferro Corporation through its allied engineering division for the design and construction of a tunnel kiln. These negotiations had required a period of years. The work was completed in 1958 and by 1961 Hood had filed for bankruptcy. The issues before the court were described as follows:

There are three major issues raised in the trial of this case which required a decision by the court. The first issue involves the construction of the contract entered into by the parties for the design and construction of the kiln.

The plaintiff contends that the defendant contracted to design and erect a tunnel kiln that should have a firing cycle of 78 hours, would operate on a schedule of one kiln car each two hours and ten minutes, and fire a minimum of 5,000 square feet of 6" x 6" x ¾" quarry tile or a minimum of 7,500 square feet of 6" x 6" x ½" quarry tile in a 24 hour period, seven days a week and 365 days a year, and that the tile thus produced would be not less than 95% standard or marketable grade.

In arriving at this construction of the contract, the plaintiff further contends that the contract is ambiguous and that parol evidence of prior negotiations is admissible in arriving at a construction of the contract. The defendant, on the other hand, contends that its obligation under the contract was only to properly design a kiln along the lines described in the specifications, in which the production schedule and quantity were only estimates, and then erect a kiln in accordance with that design.

The defendant denies that it specified that it would construct a kiln that would produce any particular percentage of marketable or standard grade tile and contends that no ambiguity exists in the contract in this respect which would render admissible parol evidence to vary or add to the specifications in this regard, but rather that Paragraph X of the contract specifically provides that the written agreement constituted the whole agreement between the parties. The defendant further denies that the parol evidence relied upon by the plaintiff would, in fact, establish any specification with regard to the production of a minimum percentage of marketable or standard grade tile.

The second major issue for decision is as to whether the evidence establishes a breach of contract by the defendant. In this regard, the plaintiff has introduced evidence which contends that only 41.25% of the tile fired through the kiln from January 1, 1958 through August 21, 1961, the date of bankruptcy, was of standard or marketable grade, with the kiln, by reason of defect of design and construction, causing cracking or other defects in the remaining tile fired through it.

The defendant, on the other hand, contends that no breach of the contract has been shown, that the evidence establishes that after the initial adjustment of the kiln in operation, the kiln operated satisfactorily, produced up to 80 to 95% standard grade tile, with cracking and defects in the tile being caused not by the design in operation, but rather by the plaintiff's other antiquated equipment and methods and by numerous other production faults and errors.

... Returning to the issue of the construction of the contract, the court is of the opinion that the specifications are ambiguous with regard to the production to be designed and constructed into the kiln and that parol evidence on this issue was properly admitted. The contract specifies, "estimated production—5,000 square feet 6" x 6" per 24 hours." Only two dimensions of the tile are given in the specification, the thickness of the tile being omitted. The thickness of the tile is significant in that approximately ⅓ or more tile of ½" thickness could be loaded upon each kiln car than would be the case of tile ¾" thickness.

The evidence reflected a tile ¾" in thickness was produced by Hood prior to the installing of the tunnel kiln and that Dr. Robson, Vice President of Ferro and manager of the Allied Engineering Division in charge of the design of this kiln, had visited and inspected the plaintiff's plant upon several occasions prior to drawing the contract and specifications and was aware that Hood produced ¾" tile. Although some contention appears to have been made on behalf of Ferro that tile ½" thick was more common in the industry, it was conceded by Dr. Robson that the reference in the specifications to 6 x 6" tile might appropriately be interpreted as referring to either tile ¾" or ½" thickness. The court is therefore of the opinion that in specifying estimated production the contract had reference to 5,000 square feet of 6" x 6" x ¾" per 24 hours. The quantity of tile which the kiln was designed to fire in any 24 hour period was therefore 5,000 square feet of 6" x 6" x ¾" tile or 7,500 square feet of 6" x 6" x ½" tile.

The parol evidence that was admitted was a letter written by Dr. Robson in the course of negotiations that read, "You will produce 5,000 square feet of tile per day, seven days a week, 365 days per year. You will produce an average of not less than 95% standard or saleable tile. Actually, our latest figures from one plant are 97% to 98% first grade ware. This ware is on uniform color and absorption so that necessary adjustments due to faulty tile and the job are entirely eliminated."

The court did rule in Hood's favor in regard to interpretation of the specifications. However, it ruled that evidence in regard to a claim for loss of profits due to the inadequacy of the new kiln did not establish such loss for the sufficient degree of certainty. Accordingly, the damages allowed were only the sum required to put the new kiln into proper working condition. Ferro was allowed to recover on its counter claim for the balance of payments due plus interest.

Reference Case 17
Collins v. Baldwin
495 P. 2d 74

This is a suit by the owner (Collins) against a contractor (Baldwin). The contractor had a dual contract with the owner. The first was to build a motel according to plans and specifications, and the second provided that the owner would sell the contractor a 25 percent interest in the completed motel. After construction, the owner brought action against the contractor alleging breach of the construction contract. The contractor sought to enforce his rights under the contract for acquisition of his 25 percent interest. The trial was held in the Oklahoma County District Court which, after receiving exhaustive evidence, ruled that the construction firm had substantially performed, even though it had failed to comply with certain specifications. The court did find damages in favor of the plaintiff in the amount of almost 20 percent of the original contract value.

The Oklahoma Supreme Court reviewed the case and discussed substantial completion, in part quoting from *Kizziar v. Dollar* (10th Cir. 268 F. 2d 914): "The law is settled in Oklahoma that when a contractor and builder has in good faith endeavored to comply with the terms of a contract, literal compliance in all details is not essential to recovery, especially where the owner has taken possession of the building." Quoting *Robinson v. Batty*, 75 Okla. 69, 181 P. 941, 942, the Oklahoma Supreme Court said: "Since the rule of exact or literal performance has been relaxed, literal compliance with a building contract is not essential to a recovery thereon, but a performance thereof in its material and substantial particulars is sufficient. There is substantial performance when the builder has in good faith intended to perform its part of the contract and has done so in the sense that the building is substantially what is provided for, and there are no omissions or deviations from the general plan which cannot be remedied without difficulty. . . ." The supreme court went on to say in reference to *Bushboom v. Smith*, 199 Okla. 688, 191 P. 2d 198,: "In such case the judgment should make monetary award to the injured party as would place him in the position he would have been in had the contract been performed, but it should not put him in a better position than he would have been had there been complete performance."

In commenting on this case Jabine (*Case Histories in Construction Law*, p. 27) notes: "It is doubtful some of the more

conservative courts would go as far as the Oklahoma Supreme
Court does in its relaxation of the old rule that specifications
must be strictly complied with, but this case is of importance
because of the weight it attributes to the good faith of the builder and the fitness of the structure for the use for which it was
intended."

Reference Case 18
W. G. Cornell Company, Washington, D.C. v. United States
376 F. 2d 299

This case involves an "or equal" portion of specifications. The United States Court of Claims has ruled that reasonableness must be applied in determining the real meaning of the contract. In doing so, the court specifically overruled the decision of various government boards who had previously denied contractor's payments from materials that the contractor contended were equal in quality to those described as the guideline perimeter in the specifications.

The subject case involved a contract for air conditioning facilities at Ft. Belvoir, Virginia. A rigid type of insulation for air ducts was required. Government engineers insisted on the rigid type, while the contractor indicated that he had assumed that a blanket type insulation would be considered equal. The contractor sued to collect the additional $3,000 it had cost to furnish the rigid insulation. Initially, the case was heard by the Engineers Board and by the Armed Services Board of Contract Appeals. Both Boards found against the contractor.

The plaintiff did not dispute the fact that the specification called for block or board type contract for insulated ducts. He depended, however, on established trade usage that has permitted the use of blanket insulation in the performance of contracts such as the one in which he bid. The plaintiff introduced specific examples of cases where the Corps of Engineers in similar cases allowed the use of blanket insulation. Specific evidence was shown that the plaintiff's contractor (General Insulation Company) had performed insulation work on approximately twelve prior contracts in which blanket insulation had always been approved and accepted by the same Corps of Engineers district office as the one involved in this appeal.

The court reversed the findings of the two boards indicating: "It is clear the plaintiff did not consider that the specifications furnished by the Government were unclear, ambiguous, or subject to a construction different to the one given to them by the plaintiff. The record shows that the plaintiff prepared its bid and planned and attempted to perform the contract work in a manner consistent with its interpretation and construction of the contract specifications. Plaintiff gave a meaning to the specifications which, in the light of its knowledge of how similar contracts had been treated in the past, was not unreasonable or in any way improper under the circumstances here."

In defending, the United States put great stress on the contention that the provision in the contract was not ambiguous and capable therefore of only one interpretation. The court disagreed:

The technical provisions and specifications incorporated in the contract are ambiguous. . . . It is apparent that more than one reasonable conclusion can be reached. . . . The phrase "other equally suitable material" could very well be meaningless if that [defendant's approach] construction were adopted. . . . Had the word "rigid" or an equivalent been inserted in the contract so that the specification read "other equally suitable rigid material" the case would take on a different appearance. . . . As noted previously, the contract and the Wunderlich statute vest discretion in the contracting officer to approve or disapprove of insulating material. It is apparent . . . that he was not justified in disapproving of blanket insulation. The contracting officer disapproved the substitution of blanket material, not because it was inferior but because he interpreted the contract as giving the Government the right to insist on rigid insulation, even though the blanket material was equal in all respects.

Reference Case 19
County of Tarrant v. Butcher & Sweeney Construction Co.
443 S.W. 2d 302

This case involves the principals governing deviations from plans and specifications. It was heard by the Texas Court of Civil Appeals. The County of Tarrant brought suit against the contractor Sweeney for a court house and jail, as well as against the architects who designed the structure and an engineer who was a member of their firm.

In 1959, the Commissioners Court of Tarrant County (Ft. Worth) decided to build a court house and jail structure. They employed architects who agreed to work for less than the full AIA fee because they would not have the obligation to regularly inspect the construction. During construction the contractor deviated from the plans and specifications in a number of ways, including: it attached shelf angles to a concrete wall with studs rather than expansion bolts as called for in the plans; it installed shelf angles with three-inch legs projecting horizontally rather than five-inch legs called for; and it did not install brick anchors twenty-four inches on centers vertically and horizontally.

The jury agreed that the contractor had deviated from the plans and specifications. However, evidence was presented to show that the engineer working for the architect had approved the changes, in accordance with the construction contract that authorized the architect to approve minor changes not involving extra cost and also not inconsistent with the purpose of the building. The jury found that before the building was finished, the project inspector and the county engineer knew of the deviations. No complaint was made at this time to the construction company because of the deviations.

In conjunction with this general situation, the county sued the architect for damages caused by negligence in failing to provide for expansion joints in the brick veneer walls. The jury agreed that the architect had failed to use the proper degree of care in regard to the weep holes and flashing. It found that the county was damaged $700 by this failure, but refused the county claim $128,722 as damages in the other changes. In affirming the judgment, the appellate court stated:

. . . The generally approved standards for measuring the owner's loss from defects in the work are two: First, in cases

where the defect is one that can be repaired or cured without undue expense, so as to make the building conform to the agreed plan, then the owner receives such amount as he has reasonably expended or will reasonably have to expend to remedy the defect. Second, if on the other hand, the defect in material or construction is one that cannot be remedied without an expediture for reconstruction disproportionate to the entity obtained, or without endangering unduly other parts of the building, then the damages will be measured not by the cost of remedying the defect, but by the difference between the value of the building as it is and what it would have been worth if it had been built in conformity with the contract.

Reference Case 20
Depot Construction Corp. v. State of New York
41 Misc. 2d 764; 246 N.Y.S 2d 527

In this case, the work was performed in a manner that had not been contemplated by the contractor when he prepared his contract. The state attempted to hold the contractor to unit prices in the contract. However, court of claims found that these unit prices did not apply, saying: "The Court agrees with the claimant and finds that this was not additional work under the terms of the contract, but that it was work outside any reasonable contemplation at the time of the contract. The State, by its own actions, caused the extraordinary conditions to arise and the claimant is entitled to be reimbursed fairly outside the general provisions of the contract."

On appeal, the Appellate Division, 3d Dep't., 23 A.D. 2d 707, 257, N.Y.S. 2d 230, noted that where there is a qualitative change in the nature of the work, as distinguished from a quantitative change, the contractor is entitled to compensation on a quantum meruit basis and that in such case the unit prices in the contract do not apply. The court said: "As previously noted, the State does not here dispute all liability, just the method of computing the amount of the award for the overrun. Since we do not find the State to have been guilty of bad faith or fraudulent misrepresentations with respect to the test borings, the test is whether the additional excavation amounted to only a quantitative change in the amount of rock to be excavated or a qualitative change in the nature of the work to be performed. If a mere quantitative change is involved the contract provisions would apply as the State contends. . . . On the other hand, if there is a qualitative change the respondent would be entitled to compensation for the extra work on a quantum meruit basis."

Depot was affirmed by this court, in 19 N.Y. 2d 100, on the ground that the work in that case involved a quantitative, and not a qualitative change, and that the contractor agreed to assume the risk of quantitative changes. This court did not change the ruling of the appellate division in that where there is a qualitative change, the contract prices do not apply, and the contractor may then recover in quantum meruit.

Reference Case 21
Joseph F. Egan, Inc. v. City of New York
17 N.Y. 29 90; 18 A.D. 2d 357

The general facts of this case are discussed in detail in chapter 2, "Construction Law". The statement of facts below is taken from the court records:

Plaintiff appeals from a judgment entered on May 8, 1963 on an order of the Appellate Division, First Department, which (1) reversed on the law a judgment of the Supreme Court, New York County, for $160,089.56 entered on June 14, 1960 upon a verdict in plaintiff's favor after trial before Mr. Justice Carney and a jury, and (2) dismissed the complaint. The jury had awarded $23,951.88, the full amount claimed for alleged extra engineering service, and $120,000, the full amount claimed for delay damages. The balance of the judgment was for interest of $15,754.68 and costs.

This action was brought by the plumbing contractor in the construction of Elmhurst General Hospital for the City of New York.

Plaintiff was one of four prime contractors who were awarded contracts on the construction of Elmhurst General Hospital. The others were the general contractor, the heating and ventilating contractor, and the electrical contractor.

The complaint stated four causes of action: (1) for extra work under the contract, (2) for work plaintiff claimed was extra work under the contract, (3) for delay damages plaintiff allegedly sustained due to defendant's acts, and (4) for breach and abandonment of the contract.

The first cause of action was settled during trial and the fourth cause of action dismissed at the close of the plaintiff's case. Except for an alleged extra of engineering services, reduced in amount claimed to $23,951.88, the items of the second cause of action were settled during the trial. Such item of engineering services and the third cause of action in the amount of $120,000 were submitted to the jury for determination.

Relative to the Delay Damage Claim

Where the contract provided for completion in 840 days but, principally by reason of the defective plans issued by defendant, plaintiff-contractor was delayed in performance of its contract work for an additional period of 383 days until its work was approved as substantially completed, and was subjected to greatly increased costs by reason of such delays and the disorganized performance caused thereby; and where, by reason of such increased costs and damages, and as a result of changes for extras not acted upon and unpaid, although years overdue, plaintiff, which had been approved by defendant on award of contract as financially capable of performing the work, and which had worked exclusively on this contract for the three years prior to substantial completion, found itself at the time of substantial performance, 383 days subsequent to the originally scheduled date for entire performance, with only $303 in its bank, and with debts for work performed under the contract in the sum of $314,079, and where its creditors were threatening steps which would result in the complete financial ruin of the plaintiff; and where, at the time of substantial completion, the contractor would normally have received a substantial completion payment of $179,000, exclusive of the extra work items improperly delayed, and such payment would have been sufficient to forestall its creditors; and where the contractor was entitled, as a matter of right, to an extension of contract time as, concededly, it was not responsible for the delays, and, pursuant to the terms of the contract, the contractor could not obtain such substantial completion payment without previously receiving such extension of time; and where the Commissioner had knowledge of the financial losses sustained by the plaintiff on the job, and the large outlays for extra work still unpaid by the defendant, did a fact question exist as to whether it was economic duress for the Commissioner, with knowledge of plaintiff's financial plight, to refuse to act upon or grant such extension of time, unless the contractor waived its intended claim for damages resulting from said delays and disorganized performance?

The following questions were posed by the counsel (Max E. Greenberg et al.) for Egan:

Where, subsequent to substantial completion of plaintiff's work, and the plaintiff's execution under economic duress of a waiver of delay claim as a condition to its receipt of the substantial completion payment, entire completion of plaintiff's contract work was further delayed, by reason of the defective plans, for a further period of 2½ years past substantial completion until entire completion, and where, in granting an extension of time, the defendant's Commissioner reserved in writing the right to impose liquidated damages for the entire delay period; and where, during this further 2½ year period after the substantial completion payment was made, there were pending undetermined claims for extras to be acted upon by the Commissioner, and there still remained due a conceded contract balance ultimately approved in the sum of $206,612.34, which was paid in several payments over the 2½ years; and where, until this sum was paid and its contract work accepted, plaintiff was in fear of the adverse actions or reprisals anticipated from the Commissioner were it to accuse him of extracting the waiver of its delay claim by coercion; and where immediately upon entire completion and acceptance of the work and the full accrual of its delay claim, and immediately prior to its receipt of its completion payment, conceded to be due by defendant, in the sum of $98,830.75, plaintiff, in disregard of its previous waiver of its delay claim, obtained under duress as aforesaid, made claim for damages due to the delays and disorganized performance caused by defendant's defective plans, can it be held, as a matter of law, that plaintiff failed to make timely disaffirmance of the waiver executed under duress?

Can the court below, as a matter of law, properly reverse the judgment based on the verdict of $120,000.00 on the delay claim, and dismiss the complaint on the ground the verdict was substantially in excess of the supporting figures and cannot be sustained, where the plaintiff offered uncontradicted proof that the defendant was responsible for 91 percent of the 383 day delay, and defendant conceded plaintiff's delay damages to be $103,224.00, plus any provable additional labor costs resulting from disorganized performance caused by defendant's faulty plans, which plaintiff, by uncontradicted testimony comparing its actual labor costs with the fair and reasonable cost of performing the work under proper plans, showed to be an additional loss of $170,926.75 above the $103,224.00 conceded sum, and the Trial Court, without exception taken, charged the jury that it could find defendant's proportionate responsibility for the conceded loss of $103,224.00 and such losses on labor productivity as it might find, but not to exceed a total of $120,000.00, the amount in plaintiff's original notice of claim?

The court found as follows:

In this contract action, the plaintiff seeks to recover the stipulated reasonable value of extra work performed on a construction job, and damages allegedly resulting from delays in the progress of the construction schedule due to the defendant's fault.

A judgment of the Supreme Court awarding the plaintiff $23,951.88 on the extra work claim, and $120,000 on the delay claim, after trial with a jury, has been reversed by the Appellate Division, and the complaint has been dismissed.

Dismissal of the extra work claim is predicated on plaintiff's failure to comply with the "notice" and "protest" provisions of the written contract. Dismissal of the delay damages claim is based on plaintiff's written waiver of any right to recover therefor in exchange for an extension of the contract completion date and a substantial completion payment.

In 1952 the plaintiff's bid for the plumbing contract in connection with the building of Elmhurst General Hospital was accepted by the defendant. From the beginning of the work, numerous necessary changes in the construction plans and problems arising out of poor co-ordination between various contractors caused delays in the construction schedule.

In regard to the delay claim, the court stated:

Plaintiff contended that economic duress practiced by the Commissioner induced it to sign a waiver of any claims for damages due to delay, in exchange for an extension of the completion date and a substantial completion payment.

The court below held that the proof did not establish duress and that, even if it did, the duress was practiced in 1956 and not disaffirmed until 1958, and thus not disaffirmed within a reasonable time. We agree.

Since an extension of the completion date was essential to obtaining a substantial completion payment, it appears that the plaintiff, in its extension application, agreed to waive delay claims because it was told that a completion payment would not otherwise be approved. Thereafter, the plaintiff spoke to the Commissioner, who persisted in demanding the waiver. Plaintiff explained his need for the money in order to pay bills, but the Commissioner was unmoved.

This fails to establish duress. There is no showing that the defendant did anything more than affirm its previously stated position, and that the defendant was in no way responsible for the plaintiff's financial distress. Moreover, under the terms of the written contract, the granting of a substantial completion payment rested solely in the discretion of the Commissioner.

Finally, if we were to reach the question, we would agree that the alleged duress was not promptly disaffirmed. Plaintiff claims that the two-year delay was born of fear of reprisals based upon other contracts it had with the defendant. Such self-imposed, undisclosed, and subjective fears do not constitute an act of duress by the defendant cognizable in law.

Fanderlik-Locke Co. v. United States F/U/O Morgan
285 F. 2d 939, 10th Cir.; 1960

The general contractor sought to invoke an owner's dispute clause upon his own subcontractor in opposition to a subcontractor's suit for extra painting work furnished in an Air Force base construction project. The court rejected the general contractor's argument, noting:

If Morgan is limited to the presentation of his claims as provided for in the disputes clause of the prime contract he has surrendered his right to the benefits of the Miller Act provisions. The findings of the administrative authorities as to the amount that he is entitled to recover would be conclusive. . . . An agreement should not be construed to bring about such a result unless it be 'manifest by plain language' of the contract. . . . Language of the subcontract references are to the general conditions of the prime contract not the general provisions and they relate generally to performance of the subcontract according to specifications not to the settlement of disputes, or the subcontractor's right to sue under the Miller Act.

The court in the decision held that the dispute mechanism clause was not incorporated into the subcontract commenting: "If a prime contractor is dissatisfied with the administrative disposition of a claim submitted under the 'disputes clause' of the prime contract, it may seek a remedy in the Court of Claims. The liability of the United States is to the prime contractor."

The court saw it as improbable that the subcontractor and the prime contractor would have intended to prescribe the procedure used in dispute settlement between the government and the prime contractor (with the subcontractor having the obligation to pursue and exhaust administrative remedies) when the U. S. Congress had established a separate procedure under the Miller Act for a subcontractor to bring suit against its contractor, a procedure the subcontractor had properly chosen.

More recently, the Fourth Circuit Court of Appeals affirmed the Fanderlik decision in a case where the subcontractor and prime contractor disagreed over the responsibility for redoing certain work.

Reference Case 23
Fanning & Doorley Construction Co. v. Geigy Chemical Corp.
305 F. Supp. 650

In this case heard in the United States District Court in Rhode Island, the contractor claimed that failure of a certain pipeline in his work was due entirely to defective specifications requiring the use of specific materials and techniques, while the defendants claimed the failure was due to defective workmanship.

In 1958, Geigy Chemical decided to build a new system of underground piping at its Cranston, Rhode Island plant. It hired Metcalf & Eddy, consulting engineers from Boston, to design the system, and to supervise the field work. The work in the proposed contract included a cast iron water piping system, concrete storm drains, a vitrified clay sanitary sewer, an industrial waste sewer, a booster pumping station. Metcalf & Eddy specified that the industrial waste system should be made of chemical stoneware bell-and-spigot pipe. The caulking material to be used in the pipe joints was a special material called Causplit. This material is a mortar made by blending a resin and powder resistant to the corrosive effects of acids, alkalis, and alcohols that were included in the plant discharge.

The contract was to start in September 1959 to be completed by February 1960, a 180-day contract period. The agreement between the parties required that the engineering firm would in all cases determine the amount, quality, acceptability, and fitness of the work. Article II stated that the contractor would do everything that the contract required "in the manner and within the time specified and that the entire work would be completed to the satisfaction of the engineer."

Fanning & Doorley began installation of the stoneware pipe and Causplit joints in December 1959. It had not previously installed this type of work. F & D did not make contact with the manufacturer, but it did seek guidance from the owner. At that time F & D was told that the work would be under the direction of the resident M & E engineer. When the first joint was made, it was done under the direction of the resident engineer who participated in the mixing and placing of the first joint. The resident engineer later testified that thereafter the recommendations of the manufacturer were carried out at all times by the contractor, that the joints were made under his (the engineer's) supervision, and backfilling was made only after approval of the resident engineer.

Some of the various measures tried at the direction of the engineer (and later the manufacturer) included:

1. December 1959—simple troweling employed at the start.
2. December 18—because of water condition, engineer directed that the pipes should be dried by the application of heat.
3. December 21—pipe was to be cradled with concrete and coated with asphalt then heated (this was further modified December 22).
4. December 31—the manufacturer replaced the Causplit mortar with one having a faster setting ingredient and recommended the use of space heaters.
5. January 13—a representative of the manufacturer suggested that more powder be added to the mix to increase the setting time. He also recommended that sulphur cement be poured around the Causplit with the understanding that this would eliminate the requirement to dewater the trenches and to apply heat to the pipes to cure the mortar.
6. January 25—reprocessed mortar was received from the manufacturer.
7. February 1—to keep mortar in the joints, manufacturer suggested placing dry ice under the mortar pan.
8. February 2—representative of manufacturer at the job site made a sample joint, and found that the mortar was not workable in that it slumped out of the joint. He recommended changes in procedures which seemed to help.
9. Febuary 26—manufacturer's representative tested a joint made under his direction and found that leakage exceeded the specifications.
10. March—the joint the manufacturer made showed an even greater percentage of leakage.

Finally, on March 10, M & E project engineer told F & D to stop laying the chemical stoneware. A factory representative of the caulking material came to the job site, and employing new techniques finally devised a procedure for making leak-free joints. Part of the new technique was the use of a different caulking material. (However, even the first joint made under the new procedures had void spaces in the top part.) It should be noted that one of the reasons for the contractors' perserverance with the changing requirements was the type of contract they were under. They were to be paid on the basis of cost plus

15 percent, however, the total amount payable was not to exceed a specific top limit.

The defendant (Geigy) argued that the plaintiff's work was defective in that, among other things, certain pipes were cracked, void spaces were found in the mortar of many joints, improper caulking and fitting of the pipes was also discovered.

The court found that this was not acceptable as proof of poor workmanship, or as a contributing cause of the leakage. Testimony showed that the cracks may well have been caused by a backhoe that was used by the defendant in excavating the ground to expose the pipes for inspection.

Findings of the court were as follows:

1. *All joints made up to March . . . were made by the contractor following the specifications and in strict accordance with the directions, orders and recommendations of the engineer and the manufacturer.*
2. *That up to March 1960, it was not possible to make a tight joint following the procedures and directions theretofore specified.*
3. *That the specifications required the contractor to do work in a manner and to a degree which could not produce the desired results as originally written insofar as the chemical stoneware system for the disposal of industrial waste was concerned. The specification requirements and all specific directions, recommendations and orders prior to March 23, 1960 were defective, inadequate and faulty.*

The court found in favor of the contractor in the amount of $103,414.

Forest Electric Corp. v. State

275 N.Y.S. 2d 917

This is a memorandum decision of the New York Court of Claims that discusses the responsibilities of the state, and its architect, in regard to coordination on a project. The memorandum is as follows:

This is a claim against the State by the claimant which was one of seven prime contractors who had bid on several specifications for the erection of the Reception Building, known as Building No. 102, at the Bronx State Hospital, Bronx County, New York. The claimant was to furnish labor and material for the electrical work. Depot Construction Corporation was the general construction contractor. Other contracts were for heating, sanitary work, refrigeration, elevator work and food service equipment.

These contracts were entered into on May 12, 1959, and were to terminate on December 1, 1961. In all the contracts it was provided that the work of each contractor was to harmonize and be installed in conjunction with the work of the other contractors, especially the general construction contractor. The State Architect had supervision of and direction over the contract work as well as authority to bring about proper execution of the contract requirements, particularly work or job coordination, in order to insure unimpeded progress of the contract.

Claimant alleges that it performed all the terms of the contract; that its part of the contract was duly accepted by the State on or about December 20, 1963; that the State breached the said contract in that it unreasonably failed to coordinate the work of other contractors with the work of the claimant, permitted delays in the construction of walls, ceilings, painting, elevators, plastering, hanging ceilings, ceramic tiling, all of which were preliminary to claimant's work and, as a result, claimant's work was hampered and delayed.

The claimant further charges that the contract required the State to provide two hoists for material and one elevator for the workmen. The State, upon removal of hoists, provided only one elevator for hoisting men and materials, all of which caused claimant to expend additional sums of money for work, labor, material and equipment.

The proof indicates that the general contractor was quite indifferent to its obligation to properly man, supervise and coordinate its work and the facilities necessary for the smooth performance of the entire job which held up the work of the claimant and that the State was lackadaisical and indifferent to the many and continuing complaints of the claimant. As an example, concrete slabs for the structure were to be laid commencing February, 1960. They were not laid until the beginning of March, 1960, holding up the related work of all other contractors, including the claimant. Nevertheless, the claimant by maximum effort and even overtime work, finished in time the work involved in that phase of the contract.

The general contractor used one superintendent for three separate jobs on the hospital site and intermingled its operations and men to the detriment of the job on which the claimant worked. The State permitted it to use one engineer for two hoists and also permitted removal of the two hoists when only one interior elevator was available and not at least two, as required by the contract. The brick work was delayed, as well as the lathing, the plastering and the painting, the setting up of door bucks, ceiling work, and the affixing of cabinets.

Hoists were not made available to claimant to the extent required by the contract. Claimant had to store on the first floor over 4,000 fixtures because hoists or elevators were not available, necessitating the use of a crane to lift the fixtures to the various floors, involving thus a double operation of equipment and manpower by the claimant.

The testimony indicated that there were various strikes during 1960 and 1961, which would affect the general operation of the general contract, but from all the evidence it would seem that had the general contractor been made to perform in timely fashion by the State, said general contractor would have been ahead of the several strikes in most instances, as claimed by the claimant. State's finding #134 concedes claimant had performed 90% of its work by June 18, 1962. Although it is difficult to assess how much could have been thus gained or lost by virtue of the strikes, the Court feels that no more than one-quarter of the time lost could or should be assessed in favor of the State in regard to this claim. Likewise, since the claim for time lost waiting for hoists and rehandling of fixtures is an estimate, the Court allows only one-half of the time claimed as a reasonable estimate of that time.

In general, by letters and intermittent oral complaints, the claimant drew the attention of the State to the delays caused by the general contractor, and the answer was almost always that the State could do nothing about these complaints, and that these were merely matters requiring job-site coordination. Behind this "job-site coordination," which is a built-in a priori protection, in such contracts the State seemed to take a cavalier, albeit benevolent, attitude towards the many requests of this claimant for use of its effective authority over this contract.

In all, only seven job coordination meetings were held on this job which lasted from May, 1959, to December 20, 1962 and, actually, to about May, 1964, because of many of the small items still to be completed after December 20, 1963.

The claimant's findings found by the Court itemize these delays and complaints, which are to be deemed a part of this decision. These specify the delays which impeded and held up the claimant's performance of the contract. The State had a duty to coordinate the entire job and failed to perform this duty.

Reference Case 25
Foundation Co. v. State of New York
233 N.Y. 177

In this case, the contractor was required to perform seven pumping operations instead of the one which he had contemplated. This caused damages due to the increased number of pumps and workmen and the maintenance of separate pumping installations. Because of these facts, it was held that the unit price for pumping (which was based on a single pumping location) would not apply to the cost of pumping. The court held: "While the bid for pumping under the original plans may have been adequate, it may have been utterly inadequate if the work were done as the changes required by the State compelled it to be done. It would be inequitable to confine the bidder to a unit bid made to meet entirely different conditions. Nor are we required, as we are required with regard to other items, to hold that such is the law. The bid price is inapplicable. The contractor may recover on a quantum meruit for the reasonable value of the work performed in freeing the seven caissons from water."

Reference Case 26

Gasparini Excavating Co. v. Pennsylvania Turnpike Commission
409 Pa. 465; 1936

Defendant had awarded plaintiff a contract to construct a section of the Northeast Extension Tollway in Luzerne County. Plaintiff could not perform the work, however, until the slushing contractor had finished his work. Plaintiff's contract specifically provided that: "No claims for damages or extra costs due to delay to the Contractor's work by the work of slushing contracts will be allowed." As required by the contract, plaintiff mobilized its equipment upon receiving the notice to proceed, only to find that the slushing contractor had not yet completed its work. The ensuing delay increased plaintiff's costs—the subject of the suit. The Common Pleas Court had applied the no damage clause to preclude plaintiff's recovery. The supreme court, however, held that: "Here there was a failure in the essential matter of the Commission not having a predetermined program and interference with appellant's performance by its exclusion from the work site from June 30, 1955 until November 30, 1955, after Gasparini received its notice of June 6 to start its operation." In the face of such interference, the court refused to apply the no damage clause.

Reference Case 27
General Building Contractors v. County of Oneida
282 N.Y.S. 2d 385

The question of responsibility for coordination of contracts on a project is a difficult one in the many states that require separate prime contracts for public construction. In the subject case, the General Building Contractor Association alleged that the state and their architect attempted to impose the responsibility for coordination of the separate prime contractors upon the contractors themselves, rather than upon the owner. The plaintiff requested that the opening of bids be held until the specifications could be reviewed by the court, and the question of responsibility resolved according to the state statutes, specifically: Section 101 of the General Municipal Law. The ruling was as follows:

The petitioner is a New York Membership Corporation known as the General Building Contractors of New York State. It consists of 180 general contractors who perform a substantial volume of the public works building construction in this state. Some of its members are residents of Oneida County. The principal respondent, the County of Oneida, is the owner of a proposed public project, a Library-Academic Building, to be constructed at Mohawk Valley Community College in Utica, Oneida County, New York. . . .

. . . The petitioner contends that the form of specifications prepared by the owner and the architect for this multiple contract project, dated March 29, 1967, violates the requirements set forth in Section 101 of the General Municipal Law. It claims that the language used in the specifications has the effect of shifting responsibilities required by the statute to be imposed upon the owner and/or architect to the contractors, resulting in confusion insofar as the orderly progress of this public work project is concerned. . . .

. . . The language used in the specifications which petitioner claims violates the statute is found at pages SC-9, SC-10 and Addendum No. 1 (1-2) of the specifications for this project. It is there provided that the contractor will "check shop drawings . . . to make sure they conform to the intent of drawings and specifications and for contract requirements. Correct drawings found to be inaccurate or otherwise in error. . . . The contractor will be fully responsible for the accuracy of such drawings and

for conformity to the drawings and specifications, regardless of the approval of the architect, unless the contractor notifies the architect in writing of any deviations at the time he furnished such drawings (SC-9). The general construction contractor shall be responsible for the proper fitting of all work. . . . Within 30 days of the execution and delivery of the contracts, the contractor for 'Contract No. 1—General Construction' shall submit to the architect for approval a satisfactory progress schedule covering total sequence and expected status of the work at any time involving the work for 'Contract No. 1, 2, 3 and 4.' (SC-10) The substance of these requirements relating to shop drawings and progress schedules is repeated in the "Special Conditions" of Addendum No. 1 at page 2. Petitioner contends that it is these provisions which are an attempt to assign supervisory work to contractors which should be the responsibility of the owner and/or of its agent, the architect, and that such are a violation of Section 101 of the General Municipal Law. . . .

. . . At the root of this controversy lies the question upon whom shall devolve the day-to-day responsibility for the orderly progression and coordination of the public project. The provisions contained on Pages SC-9, SC-10 and Addendum No. 1 relative to the general contractor's responsibilities for shop drawings and progress schedules, particularly that expression which makes the general contractor "fully responsible for the fitting of all work" appears to this court to impose upon the general contractor responsibilities and obligations as to supervision and coordination not envisioned by the statute and which should be borne by the owner and/or the architect.

Section 101 of the General Municipal Law provides in substance that in any project which exceeds the sum of $50,000 the owner will prepare separate specifications for the three subdivisions, plumbing, heating and ventilating, and electric wiring (subdivision 1). While the statute is silent as to whether the municipality may assign the work of such supervision to the successful bidder, it appears to this court that had the Legislature intended such assignment where separate bidding is required, it would have so provided. . . .

. . . The state recognized the increase in administrative problems imposed upon it by the multiple bid contract system but accepted this burden in view of the over-all savings.

The interpretation of the statute [General Municipal Laws, Section 101] must be read and given effect as it was written by the Legislature and not as this court thinks it might have been written if the Legislature could have imagined all of the problems which might arise under it. Here, it appears that the County is attempting to exercise powers not expressly granted it under the statute and which can be exercised only where it is "so essential to the exercise of some power expressly conferred as plainly to appear to have been within the intention of the Legislature." The implied power must be necessary, not merely convenient, and the intention of the Legislature must be free from doubt. . . . It does not appear that the shifting of responsibility for coordination and supervision from the County or its agents, in these cases its architects, may be shifted to any of the prime contractors. The power which the county seeks to imply into the language of the statute is not a necessary one, but merely a convenient one.

Reference Case 28
Hammermill Paper Company v. Rust Engineering Co.
243 A. 2d 389

Hammermill Paper Company retained Rust Engineering Company to construct additional facilities at the Hammermill Erie, Pennsylvania, plant. The court described the situation as follows:

> The instant controversy involves the construction and later collapse of a brick curtain wall, 14' 8" high and 165' in length, which was erected as a "vertical extension to a third story height of the existing east wall of Building No. 75." Hammermill contends the wall collapsed because of faulty and negligent construction, while Rust's pleaded position is that the cause of the collapse was an "Act of God" (excessive rains), that Hammermill had paid Rust for and accepted the work involved in constructing the original wall and in reconstructing it after collapse and was, thereby, stopped from further complaint, and finally that Hammermill has been adequately compensated by its insurance carrier for any "use and occupancy" loss incurred by the collapse of the wall. Said "use and occupancy" loss in the averaged amount of $70,392.56 arose because of the interruption of Hammermill's paper-making operation caused by the collapse of the wall through the roof of the Building No. 75 and onto the machinery in the operation and there is an additional averred loss of $11,757.53 for clean-up, maintenance and reconstruction costs involving machinery and Building No. 75, making a total of claimed loss of $82,150.09, which amount was apparently paid to Hammermill by its insurance carrier under a binder to its fire insurance policy.
>
> Hammermill's insurance carrier in the name of Hammermill instituted this assumption against Rust in the Court of Common Pleas of Erie County to recover $82,150.09. Rust filed an answer containing new matter. Hammermill filed a reply thereto and Rust moved for judgment on the pleadings, which motion was granted. The court below, granting Rust's motion for judgment on the pleadings, concluded that Rust was ... "an employee agency under the direct control of Hammermill" and that Hammermill was alone at fault, having retained control and responsibility for the construction of the wall. With that conclusion of the court below we do not agree. ...

. . . Nowhere in the agreement is there any specific language which gives Hammermill the responsibility for final approval of the design and specifications to be supplied by Rust, nor any indication that Hammermill, following the guidelines of such design and specifications, was to supervise, inspect and approve as the work progressed. In this agreement, Hammermill contracted to engage the independent services of Rust to accomplish a particular result. Hammermill was interested, primarily, in the result and, secondarily, in keeping an eye on the costs incurred. It is apparent from a reading of this agreement in its entirety that a certain modicum of control was agreed upon by the parties, but such control was to enable Hammermill to regulate the costs of the project.

While no hard and fast rule exists to determine whether a particular relationship is that of employer-employee or owner-independent contractor, certain guidelines have been established and certain factors are required to be taken into consideration:

> "Control of manner work is to be done; responsibility for result only; terms of agreement between the parties; the nature of the work or occupation; skill required for performance; whether one employed is engaged in a distinct occupation or business; which party supplies the tools; whether the payment is by the time or by the job; whether work part of the regular business of the employer, and also the right to terminate the employment at any time." [Stepp vs. Renn, 184 Pa. 634, 637, 135 A. 2d 794, 796; 1957 and additional citation.]

The fact that Hammermill retained control necessary to supervise and exercise direction over the costs feature of the work; that it secured the necessary work permits and that it retained the right to add or subtract from the work to be done, does not convince us that Hammermill thereby occupied the status of an employer of Rust. Naturally, Hammermill was interested in the result and the cost of attaining such result but the indices of such interest as delineated in the agreement do not constitute a responsibility for the manner in which the work was to be done by Rust. Rust was a specialist and possessed expertise in the construction field and . . . was certainly cognizant of the application of building codes to actual jobs and the standards or strength and quality to be put into a particular job, taking into consideration the owner's needs, local surface and sub-surface conditions and the effects of weather on the resultant construction. Between the parties, Rust and only Rust, had the necessary skill to perform the required work. . . . Rust, apparently, was to supply the tools, *labor and materials to complete the work and was to be paid on a cost plus 4.2% basis for construction and erection of the required structures. Rust controlled its own workers, it assumed possession of the job site and it, necessarily, had to have control of the manner in which the work was to be done. . . .*

. . . The reservations of control in the case at bar, upon which the court below predicated its conclusion that an employer-employee relationship existed, were aimed toward keeping the costs of the project within bounds, toward reserving the right to expand the job if the work was found less costly than imagined, and toward reducing the cost of the work if the costs became greater than anticipated. We fail to find, on the basis of the contract between parties, that Hammermill was insisting on retaining and reserving such a broad scope of control as to deprive Rust of the freedom of decision it would normally employ as an independent contractor and to so restrict Rust's exercise of judgment in construction matters that Rust would be considered an employee. Such a state of affairs might be shown if and when testimony was taken; however, the pleadings do not warrant such a conclusion so as to justify the entry of this summary judgment. . . .

Moreover, there are other issues of fact relative to the scope of Hammermill's control which arise from the pleadings. Rust pleaded that Hammermill had "examined and approved the construction plans for the project." Hammermill's answer to this was that it "approved the construction plans for the project in the sense of approving the result of the construction . . . but it specifically denied that it in any way approved or had control of the method of construction by [Rust]." And, when Rust alleged that Hammermill had daily inspections of the construction site and approved said construction during the course of construction, Hammermill replied that Rust "was in complete charge of the method of performance of the terms of the construction contract and that [Hammermill's] inspections were limited to approval only to the result of [Rust's] construction activities." Such issues of fact as to the extent of Hammermill's control of the job and approval and/or acceptance of the result arise from the pleadings and these issues can only be resolved at trial and not at the pleading state.

The court limited its review to the contention that Hammermill was responsible because of its measure of control over the job. The court did discuss the right to damages on the use and occupancy issue. It pointed out that the engineering firm could escape liability if it could prove to the satisfaction of the court or jury that the collapse of the wall was as it alleged an act of God, and not as a result of faulty or negligent construction.

Reference Case 29

Harper Drake & Assoc. Inc. v. Jewett & Sherman Co.
182 N.W. 2d 554

This case demonstrates the importance of documentation in furnishing a reasonable basis for damages. The situation involved a design assignment in which architect, Harper Drake & Associates, contracted to design a new plant and warehouse for food processor and distributor, Jewett & Sherman Co. (J & S). After preliminary discussions, on July 12, 1966, the Chairman of the Board of J & S telephoned Harper and told him that the building committee wanted him to do the design, and that he should get started on the work. From that date through September 22, Harper and his associates devoted time to the proposed design. In this period, on August 10, 1966, Harper tendered the AIA Standard Form of Agreement between owner and architect to J & S. The contract called for a 5 percent (of construction cost) design fee. Neither party signed the contract.

By September 22, the corporate engineer for J & S felt that the design was not moving rapidly enough. J & S contacted Harper and advised him to stop all work. Harper was told that he would be paid for his services and that he should submit a bill. Harper submitted a bill in the amount of $21,875. His derivation was based upon an estimated project cost of $1,250,000. On the basis of that figure, his design fee at 5 percent would have been $62,500. Harper estimated that his work up to December 22 amounted to 35 percent of the total design effort, and he thereby arrived at the figure of $21,875. J & S refused the bill on the grounds that it was based on a contract neither party had signed. They instructed Harper to submit a statement of time that he and his associates had put in on the project. Everyone in his office, and in the associated engineering offices, kept track in writing on a regular basis of the time spent on each job. Harper estimated his time on the basis of an appointment book and his calendar pad.

Harper filed a complaint that alleged that he should receive payment on the basis of quantum meruit or the unsigned contract. The case went to trial, and the jury returned a special verdict in the sum of $19,448.50. The defendant moved for a new trial on grounds that the verdict was excessive and not supported by evidence. In the supreme court hearing of the appeal, the court considered a previous case, *Barnes v. Lozoff* (20 Wisc. 644; 123 N.W. 2d 543), that had approved the percentage-of-cost method. The court pointed out a substantial difference as follows:

In the case at bar, Harper explained at a preliminary meeting that, if hired, his fee would be five percent of the total cost of construction. Much later, on July 22, Gardner called him and said words to the effect, "Come on down and get started on the job." A month later Harper rendered the A.I.A. contract. Gardner's phone call amounted to an offer, and Harper's subsequent part performance amounts to an acceptance of the offer. But at this point, there is no valid contract because the parties never agreed to what the consideration would be. It cannot be argued that the parties impliedly agreed to use Harper's initial five percent statement for the element of consideration because that would still leave the term of consideration too indefinite to be enforceable. This is so because at the time of the phone call, no dollars and cents figure as to the total cost of construction had yet come into existence. Without such a figure, the amount represented by five percent of the cost is unknown. It would abuse the fundamental precepts of contract interpretation to hold that Gardner bound himself and his company to pay five percent of whatever Harper should later decide would be the actual cost of the building.

Therefore, since the oral agreement never embodied the element of consideration and since the subsequent written contract was never executed by either party, it is clear that no agreement was ever reached between Harper and Jewett & Sherman Co. as to what Harper's fee should be. For that same reason [the absence of consideration], there was never an enforceable contract at all reached by these parties. Therefore, we think the appellant should not be allowed to recover on a percentage basis in this case.

Having rejected the percentage-of-cost-of-total-construction-cost method of computing damages, the court then turned to the sufficiency of evidence to support the verdict of the jury. Harper's testimony according to court records, was as follows:

Harper testified that he personally spent 156 hours on the Jewett & Sherman [project] and that his time was worth $37.50 an hour and this amounted to $5,850. As mentioned earlier, Harper, unlike his employees, kept no record of what hours on what days he spent on the various projects in his office. He was accustomed to working on several projects at the same time. Harper's conclusion that he worked 156 hours on the Jewett &

*Sherman job was based on the appointment book and desk
calendar pad which he kept during the period in question. . . . It
is not clear exactly what information was recorded in the two
sources, but, by Harper's own testimony, his actual hours were
not reflected therein. Apparently, [the process was not
explained at the trial] he would find a notation of a
conference or other activity connected with the Jewett &
Sherman project on a given day and then estimate how
many hours that activity must have taken up. Harper
testified that he had no independent recollection of what
hours he worked on what days but that nevertheless he was
sure that Exhibit 12 was an accurate reflection of the time he
put in.*

Exhibit 12 was similar to Exhibit 10. Exhibit 10 listed the
employees hours by job and date. Exhibit 12 presented Harper's
reconstructed time in the same format. However, Harper had
not been able to produce his appointment book or desk calendar pad upon which Exhibit 12 was purportedly based. The
court concluded that Exhibit 12 (which was an extension of or
part of Exhibit 10) was improperly admitted into evidence by
the trial court:

*The admission of Exhibit 12 was highly prejudicial to appel-
lant, because on that exhibit Harper's hours were depicted in
exactly the same manner and format as the hours of all other
employees listed on Exhibit 10. Thus the jury could easily have
been misled into thinking that Harper's hours rested on the
same foundation as all the other hours on that sheet (i.e., valid
business records).*

*Since the Harper portion of Exhibit 10 was erroneously ad-
mitted into evidence there is no evidence of any kind in the
record which would support an award for Harper's services.*

*The amount of work Harper performed and therefore the
compensation to which he was entitled must rest upon a foundation of rational and credible evidence, not speculation and
guesswork.*

*We conclude that in the absence of the Harper portion of
Exhibit 10, the evidence does not support the verdict. Consequently, the amount of the verdict must be reduced by the
sum of $5,850. This amount was submitted by Harper as the
reasonable value of his services based on an hourly rate times
2.5 the overhead factor.*

While the monies involved are not monumental, the principles are very important in the development of a supportable

claim for damages. Further, the claim for damages must be such that if a favorable award is achieved, it will be demonstrably supported by the evidence, so that it will stand up through appeal.

Reference Case 30
Herbert v. Aitken
5 N.Y.S. 839; 25 N.E. 954; 1890

This case had to do with the responsibilities of a supervising architect. The court recognized the definition that indicates that a supervising architect is not required to spend all of his time at the site of construction. The court described the responsibility of the supervising architect as follows:

The counsel would not contend that the architect is an insurer of the perfection of the mason work, the carpenter work, the plumbing, etc. He is bound only to exercise reasonable care, and to use reasonable powers of observation and detection, in the supervision of the structure. When, therefore, it appears that the architect has made frequent visits to the building, and in a general way has performed the duties called for by the custom of his profession, the mere fact, for instance, that inferior brick have been used in places, does not establish, as a matter of law, that he has not entirely performed his contract. He might have directed at one of his visits that portions of the plumbing work be packed in wool; upon his next return to the building the pipes in question might have been covered with brick in the progress of the building. If he had inquired whether the wool-packing had been attended to, and had received an affirmative answer from the plumber and the bricklayer, I am of the opinion that his duty as an architect, in the matter of the required protection of said pipes from the weather, would have been ended. Yet, under these very circumstances, the packing might have been intentionally or carelessly omitted in fraud upon both architect and owner, and could it still be claimed that the architect had not fully performed his work? An architect is no more a mere overseer or foreman or watchman than he is a guarantor of a flawless building, and the only question that can arise in a case where general performance of duty is shown is whether, considering all the circumstances and peculiar facts involved, he has or has not been guilty of negligence. This is a question of fact, and not of law.

Reference Case 31

Hersey Gravel Co. v. State

Supreme Court of Michigan, 305 Mich. 333; 9 N.W. 2d
567;1943

From the court records:

This is an appeal by defendants State of Michigan and
Michigan State Highway Department from a judgment entered
in the Court of Claims in favor of plaintiff Hersey Gravel Company in the sum of $16,155. The total amount claimed by
plaintiff is $59,622, and it has taken a cross-appeal.

On July 7, 1938, the State advertised for bids for the construction of 5.17 miles of highway . . . vice-president and manager of
plaintiff . . . obtained plans and specifications from the Highway Department and spent two days examining the proposed
right of way and "borrow pits." The blueprints which he
examined contained notations of soil conditions upon which
he claims his company based its bid, which was filed and
opened on July 20th. This bid in the sum of $266,324, being the
lowest of those tendered, was accepted. . . . The contract required the work to be completed by July 1, 1939. Delays were
encountered and the work was not actually completed and
accepted until July 1, 1940, but no delay penalty was exacted
by the State.

The contract called for 373,086 cubic yards of earth excavation and 17,007 cubic yards of rock excavation, but an extra
construction estimate shows that the contractor completed an
additional 32,175 cubic yards of earth excavation and
11,390.08 cubic yards of rock excavation. The amount allowed
plaintiff for additional construction, including these items and
others, totalled $35,111.

The verified claim filed by plaintiff in the Court of Claims
states that: "If the material to be encountered had been of the
character indicated by the drawings and as represented directly or impliedly, the claimant could have completed the
work at the contract price and would have earned a reasonable
profit. By reason of the fact that the material actually encountered was not the kind indicated in the drawings and directly
and impliedly represented to be, but of a kind vastly more
difficult and expensive to move as above set forth, the cost of
completing the work of the contract was $59,622 in excess of
the cost anticipated."

... The soil notations on the blueprints were made as a result of investigations conducted under the supervision of the district soils engineer of the Highway Department in the winter of 1937, when a crew of men dug test holes down to the ditch grade and took soundings at points where cuts were shown on the plans.

Plaintiff's testimony is that the actual soil conditions encountered were of an entirely different character from those indicated on the plans, far more difficult and costly to handle, and destructive to its equipment. For example, although plaintiff claims its equipment was in good working order, 17 sets of steam shovel dipper teeth were used in the west "borrow pit" in three months, and 16 sets in other pits in less time, although it takes, ordinarily, only one set of dipper teeth a season to handle 200,000 yards of material.

The State denies that the material encountered was more difficult and expensive to handle than that described in the plans, and, although it maintains that the notations thereon were accurate, insists that the plaintiff should have been aware of the difficult and rocky nature of the terrain because of the outcroppings of ledge rock and boulder formation readily discernible to prospective bidders. The State admits that the work progressed slowly, but charges that this was because of the dilatory methods employed by plaintiff and its lack of enough good equipment. It is asserted that, if plaintiff's representative had made the proper kind of investigation, the exact nature of the soil could have been ascertained and its bid made accordingly.

The trial judge held . . . that plaintiff was entitled to rely upon the contract, blueprints, plans and specifications prepared by the State, and upon the engineering practice in that connection, and he stated that it was the duty of public authorities, when preparing proposals, to provide all available information and data in unmistakable and clear-cut terms. He absolved the State and the Highway Department of any bad faith, but held that, so far as the excavations along the length of the highway were concerned, there was a warranty in connection with the nature of the subsoil, and that this warranty had been breached because of a misstatement of the conditions actually existing. He declined to hold that an implied warranty existed with respect to the nature of the soil in the "borrow pit," or that there was any conclusive testimony that plaintiff's equipment was not in good condition. . . .

The State . . . relies upon the accuracy of the representations on its plans and specifications, and also insists that plaintiff is precluded from recovery because the blueprints upon which its bid was based are supplemented by specifications which say: "Soil notations shown on the plans are for information only and shall not be construed to relieve bidders of their responsibility to satisfy themselves by examining the site of the proposed work as to actual soil conditions."

This provision put plaintiff on notice, but the notations on the plans had the effect of also advising plaintiff that an investigation had been made by the Highway Department of the character of the soil along the entire proposed highway. The testimony shows that this investigation extended over a considerable period of time. The period between the time the advertisement appeared asking for bids and the date upon which bids were to be submitted and opened, would not suggest to any reasonable bidder that it was necessary for him to make a more extended investigation of soil conditions than was made by plaintiff's manager, Allswede, who spent two days examining the proposed right of way. Plaintiff complied with the requirements of the proposal and carried out the responsibility to satisfy itself as to actual soil conditions by the examination of its manager of the site of the proposed work.

Undoubtedly the commission's knowledge of subsoil conditions was superior to that of the plaintiffs, and they tried to acquire this knowledge from it. It is equally true that these facts were not within the fair reasonable reach of the plaintiffs, and there was lack of time for them to obtain this information by an independent investigation before the letting.

Plaintiff's cross-appeal is from the trial court's refusal to allow its claim in connection with material excavated from "borrow pits." The court held: "As to the claims in connection with the borrow pits, I can find no ground for raising any implied warranty in this contract except the one that the material from those pits were reasonably suited to use as fill material in the making of grades. In point of fact the material was suitable for that use as such material. It was difficult to excavate with shovels but it was excavated with shovels. One pit became impracticable after about 14,000 cubic yards were removed but another pit was substituted. One pit was difficult to excavate and presented some compacted formation that could not be excavated after some 97,000 cubic yards had been taken from the pit with the equipment claimant had. I am not able to see where there is any implied warranty to be drawn from the contracts in connection with the borrow pits which has been violated. The conclusion that I do reach is that the petitioner is entitled to compensation for highway excavations, but not for excavations in the pits.

Reference Case 32
Hollerbach v. United States
233 U.S. 165; 1914

In this case, the contractor bid for the repair work at an earthen dam based upon specifications that turned out to be incorrect. The specifications purported to give only appproximate quantities, and directed that the bidder should visit the site to determine the nature of the work.

However, the specifications included the following: "the dam is now backed for about 50 feet with broken stone, sawdust and sediment to a height within 2 to 3 feet of the crest."

After accepting the contract, the contractor proceeded to excavate, with the result that the specifications had not even been close to accurate. The dam was not backed with broken stone, sawdust, and sediment. Instead, the contractor encountered a sound log cribbing filled with stone. The cribbing was more expensive than the specified material would have been. The contractor filed a claim against the U. S. Government. The court ruled in favor of the contractor stating:

> True, the claimant [the contractor] might have penetrated the 7 feet of soft slushy sediment by means which would have discovered the log crib work filled with stones which was concealed below, but the specifications assured them of the character of the material—a matter concerning which the government might be presumed to speak with knowledge and authority. We think the positive statement of the specifications must be taken as true and binding upon the government, and that upon it rather than upon the claimants, must fall the loss resulting from such mistaken representations. We think it would be going quite too far to interpret the general language of the other paragraphs as requiring independent investigation of facts which the specifications furnished by the government as a basis of the contract left no doubt. If the government wished to leave the matter open to the independent investigation of the claimants, it might easily have omitted the specification as to the character of the filling back of the dam. In its positive assertion of the nature of this much of the work it made a representation upon which the claimants had a right to rely without an investigation to prove its falsity.

Reference Case 33

Johnson, Inc. v. Basic Construction Co.
429 F. 2d 764, D.C. Cir.; 1970

The court was faced with a subcontractor's failure to adhere to the disputes procedure established in the prime contract, allegedly applicable by virtue of a general incorporation by a reference clause in the subcontract: "The subcontractor agrees to perform all work required by the above-mentioned contract in accordance with the requirements of the prime contract documents, plans, specifications, general conditions, special conditions." (pp. 775–776)

Johnson, the subcontractor, brought suit against the general contractor, Basic Construction, claiming that Basic was obligated to give it a commitment for payment for extra work *even though Basic had received no commitment from the owner.* In the absence of such a commitment, Johnson argued that it was justified in abandoning its work and in being compensated for the work it had performed. Basic argued that it was relieved of the obligation of giving a commitment to the subcontractor on the extra work because the subcontract integrated the terms and conditions of the prime contract thus binding Johnson to a disputes clause in those documents that would preclude Johnson from recovering. The court held that:

We do not so construe either the prime contract or the subcontract for two reasons. First because Basic never satisfied the requirement of Article X that there be a 'supplement' to the contract providing that the contract consideration be increased. Second, because even if the prime contract were fully incorporated into the subcontract, its general provisions would not overcome the specific provision of the subcontract dealing with "Changes" which required Basic to give a written order for the work which made "allowance" for the increased cost.

After making the above ruling, in further discussion, the court indicated that the disputes clause was incorporated into the subcontract only insofar as it was applicable to the work performed and that the clause by its terms did not extend to require an adherence by a subcontractor to an administrative remedy designed to be used only by the parties to the prime contract.

The limited application given the incorporation clause by the court in this case is explainable. First, the subcontract incorporation clause made no mention of binding the subcontractor to the general contract provisions containing the disputes clause to the same extent that the prime contractor was bound. In *Johnson v. Basic Construction*, the incorporation clause only stated that: "The subcontractor . . . agrees . . . to . . . perform all work required by the above mentioned contract [the prime contract] . . . for furnishing and performing painting, finishing, vinyl wall covering work, etc., in accordance with the requirements of the prime contract documents, plans and specifications, general conditions, special conditions, . . . and alternates . . . and as described more completely in Exhibit A."

The court refused, on the basis of such a clause, to presume a relinquishment by subcontractor of his commonlaw right to abandon the work:

So we consider the disputes clause in a slightly different context from the extra work provision, i.e., the disputes clause was not specifically incorporated by reference and it relates to a procedural matter which is further removed from the work contemplated by the contracts. However, since there is no clear contractual language requiring Johnson to relinquish its rights of abandonment in return for its questionable right to recover its extra costs through hazards of litigation and since the contract was drafted by Basic and ambiguities are to be construed most strongly against it, and since the disputes clause by its terms relates to administrative remedies between the owner and the prime contractor without any reference to the subcontractor, we conclude that the disputes clause is not applicable to disputes between Basic and Johnson.

The court in *Johnson v. Basic* refused to presume that subcontractor waived a common law contract right on the basis of a general incorporation clause. Other courts confronted with the same question in the context of government contracts have all but unanimously agreed that a general incorporation clause will not constitute a waiver of a known statutory right. Pursuant to the Miller Act (40 U.S.C.A. 270b; 1935) subcontractors on government contracts are given a statutory right to sue the general contractor and his bondsman. General contractors have sought to preclude such suits on the grounds that the disputes clause of the prime contract applied to the subcontractor by virtue of an incorporation by reference clause in the subcontract.

Reference Case 34
Johnson v. Fenestra, Incorporated (Erection Division)
305 F. 2d 179, 181, 3rd Cir.; 1962

A subcontractor sought damages from its prime contractor for the late delivery of certain wall panels that were to be installed by the subcontractor. Plaintiff sued for the extra costs incurred complaining that a crew of workmen had to be kept available and inactive waiting for the materials.

The district court denied recovery on the claim predicated on the reasoning that "the possibility of delay in furnishing material was merely one of the calculated risks which constitute a normal feature of the contracting business". Disagreeing, the Third Circuit Court of Appeals, applying Pennsylvania law, overruled the district court decision, stating: "It is a familiar rule of the contract law, adopted and applied by the courts of Pennsylvania, that a party breaches a bilateral contract when he does improperly or fails to do something which he has expressly or impliedly undertaken to do to facilitate the performance of the other party."

The court noted further that the contract expressly required the prime contractor to supply the panels that the subcontractor had agreed to install, and that the subcontractor's performance was to begin seven days after execution of the contract. Based thereupon, the court, again applying Pennsylvania law, stated: "The conclusion is inescapable that the bargain as made necessarily implied and gave the subcontractor assurance that the prime contractor would perform his obligation to supply panels at times and in quantities consistent with the understanding of the parties as to the prompt beginning and early completion of this installation." The court, therefore, reversed the district court decision and remanded the case to the lower court for an award of plaintiff's "additional costs of performance".

Reference Case 35
Peter Kiewit Sons' Co. v. Iowa Southern Utilities Co.
355 F. Supp. 376; 1973

The court held that the construction schedule G-1 prepared by the owner, Southern Utilities Co., for the completion of the various elements of the construction, was not binding upon the owner. The purpose of the construction schedule was to give all contractors a basic idea of when various phases of the work would start and how rapidly it would be prosecuted in order for everyone to make the completion deadline and that, accordingly, the owner did not breach its contract with the general contractor because of deviations in the actual construction dates from those set forth in the construction schedule. The court stated:

Viewing the contract document as a whole, the Court concludes that Iowa Southern did not breach its contract with Kiewit because of the deviations of the actual construction dates from the construction schedule, G-1. . . . In this contract, there is no doubt that the completion date of the power station was of the essence; myriad provisions of the contract so state. As to the intermediate dates contained in G-1, however, there is no express provision in the contract which makes these dates absolutely binding upon Iowa Southern. . . . Schedule G-1 was intended by the parties to give a basic idea of when the various phases of Kiewit's and the other contractors' work should start and how rapidly it should be prosecuted in order for everyone to make the completion deadline of May 1, 1968.

Reference Case 36

Lichter v. Mellon-Stuart Company
305 F. 2d 216, 3rd Cir., 1962

This case involved an action by a masonry subcontractor to recover from its prime contractor the balance due on the subcontract and damages for the general contractor's alleged delays to the subcontractor. The prime contractor counterclaimed.

Prior to the subcontractor coming on the job it had become increasingly apparent that the general contractor was deviating from the progress schedule received by the subcontractor at the start of the work. The subcontractor claimed that the general contractor breached its subcontract by causing delays that affected other phases of the overall construction and that these delays in turn created a condition of unreadiness for the orderly and systematic performance of the subcontractor's masonry work. The subcontractor additionally claimed that the general contractor's breach was established in the record by testimony that the subcontractor's workmen were required to perform an average of thirteen separate operations on each floor of the ten–story structure, when normal procedure would have involved not more than two or three operations on each floor. The lower court found that the building was not readied for the subcontractor's masonry work as set forth in the schedule, that the subcontractor was required by the general contractor to perform its masonry work piecemeal and in a haphazard and disorderly manner, and that: " . . . this required Southern [the subcontractor] to perform the masonry work over a longer period of time than if it had been performed in sequence, floor by floor, and increased its cost considerably."

The lower court found that the subcontractor's work had been delayed by a number of factors, including change orders, delays by other trades, strikes, and interferences by the general contractor. The court held that because a substantial amount of the lump sum, which the contractor proved as its extra costs to perform the masonry work, was the consequence of factors other than a breach or breaches of contract by the general contractor, and the general contractor was not liable to reimburse the subcontractor for its increased costs caused by the delays. The subcontractor took an appeal and the appeals court affirmed the lower court's decision, finding:

> But even if Southern [the subcontractor] is correct in its contention that Mellon breached the contract by insisting that the

subcontractor proceed under conditions necessitating piecemeal performance of the masonry work, we think there is an insuperable obstacle to recovery on this record. In the opinion of the court below, on Southern's motion for denying a new trial, this difficulty is stated as follows:

Even if one could find from the evidence that one or more of the interfering contingencies was a wrongful act on the part of the defendant, no basis appears for even an educated guess as to the increased costs suffered by plaintiffs due to that particular breach or breaches as distinguished from those causes from which defendant is contractually exempt from responding in damages.

In proving damages, Southern had introduced testimony as to what it would have cost to perform all of the masonry work if that work had been performed without delays. The subcontractor then proved the actual cost of the entire masonry job as delayed, interrupted, and hindered by all causes. Even though there were causes for delays to the subcontractor other than those caused by the prime contractor's activities, the subcontractor claimed the entire difference as damages without offering sufficient testimony to itemize what delays of the total delays were attributable solely to the contractor and which delays were not; e.g., those attributable to change orders, periods of long waiting while the architect held under advisement questions that arose concerning work and materials, all of which involved no breach of the contract by the general contractor.

The court, therefore, concluded: "In these circumstances Southern's inability to break down its lump sum proof of extra costs justifies the denial of any recovery if on the record any substantial part of the added cost of the performance was chargeable to non-actionable causes rather than to any breach of contract by Mellon."

Reference Case 37
Luria Engineering Co. v. Aetna Casualty and Surety Co.
206 Pa. Super. 333; 1965

A roofing subcontractor refused to perform after a long delay due to labor difficulties, without some increased compensation. Plaintiff general contractor hired a new roofer and sued defendant surety company for the increased cost incurred by the original roofer's failure to perform. In assessing the original roofer's excuses for nonperformance, the superior court noted: "We believe the present rule in Pennsylvania to be the acts of a third party making performance impossible or causing a delay resulting in substantial increase in expense to the contracting party do not excuse failure to perform if such acts were foreseeable because it was the duty of the contracting party to provide for that situation in his contract. . . . While the word 'foreseeability' does not appear in the Moore case [Reference Case 42] it is clear that the rationale of the decision is that a contingency, if foreseeable, must be covered by the contract or the happening of the same will not excuse non-performance."

Reference Case 38
Luria Brothers & Co. v. United States
369 F 2d 701

Luria was contractor on a job calling for the construction of aircraft maintenance facilities for the U.S. Government at Willow Grove, Pa.

The chief basis for this claim was the fact that completion was 518 days beyond the scheduled completion date. (The contractor had extended the completion date by 518 days, but the Government did not attempt to exact liquidated damages provided for in the contract.) The contractor sued on the basis that the specifications were defective and caused the delay and additional work that it had to perform. The contractor had gone through the cycle of appealing to the contracting officer, the General Accounting Office, the Secretary of the Navy, the Armed Service Board of Contract Appeals—all of which had rejected his claims.

The contractor's allegations were typical of many contracts. Their petition included the following assertions:

1. The orginal plans were defective and faulty;
2. Defendant was dilatory in making necessary contract changes and taking other action;
3. A trial and error method was imposed upon plaintiff by defendant to accomplish certain items of the construction.
4. The magnitude and nature of some of the changes were beyond the scope of the original contract;
5. The frequency and extensiveness of the revisions to other phases of the construction work were also unreasonable and beyond the scope of the contract.

An extensive trial followed. At the conclusion of the recital of facts, the court said:

That the original specifications were defective is beyond dispute. They misrepresented the nature of the bearing value of the material underlying the foundation of the structure at the prescribed elevations, and hence, the dimension and depth at which the arch-column footings were to rest to such an extent that the changes required to complete the structure were beyond the scope of the original contract.

It is well settled that when the government orders a structure to be built, and in so doing prepares the specifications prescribing the character, dimension and location of the construction work, it impliedly warrants that if the specifications are complied with, satisfactory performance will result. When, as here, defective specifications delay completion of the contract, the contractor is entitled to recover damages for defendant's breach of this implied warranty.

In addition, the defendant was dilatory, both in recognizing the need for and in making appropriate revisions to the defective foundation plan. Defendant should have determined whether the sub-grade rock had adequate bearing capacity prior to approving the pouring of the first D-line footings. Upon finally recognizing that the subgrade rock was unsatisfactory, defendants or its agents should have completed the re-design of the foundation with all due haste so that plaintiff could have continued the foundation work without any significant delay.

Furthermore, the defendant should not have imposed upon the plaintiff beyond reasonable trial and error method of excavation once the revised design had been completed. This requirement, together with the extremely slow recognition and correction of the defective plans, constituted a breach of the implied obligation contained in every contract, that neither party will do anything that will hinder or delay the other party in performance of the contract.

That these breaches of contract by defendant caused considerable delay in connection with the foundation work is clear from the foregoing. Plaintiff is, of course, entitled to receive the damages it incurred because of this delay.

Upon consideration of the evidence, our trial Commissioner has determined that the defendant unreasonably delayed the progress of the foundation work for a period of 330 days of the total 420 days delay. This finding is fully supported by the record.

The defendant government attempted to have the finding of 330 days reduced by 30 days which they claimed would have been a reasonable length of time to make the necessary design changes. The court said:

Ordinarily, defendant is entitled to make necessary changes, and where the change is necessitated by defective plans and specifications, defendant must pay the entire resulting damage without any reduction for time to make changes, as would be the case if the redesign was necessitated by a changed condition or the like.

In fixing the damages, the court ascertained the cost of the entire 518-day overrun, and awarded the fraction of the cost attributable to 420 days. These damages were made up of the overrun costs for idle equipment, field supervision, winter protection, maintaining excavations, and wage and material increases—plus the full insurance premium required.

The trial commissioner had found that the plaintiff contractor was not entitled to home office overhead, but the court reversed this finding. They indicated that home office overhead is a well-recognized item of damage for delay, and that the plaintiff should be able to recover. On a $1,700,166 (including changes) contract, the court awarded the following delay costs:

1. All field delay		$85,545
2. Home office overhead		$62,948
	Total	$148,493

Reference Case 39

MacKnight Flintic Stone Co. v. The Mayor

160 N.Y. 72; 54 N.E. 661

The case, decided in 1899 by the New York Court of Appeals, is a classic decision that is still a construction guideline.

The MacKnight Flintic Stone Company was the lowest bidder on a contract to complete a district court house and prison for the city of New York. MacKnight Flintic was to furnish "all materials and labor for the purpose and make tight the boiler room, coal room . . . of the Court House and prison . . . in the manner and under the conditions prescribed and set forth in the annex specifications which are hereby made part of the contract." The plans and specifications had been prepared by the city itself. The contract indicated that the city would inspect the work as it progressed to insure that the specifications were followed.

The design documents contemplated a water problem, because the floor of the boiler room was some twenty-six feet below curb level. The specifications described in detail the manner in which waterproofing was to be accomplished, including column jackets and a waterproof lining over the floor and lower walls. The specifications required that the facility be "turned over to the City by him in perfect order and guaranteed absolutely water and dampproofed for five years from the date of acceptance of the work." There were serious leaks, and the city refused payment for the work. The contractor brought suit on the basis that he had followed the specifications exactly, and that nevertheless, leaks developed around the column jackets and in other places. The contractor utilized a water ejector to pump out the boiler room and keep it dry. He also proposed to do additional work to seal off the water, but his suggested plan was rejected. In his suit, the contractor stated that it was impossible to obtain a dry cellar if the specifications prepared by the city were followed.

At the first trial, the complaint was dismissed. The Appellate Division of the State of New York affirmed the dismissal. The contractor appealed to the Court of Appeals, and the lower courts were reversed. Some portions of the opinion follow:

The agreement is not simply to do a particular thing, but to do it in a particular way and to use specified materials, in accordance with the defendant's design, which is the sole guide. The promise is not to make watertight, but to make watertight by following the plan and specifications prepared by the defendant from which the plaintiff had no right to depart, even if the departure would have produced a waterproof cellar.

If the contractor had designed and executed a plan of its own which resulted in a tight cellar, it would not have been a performance of the contract, for it was to produce a waterproof cellar by following the plan and specifications made by the defendant and not otherwise. The plaintiff was not allowed to do additional work, according to a plan of its own, although it claimed it would prevent all dampness, and the defendant did not attempt to remedy defects at the expense of the plaintiff, as authorized by the contract.

There was no discretion as to the materials to be used or the manner in which the work should be done. The plaintiff had no alternative except to follow the plan under the direction of the defendant's officers in charge. The defendant relied upon the skill of its engineer in preparing the plan, with the most minute specifications, and bound the plaintiff to absolute conformity therewith. . . .

This is not the case of an independent workman, left to adopt his own method, but of one bound hand and foot to the plan of the defendant. The plaintiff had no right to alter the specifications, although the defendant had a qualified right to do so. If the plan and specifications were defective, it was not the fault of the plaintiff, but of the defendant, for it caused them to be made, and it alone had to power to alter them. It relied upon its own judgment in adopting them, not upon the judgment of the plaintiff. It decided for itself out of what materials and in what manner the floor should be constructed, and not only required the plaintiff to use precisely those materials to do the work exactly in that manner, but also inspected both as the work advanced without complaint or questions to either.

Reference Case 40

Meads & Co. v. City of New York
191 App. Div. 365, N.Y.; 1920; 181 N.Y.S. 704

In this case, the contractor according to the specifications had an option, to either sheath from the grade level to the bottom of the excavation, or to pitch back the banks in an open cut.

The contractor chose the method of pitching back the banks. This pitching back was to meet a requirement that adjacent material could not fall into the excavation, and that a specified clearance had to be maintained from the property line. During the work, a slide occurred. At that time, the architect ordered the contractor to install sheathing and shoring instead of the pitch-back method. The contractor protested the change in method, but continued to perform as directed by the architect. The court said: "The contract expressly gives to the contractor the option to choose his method. The architect deprived him of his choice and compelled him to adopt a more expensive one. . . . The architect could undoubtedly require an adequate use of the method; but the contract did not give him the power to prescribe a method much more expensive, and not contemplated by the contract."

In *Horgan* v. *The Mayor* (160 N.Y. 516) the court stated: "I think the law is that, so long as a contractor produces work which satisfies the specifications, he can, in the interest of economy, choose his own methods. This is not only law but common sense; for when a contractor bids, his estimates, which influence the bid, are necessarily based on his own methods of work, so long as those methods are not controlled by the specifications."

Reference Case 41
Meyers v. Housing Authority of Stanislaus County
50 Cal. Reptr. 856

Meyers, a California contractor, claimed that the County of Stanislaus had required him to do extra work on a housing project, and demanded extra payment for the work.

Evidence indicated that the drawings were, indeed, ambiguous, but the trial court ruled against the contractor. On appeal, the Fifth District Court of Appeals of California upheld the ruling of the trial court. In the discussion of the appeal, the court said:

. . . *Defendant, Housing Authority, of Stanislaus County, called for bids for the construction of housing units at two sites within the County. Plaintiffs were the successful bidders and entered into a single contract with defendant covering both projects. Although details differ for the work involved at each project, only one legal question is presented: under the contract, are plaintiffs required to install sewer and drainage lines and manholes beyond the project limits? The Trial Court found that plaintiffs must make all plumbing installations shown in the drawings or mentioned in the specifications, necessary to make the projects useable.*

The question arises because part of the sewer and drainage lines, connections and manholes shown in the drawings and necessary to connect the dwelling units to existing main lines, extend beyond the "contract limits," "property line," and "project limits" shown on the architectural plans. Plaintiffs contend that the drawings delimit their responsibilities to the designated boundaries. However, the lines and manholes are clearly shown in the drawings, and the plans indicate where existing 6" lines are to be replaced by 8" pipe. Futhermore, the fall or grade of the drainage line is indicated on the drawings and a detail of the "off site" storm drain anchor block is shown.

The drawings, standing alone, are ambiguous since they not only designate the limit lines upon which the plaintiffs relied, but also designate sewer lines and installations necessary to complete each unit, that extend beyond the limits. However, the drawings constitute only one document in an integrated contract that provides: "the contract shall consist of the following component parts: (a) This instrument (b) general condi-

tions, (c) special conditions, (d) technical specifications, and
(e) drawings." ·

In determining the meaning of a contract, all documents that
are parts thereof must be construed together. Hence, the drawings must be interpreted in light of the other documents incorporated in the agreement.

. . . The trial judge also noted that by the first paragraph of
the contract, plaintiffs agreed to furnish: "all labor, material,
equipment and services, and to perform and complete all work
required for the construction of low rent housing projects . . .
Paterson consisting of ten dwelling units, and . . . Westley consisting of twenty dwelling units, together with necessary site
development including, but not limited to grading; paving;
sewers. . . . "

. . . Special conditions in the specifications delineate work to
be done by others at no expense to the contractor. The exempted work, including the electrical distribution system to and
including meters and streetlighting systems, but not "off site"
plumbing, sewer or drainage facilities. Failure to include "off
site" plumbing in this itemization of facilities the contractor is
not required to install means, conversely, that he is required to
furnish them.

Reference Case 42
Moore v. Whitty
299 Pa. 58; 1930

Plaintiffs had been hired to install bath fixtures in two buildings being constructed by the defendant. Although the contract originally called for union labor only, defendants agreed to delete such provision after negotiations with the plaintiffs. Labor disputes ensued when plaintiffs' nonunion crews arrived and defendants terminated plaintiffs' contract, seeking to excuse their actions on the grounds that the union reaction was unexpected. Rejecting this excuse, the court noted: "Contingencies not provided against will not ordinarily excuse performance. . . . Both parties to the contract realized the uncertainty of the labor situation. . . . Defendants were fully informed of all the circumstances and agreed to omit the clause requiring employment of union workmen. Having failed to provide against the very contingency which both parties were aware might occur, the happening of such contingency cannot be set up as an excuse for failure to perform."

Reference Case 43
Mullinax Engineering Co. v. Platte Valley Construction Co.
F. 2d 533, 10th Cir.; 1969

Plaintiff had been hired by defendant general contractor to do the asphalt and paving work on a highway construction project. The defendant was to perform the grading and dirt removal work that had to be completed before plaintiff could begin its operation. Plaintiff was directed to begin work as soon as defendant had a sufficient portion of grade ready "so that subcontractor can continue his operations without delay." After commencing work, plaintiff was delayed eighteen days by intermittent suspension and resumption of grade work by defendant. The court upheld plaintiff's right to recover the costs of its idled crews, stating that: "It follows then that where a prime contractor fails to prepare the premises in a state of readiness so that the subcontractor can proceed with the work at the time contemplated by the subcontract, and the subcontractor is damaged thereby, the prime contractor is liable for the damages caused by the delay."

Reference Case 44
Nathan Construction Company v. Fenestra Inc.
409 F. 2d 134

The question of what is substantial performance as compared with complete performance was important in the subject case. Fenestra Inc. was subcontractor for the windows and curtainwall for a building in Omaha. It sued Nathan Construction contractor, a general contractor, to recover approximately $50,000 that it claimed Nathan owed it.

Nathan asserted that the curtainwall was not in conformance with the specifications because it permitted excessive infiltration of air, water, and dust; did not move freely with changing temperatures, creating excessive stresses and distortions; and was improperly sealed. The sum total effect was to produce abnormal deterioration.

Nathan filed a counterclaim for almost $400,000 in damages based upon its inability to meet the obligations to the building's owner or to indemnify against any potential liability to the owner. (The owner was permitted to intervene in the case under Civil Rule 24(b) as having a claim with questions in law and fact in common with the contractor.)

The case was heard without jury before the chief justice of the Nebraska District Court. He found that Fenestra had demonstrated substantial performance of its obligations, and that having so shown substantial performance it was the burden of the contractor and owner to prove that any damages had incurred. Since they did not sustain this burden, judgment was found in favor of Fenestra and the counterclaim was dismissed. The owner and contractor appealed to the Eighth Circuit Court.

The building involved was to be remodeled into a luxury apartment house-office building. Curtainwall was not a new feature in Omaha at this time. Other renovation work in the area had utilized a curtainwall approach. The exterior design was by the owner's architect, and was determined before Fenestra acquired the subcontract. Fenestra prepared shop drawings and adjustments in these were made in accordance with conditions encountered on the site. The Fenestra superintendent on the job site worked with the contractor's superintendent. Their work was open and obvious. Fenestra was never told to stop its work, and representatives of both the contractor and the owner inspected the project frequently.

Fenstra indicated that it had completed its work in June 1963. It conducted a final inspection and detected no infiltration of air or weather. However, the contractor refused to pay the balance due on the subcontract. Representatives of the owner, contractor, and Fenestra met several times to ascertain the basis of complaints and what might be done to remedy them. At a meeting held in January 1964, the group inspected the building and no evidence of leakage was found.

There was an agreement to weatherstrip aluminum vents which was approved by the contractor and started and concluded at his direction. Other meetings took place in the summer of 1964. Fenestra did not believe that the complaints were specific enough to indicate that water and air infiltration had really occurred. Further meetings took place in which caulking was reviewed as well as gaskets. A final meeting took place in November 1966 almost three and a half years after the work had been completed. In the meanwhile, the apartments were rented and the vacancy rate was as low as 6 percent.

The appeals court ruled in favor of Fenestra on the main issue of the case. It also ruled that if a legal counterclaim did exist, the defendant had failed to prove the amount expended, and so could recover nothing. In general, the court made the following points:

Intent of the parties. The defendant and the intervenor argue that weather protection was important for this reconstruction job and was deemed necessary and highly desirable by them. There is little question as to this. . . . However, we do not read the subcontract as one that required the building to be absolutely water- and weather-tight, with nothing due Fenestra if that high standard was not fully met. . . .

Fenestra's posture. Plaintiff Fenestra at all times has taken the position not that it rendered only substantial performance of its subcontract with Nathan but that it fully performed its obligations under the agreement and that it is therefore entitled to recover the balance of the stated contract price. . . . Thus it was the trial court which advanced the concept of substantial performance into the decision of the case. It has been said that American courts are united in holding that a substantial performance of a building or construction contract will support a recovery either on the contract, or in some jurisdictions on a quantum meruit basis. Three reasons for this have been advanced:

1. *That work on a building is such that, even if the owner rejects it, he receives the benefit of it and it is equitable to require him to pay for what he gets;*

2. Literal compliance with every detail of specifications is impossible; and

3. The parties are assumed impliedly to have agreed to do what is reasonable under all the circumstances with respect to performance.

Substantial performance, of course, is not easily defined. Fortunately for us in this diversity case, the Nebraska Supreme Court has announced its definition of the concept and has recognized substantial performance and litigation of building and construction contracts.

> While it is difficult to state what the term substantial performance or substantial compliance as applied to building and construction contracts means, it seems that there is substantial performance of a contract for all of the essentials necessary to the full accomplishment of the purpose with such an approximation to complete performance that the owner obtains substantially what is called for by the contract." (Jones vs. Elliot, 174 Neb., 96, 108 N.W. dd 742, 748; 1961.)

Reference Case 45

New England Foundation Co. v. Commonwealth

327 Mass. 587; 100 N.E. 2d 6; 1951

The contract required the contractor to cast-in-place concrete piles with a safe working load capacity of twenty tons. Further, the specification indicated that the "safe value of piles shall be determined by the following formula:

$$P = \frac{2\ WH}{S + 0.1}$$

Where P equals the safe load in pounds, W equals the weight of the striking part of the hammer in pounds, H equals the fall in feet of the striking part of the hammer, as equals the average penetration per blow in inches under the last five blows. The engineers may modify the required value of S on the basis of the load tests." The theoretical value for S was 0.65 in., W=5,000 lbs., P=40,000 lbs. and H=3 ft. According to this formula, a pile driven with the penetration of 3.25 in. or less during the last five blows would be driven in accordance with the formula. Test piles were driven according to the formula and loaded with twenty tons. At this point in time, the contract had not been awarded. Had the engineers desired to change the value of S, presumably the contractor would have had an opportunity to renegotiate his price.

A total of more than 4,000 piles were driven by the contractor, under the supervision of the engineers. Each pile was driven according to the formula. No further load tests were made until 4,325 piles had been driven. At this point, a load test indicated that the piles would not hold a twenty-ton load within proper settlement criteria. The owner insisted on driving an additional number of piles to make up the deficit in load capacity. On completion of the job, the owner deducted $69,844 from the final payment to the contractor. The contractor entered suit on the basis that the additional piles were extra work. The owner argued that the additional piles were required for the contractor to fulfill his requirements under the original contract.

The court found that the contractor was entitled to rely on the formula to define the means of achieving the contractual requirements. They disallowed the owner's position that the inclusion of the formula was for information purposes only.

Reference Case 46

Race Company v. Oxford Hall Contracting Corp.

268 N.Y.S. 2d 175

The question of literal performance of the contract terms can be important; similarly, the question of waiver of literal performance can become equally important.

This was a factor in this case decided by the Appellate Division of the Supreme Court of New York, Second Department:

[From the prevailing memorandum] On November 14, 1962 Plaintiff and the corporate defendant Oxford signed a contract for the installation of the central heating and cooling plant in defendant's building in accordance with certain plans and specifications, all work to be done in accordance with plaintiff's letter of October 26, 1961.

The contract contained an arbitration clause. It also provided that the contract was not to become effective until the plans and specifications were signed by the contracting parties.

Thereafter, plaintiff completed the job except for certain work which was not completed at defendant's request. When plaintiff commenced this action, defendants moved to compel arbitration, which plaintiffs opposed on the grounds that the plans and specifications had never been signed. It is conceded that plaintiff completed the work in accordance with the plans and specifications. Under these circumstances, both parties by their conduct adopted the plans and specifications, the failure to sign them is inconsequential, there was compliance with a valid agreement, and plaintiff should be compelled to arbitrate.

[From the dissenting opinion filed by two justices] We hold, as does the majority, that completion of the work constitutes the waiver of the provision that the contract should not become effective until both contracting parties signed the architect's plans and specifications, is to extend the contract, and necessarily, the arbitration provision thereof, which may not be done. If a party wishes to bind another in writing to agreement to arbitrate disputes, this purpose should be accomplished in such a way that each party to the agreement will fully and clearly comprehend that the agreement to arbitrate exists and binds the parties thereto.

Here the plain meeting of the conditioned precedent is that the contract and its arbitration provision do not effectively *exist and do not bind the parties unless and until they both have signed the architect's plans and specifications. Consequently, if plaintiff's completion of the work amounted to a waiver at all, it was a waiver of the written agreement in toto, and not just in part.*

Reference Case 47

Roanoke Hospital Association v. Doyle Russell, Inc. and Federal Insurance Company

Cir. Ct., Roanoke, Va.; Review by Supreme Court of Virginia, Record #740212; 1975

In 1967, Roanoke Hospital Association (the owner) advertised for bids on construction of a fourteen-story addition to its facilities. Bids were received upon a commitment for completion by January 1, 1970, and upon the condition that a bid could not be withdrawn for thirty days after submission. Bids were opened on July 17, 1967, and ten days later the owner entered into an $11 million lump sum contract with Doyle & Russell, Inc. (the contractor). Federal Insurance Company was the performance surety.

Before bids were opened, the owner had obtained a loan commitment at 6¼ percent interest. When the bids showed that the commitment was insufficient, the owner obtained, on the date the contract was signed, a letter of commitment for a $5.5 million, fifteen-year loan at 6⅜ percent interest, contingent upon completion by June 30, 1970. The completion date in the commitment was later changed to October 31, 1970. In addition to the loan, financing arrangements included a $3 million Hill-Burton grant and funds provided by the owner.

Witnesses for the contractor testified that the contractor had no knowledge of the details of the owner's financing arrangements when the contract was executed and acquired none for more than three years. Flannagan, the hospital administrator, testified that he told the contractor's representatives when the bids were opened "that the building must be completed by the date specified in the contract or else our financial arrangements would have to be redone or rearranged and would cost . . . the hospital a higher rate of interest", but that he told them nothing about the details of the arrangements because he "didn't think it was their business."

For various reasons, including the need to redesign the foundation (see *Doyle & Russell v. Roanoke Hospital*, 213 Va. 489, 490-91, 193 S.E. 2d 662, 664; 1973), construction progress was delayed, and in October, 1969, the contractor issued a revised progress schedule projecting completion by September 30, 1970. Progress lagged behind the revised schedule, and on January 17, 1970, the architect wrote to the contractor advising it that the lending agency, which had accepted the new projected completion date, had notified the Board of Trustees that it would grant no further extensions of that date.

In October, 1970, it was apparent that the project would not be completed by the October 31, 1970, loan commitment deadline. The two options for the permanent loan commitments were due to expire on October 30, 1970. The owner decided to exercise the option for a commitment for a $5.5 million, fifteen-year loan at 8½ percent, conditioned upon completion by June 30, 1971.

The hospital addition was ready for occupancy on April 14, 1971, and was completed on September 3, 1971.

In its motion for judgment, the owner sought a total of $3 million in compensatory damages for "Defendant's failure or refusal to complete the work within the time stipulated, or within any requested allowable extension of time for completion . . . " and elected "to recoup the sum of $956,000 held by Plaintiff as retainage". The contractor filed a counterclaim for the retainage.

The evidence showed that the interest expense the owner will incur over the life of the 8½ percent permanent loan will be $1,185,159.95 greater than the expense it would have incurred over the life of the 6⅜ percent loan; that the sum of $832,300 invested at 5 percent annum for the period of the loan would generate funds equal to those additional interest costs; and that 5 percent was a proper investment factor to be used in computing the return on investment a charitable institution could reasonably expect to earn.

For damages sustained during the period of construction delay, the owner claimed a total of $730,698, including $690,287 for interest expense incurred and interest revenue lost and $40,411 for expenses incurred for utilities, storage costs, and insurance premiums.

The trial court entered final judgment on January 29, 1974, confirming the verdict of a three-man jury. The verdict denied the owner's $832,300 claim and allowed the contractor's $956,000 counterclaim, with interest from September 3, 1971. On the owner's $730,698 claim, the verdict awarded $552,500 with interest from April 14, 1971. That award included $522,500 for what the verdict termed "temporary . . . interest costs" and $30,000 for the expenses included in the owner's $40,411 claim.

The Supreme Court of Virginia then reviewed the case stating, in part:

The questions presented by the owner's assignments of error are:

1. *Whether the owner is entitled to damages for added interest costs for the permanent loan attributable to higher interest rates;*

2. Whether instructions "D" and "E" erroneously induced the jury to disallow the owner's claim for those damages;
3. Whether the trial court erred in awarding the contractor the contract retainage, with interest from the date of completion.

The question presented by the contractor's assignment of crosserror is whether the trial court erred in allowing the owner damages for any added interest costs during the period of unexcused delay. On appeal, the contractor concedes liability for the $30,000 award.

There are two broad categories of damages ex contractu: direct (or general) damages and consequential (or special) damages. Washington & Old Dominion R.R. Co. v. Westinghouse Co., 120 Va. 620, 627, 89 S.E. 131, 133 (1916). See also Sinclair v. Hamilton & Dotson, 164 Va. 203, 209, 178 S.E. 777, 779 (1935). Direct damages are those which arise "naturally" or "ordinarily" from a breach of contract; they are damages which, in the ordinary course of human experience, can be expected to result from a breach. Consequential damages are those which arise from the intervention of "special circumstances" not ordinarily predictable. If damages are determined to be direct, they are compensable. If damages are determined to be consequential, they are compensable only if it is determined that the special circumstances were within the "contemplation" of both contracting parties. Whether damages are direct or consequential is a question of law. Whether special circumstances were within the contemplation of the parties is a question of fact. . . .

As a general rule, contemplation must exist at the time the contract was executed. . . . However, that rule is not absolute. When the breach alleged is an unexcused delay in completion, if the completion date has been altered by consensual amendment, contemplation is to be determined as of the date of amendment.

Here, the damages claimed by the owner involved three types of interest costs: (1) added interest costs (including expenditures on borrowed funds and interest revenue lost on invested funds) during the construction period arising from the longer term of borrowing neccesitated by the contractor's unexcused delay (hereafter, "extended financing costs"); (2) added interest costs during the construction period attributable to higher interest rates during the extended term (hereafter, "incremental construction interest costs"); and (3) added interest costs for the permanent loan attributable to higher interest rates (hereafter, "incremental permanent interest costs"). . . .

In pertinent part, instruction "D" read as follows:

The court instructs the jury that one element of damage for which the Hospital seeks to be compensated is the sum which it contends it has expended for increased interest costs for both construction financing and permanent financing resulting from the delay in the completion of the project.

The court instructs the jury that the claim of the Hospital for damages resulting from increased interest rates is not a direct damage naturally flowing from Doyle and Russell's alleged breach of contract in failure to complete the project on time, but is, instead, a consequential damage.

... The owner argues that all three types of interest costs are direct damages and that instruction "D", insofar as it classified the latter two types as consequential damages, was erroneous. The contractor argues that all three types are consequential damages. We agree with the owner and the trial court that the extended financing costs are direct damages. Customarily, construction contracts, particularly large contracts, require third-party financing. Ordinarily, delay in completion requires an extension of the term of construction financing. The interest costs incurred and the interest revenue lost during such an extended term are predictable results of the delay and are, therefore, compensable direct damages. ...

The measure of direct damages caused by unexcused delay in contract completion is either the rental value of the completed structure for the period of delay, or the reasonable return on the completed structure treated as an investment for the period of delay. ... The owner elected to seek the latter. Instead of applying an arbitrary interest rate to total value, the jury adopted the owner's more precise formula and applied the construction loan rate to the loan receipts and an imputed rate to the Hill-Burton funds and the owner's funds invested in the project.

We agree with the trial court that the damages resulting from increased interest rates are not direct damages. Increases in interest rates are not caused by delays in completion of construction contracts. Rather, they are caused by variable pressures and counterpressures affecting supply and demand in the money market. Although interest rates on short-term borrowings are characteristically more volatile than those on long-term borrowings, both are usually unpredictable. For that reason, increases in interest rates are "special circumstances", and damages resulting therefrom are consequential and not compensable unless such circumstances were within the contemplation of the parties. Instruction "D" correctly advised the jury that both incremental construction interest costs and incremental permanent interest costs are consequential damages.

Instructions "IV" and "D" told the jury that such consequential damages were compensable if the parties had them in contemplation at the time the contract was executed or when "thereafter amended". The quoted language was inserted by the trial court over the objection of the contractor. We hold that this language was without evidence to support it. Although the record indicates that the parties agreed upon a host of change orders, there is no evidence of a meeting of the minds upon an amendment altering the completion date first fixed in the contract. Consequential damages, then, were compensable only if the "special circumstances" from which they resulted were contemplated by the parties on the date the contract was executed, and there is, therefore, no merit in the owner's complaint that instruction "E" improperly emphasized that date. . . .

The jury's verdict, signed by the foreman, expressly awarded $522,500.00 in damages for "temporary" interest costs. In response to the foreman's earlier inquiry, the trial court had explained that temporary interest costs included those incurred "during the completion of the job." Manifestly, temporary interest costs as explained by the trial court and reflected in the language of the verdict included what we have denominated as "extended interest costs" and "incremental construction interest costs". Indeed, from the evidence adduced in support of the owner's $690,287.00 claim, it was impossible for the jury to separate the two so as to award one and deny the other.

. . . Although we cannot make a reliable computation from the record, it is clear that some portion of the $522,500.00 award represents incremental construction interest costs which, as we have said, are consequential damages. That portion of the award can stand only if the jury made a factual determination that the "special circumstances" from which such damages arose were within the contemplation of the parties. On the other hand, the jury denied the owner any award for incremental permanent interest costs, also consequential damages, and this can only indicate that the jury made a factual determination that the "special circumstances" were not within the contemplation of the parties. Since there is nothing in the evidence to justify such contradictory factual determinations, we hold that the verdict is irreconcilably inconsistent and cannot stand. . . .

. . . To the extent that the verdict awarded the owner direct damages and the contractor the contract retainage, the judgment is affirmed. To the extent that the verdict awarded the owner consequential damages for incremental construction interest costs and denied the owner consequential damages for incremental permanent interest costs, the judgment is reversed. The case is remanded for a new trial, and the trial court is directed to instruct the jury to fix the quantum of direct damages; to determine whether, at the time the contract was executed, the parties contemplated "special circumstances" justifying consequential damages; and to award or deny consequential damages accordingly.

Reetz v. Stackler
24 Misc. 2d 291; 201 N.Y.S. 2d 54; 1960

A contractor undertook to provide an acoustical ceiling in a bowling alley.

1. Contractor is to furnish without extra charge any work or materials required to conform the buildings to all laws, the rules and regulations of all municipal departments and the Board of Fire Underwriters.
2. If there is any conflict between drawings and specifications, and the law, the law is to be followed.
3. The contractor will perform without additional cost all work necessary to obtain approval from all municipal authorities having jurisdiction.

The town building department required a two-hour fire rating for the ceiling, and a change to the contract was executed to that effect. After completing the work in conformance with the building department's instructions, the contractor submitted a claim for extra work citing the fact that the final ceiling was different than that described in the contractual plans and specifications.

However, the court found for the owner stating:

The plaintiff specifically assumed the obligation of erecting a ceiling with a 2-hour fire rating. The provision of the rider in itself was sufficient to obligate the plaintiff to put in a ceiling meeting the requirements of the town . . . despite additional expense.

The mere fact that the performance of a contract becomes economically unprofitable is insufficient to relieve a party from his contractual obligations. . . . This is so even though the increased cost and expense result from the interference of law or government regulation.

Reference Case 49
C. W. Regan Inc. v. Parsons, Brinckerhoff, Quade, & Douglas
411 F. 2d 1379

The question in this case is the responsibility of the engineer for contractor actions or operations. The project involved the constructions of a tunnel under the Elizabeth River between Norfolk and Portsmouth, Virginia. During construction an unprecedented high tide flooded the tunnel causing extensive damage.

The plaintiff, Regan, brought action against another contractor, Diamond, and the engineering firm that had designed the tunnel. The initial trial in U.S. District Court for the Eastern District of Virginia resulted in a judgment of almost $200,000 against the engineers, but absolved the defendant contractor. The engineering firm appealed, and the plaintiff contractor appealed the portion of the verdict that held the other contractor not liable.

The project was initiated in 1960 by the Elizabeth River Tunnel Commission. The project involved a tunnel almost one mile long that had three separate sections: access roads, cut and cover sections, and a central tube. There were two ventilating buildings or towers near each end about 200 feet offshore. The defendant Diamond had a base contract to build the access roads, retaining walls, install the tunnel roadway, finish the ventilating buildings and install electric and drainage systems in the tunnel. Plaintiff Regan had a number of responsibilities including the electrical cables within the tunnel between the two ventilating buildings.

At the Norfolk end, a steel tide gate was installed, for the purpose of sealing off possible flooding through the open cut area during construction. The Portsmouth side was higher than the Norfolk side and the plan called for retaining walls and approaches (to be built by Regan) to be above the level of any previously recorded or anticipated tide or flood. Therefore, a tide gate was not planned for the Portsmouth side.

By November 1961, the steel tide gate was in place at the Norfolk end. There was one remaining metal bulkhead inside the tunnel tube about 500 feet in from the Portsmouth end. This bulkhead was interfering with the work of both contractors, most specifically, Regan's pulling of cables from one ventilating building to the other.

Diamond requested permission to remove the steel bulkhead,

and replace it with a wooden bulkhead at the portal between the ventilation building and the shore, where it would not interfere with Regan's work. The purpose of the wooden bulkhead was to keep out ground water and seepage, a flood tide not being anticipated from the Portsmouth end.

Diamond's plans for the wooden bulkhead were examined by the engineer. Certain adjustments were made in conformance with the engineer's recommendation.

By March 7, 1962, the date of the high tides, Diamond had completed the basic heavy structural work. The tunnel was open from end to end except for the wooden barricade at the Portsmouth portal, and the tide gate at the Norfolk portal. Plaintiff Regan was the contractor with the majority of work remaining. (Regan was several months behind the contract schedule and had not installed the retaining walls on the Portsmouth side.) A combination of winds and high tides produced a water level three feet higher than any previous recorded spring tide. Flood water began entering the tunnel from three sources: the Norfolk end, the Portsmouth end, and the Portsmouth ventilating building.

An attempt to close the steel tide gate failed because of three lines passing through it (two belonging to Diamond and one belonging to Regan). Diamond personnel refused to cut or remove the lines because they served air lines and pumps inside. Finally, after more than six hours, during which time a substantial amount of water had entered the tunnel, the tide gate was opened, pipes and lines were cut, and the tide gate was closed.

Calculations indicate that the water entering from the Portsmouth side was at least equal to that from the Norfolk side. It entered through both the wooden bulkhead and the holes in the foundation of the ventilation building. In both cases, a number of the holes had been made by Regan in preparation for pulling cables and conduits.

In summarizing the situation, the appeals court said:

A great quantity of water came into the tunnel and caused damage. The water came from three sources. The plaintiff was in sole control of the second source—the open ventilating building. The plaintiff was partly responsible for the third source—the leaky wooden bulkhead—because of holes he had drilled in it for pipes and wires. The defendant Diamond had done the planning and the building of the wooden bulkhead; making it watertight was Diamond's duty. The engineer, Parsons, was alleged to be responsible for the leaks around the wooden bulkhead because of Parsons' approval of the struc-

tural soundness of the plans drawn and submitted by
Diamond. Each of the three independent sources of water could
be found from the evidence to have contributed equally to the
damage plaintiff complained of.

The engineer Parsons had no written contract with anyone.

The Contract Documents . . . consisted of the formal contracts between the Tunnel Commission on one hand and Regan
and Diamond on the other, which contracts incorporate the
Plans and Specifications of the Virginia Dept. of Highways as
modified and supplemented by the Plans and Specifications.

In the contract documents Diamond, Regan and the Tunnel
Commission agreed that Parsons, as the owner's representative, should have certain authority to supervise and inspect
and reject so as to procure for the Tunnel Commission the
ultimate permanent result called for by the contracts; but the
documents do not impose upon the engineer, not a party to the
contracts, any duty towards the contractors of their personal
property. To the contrary, Section 107.13 requires the contractor to indemnify the engineer against claims and suits arising
out of the contractor's "operations," negligent or otherwise;
and Section 107.17 expressly provides that the engineer, as the
agent and representative of the Commission, shall have no personal liability in carrying out any power and authority under
the contract or the specifications.

Independent of the contract documents, but corroborating
them, the uncontradicted testimony is that Parsons' mandate
from the Tunnel Commission was to supervise, inspect and
reject for the purpose of seeing to it that the permanent construction was built in accordance with the plans and specifications. As to temporary structures, the uncontradicted testimony is that the engineer's inspection is confined to structural soundness; that approval of the contractor's working
drawings for the temporary bulkhead meant simply, "that at
the time the engineer knows of no good reason for objecting
thereto"; that each contractor had the duty of protecting his
own work; and that fitting the wooden bulkhead against the
masonry and caulking it against leakage were all field construction details which were the contractor's—not the
engineer's—responsibility. No duty to inspect the details of
temporary construction nor to protect the property of one contractor from negligence of another contractor was shown.

In finding for the engineer, the court also pointed out that the
express provisions of the contract did not support a theory
invoking a duty on the part of the engineer to insure that one

contractor's negligence does not damage the property of another contractor. Also, the court indicated that there is not an implied continuing duty created to inspect temporary details of construction of a temporary structure. However, the court did note that it is possible: "for an engineer to assume such sweeping duties of supervision and control over all details of construction that nothing else appearing he may be held to have assumed a duty to parties outside his contract."

Reference Case 50
Kirk Reid Co. v. Fine
139 S.E. 2d 829

This case involves a contract for installation of air conditioning and heating systems valued at approximately $253,700 in Norfolk, Virginia. The complaint was made by the contractor, and defended against by the owner. The Virginia Supreme Court ruled that the contractor was guilty of an unauthorized deviation from the plans and specifications. However, that court found that the trial court had imposed an unfair penalty by refusing to award him the unpaid balance of the contract price. Extracts from the court opinion follow:

The contract, which was on a form approved by the American Institute of Architects, required the complaintant to furnish all of the material and perform all of the work in accordance with drawings and specifications, made a part of the contract, which were prepared by Oliver & Smith, architects employed by the defendant. The architects and an independent engineer, James E. Hart, employed by them for this project, were, according to the contract, to have general supervision of the work.

The complaintant presented evidence tending to show that as soon as the work commenced, it was discovered that the ducts, through which the air was to be carried from the conditioning unit to the upper floors of the building, could not be installed as prescribed in the drawings because of the presence of existing electrical conduits.

It was also asserted by the complaintant that the room which was designated to house some of the necessary equipment was of inadequate size. The complaintant contended, in the trial court, that these difficulties rendered the contract impossible of performance and necessitated changes in the work and equipment to be installed, resulting in charges for extra work in excess of the contract price. On the other hand, the defendant presented evidence to show that the plans and specifications could not have been complied with as originally prepared.

There was a serious conflict in the evidence relating to the complaintant's authority to make changes in the work.

The complaintant presented evidence in the form of statements contained in a letter written by the complaintant to defendant after the work was accomplished to the effect that the defendant was informed of the necessity for the changes before they were made. However, the complaintant's representative admitted on the witness stand that the defendant did not approve the changes, and the latter denied emphatically that he knew of any changes "until after the work had been completed, and when I had paid almost every cent under the contract."

This case was heard by a Commissioner and Chancery who, after hearing the evidence, filed a report finding that the air conditioning system failed to meet the contract requirements because it was 46–50 tons short of capacity required, the primary air handling unit was lower than the requirement by almost 8000 CFM, the condenser water pump was 120 GPM short and cited other instances where piping and valving was less than the quality required.

Based upon his findings, the Commissioner ruled that the equipment installed was much less expensive and smaller in size and capacity required by the specifications. Noting that the defendant's consent had never been obtained for these changes, the Commissioner found that there was no substantial compliance with the terms of the contract, and that the difference in cost between equipment contracted for and that installed amounted to $24,253, which amount he awarded in favor of the defendant, while dismissing the bill of complaint.

In addressing the appeal, the appeals court discussed the authority of the architect in terms of his activity as a general agent of the owner when he is engaged to supervise work: "Thus, it is clear that the authority of the architect and the engineer to act as agents of the defendant was of limited scope confined to those areas set forth in the contract, and where, in special instances, their powers might be broadened. It is equally as clear that changes in the work, except of a minor nature, could only be made on the written order of the defendant or on the written order of the architects or engineer stating that the defendants had authorized such changes."

After it had been shown that the defendant, the architect, or the engineer had not authorized or approved such changes, the contractor attempted to search out phrases of the contract with which it contended the architects and engineer had power to authorize changes. The court rejected these contentions as follows:

... Whatever may have been said or done by the architects or engineer to lead the complaintant to believe that they had approved the changes, their actions were in direct conflict with the provisions of the contract which required that written approval should be had before major changes could be made.

These contractual requirements were as well known to the complaintant, and equally as binding upon it, as they were to the defendant, architects and engineer. To the extent that the actions of the architects and engineer were in conflict with the provisions of the contract, such actions were in excess of the authority of these limited agents, and, unless ratified by the defendant, not binding upon him.

The complaintant says, however, that the defendant did ratify the revision on the part of the engineer and architect by remaining silent and not insisting on the revision of the plans being referred to him for prior approval. . . .

. . . This contention flies in the face of the evidence, accepted and acted upon by the Commissioner and the Chancellor, that the defendant never authorized the complaint, the architects or the engineer to make any changes, that he never approved such changes and he "did not know there was any change in the plans and specifications until after the work had been completed."

Knowledge is the essential ingredient upon which the theory of ratification rests. One cannot be held to have ratified that about which he has no knowledge. The record before us simply does not support the contention that the defendant knew about the changes while the work was in progress, and he certainly did not ratify them after he was given such essential information.

We must conclude that the complaintant made the changes in the work without proper authority and that it deviated substantially from the requirements of the contract, to the damage of the defendant.

. . . It is clear from the records that the sum of $24,253 awarded on the cross-bill was considered by the Commissioner and the Chancellor to be the outside amount of the damages caused by the changes in the work. The evidence in this case requires that the complaintant be allowed a credit for the unpaid balance of the contract price against that figure. To hold otherwise would put the defendant in a better position than he could have occupied if the contract had been performed with precise exactness.

Furthermore, there is nothing in the records that suggests, and the Commissioner did not so find, that the action of the complaintant even approached the modicum of bad faith which would, in effect, visit upon it the imposition of a penalty for its departures. The record would indicate that, rather than setting out to save money on the contract by its wrongful bet-

terment, the complaintant spent more to perform the work than it was called upon to do.

Thus, the appeals court awarded the unpaid balance to the contractor, but a penalty remained since the figure of $24,253 was reduced only by the amount of the unpaid balance leaving a net amount of $9,780.

Reference Case 51

L. Rosenman Corporation v. United States

U.S. Ct. Cl., #211-65

In finding for the plaintiff, the court stated:

Although the specifications and drawings may have been clear as a bell in the mind of defendant's architect, it is not the subjective intent that is the legal determinant. . . . Rather, it is the representations of the specifications and drawings themselves which represent defendant's intent. And these were not so clear as to compel plaintiff to seek clarification, or as to make defendant's interpretation binding upon plaintiff. See, Tufano Contracting Corp. & Anthony Grace & Sons, Inc., Joint Venture v. United States, 174 Ct. Cl. 398, 405, 356 F. 2d 535, 539 (1966). 'The Government as the author [of the contract] has to shoulder the major task of seeing that within the zone of reasonableness the words of the agreement communicate the proper notions—as well as the main risk of a failure to carry that responsibility.' WPC Enterprises, Inc. v. United States, 163 Ct. Cl. 1, 6, 323 F. 2d, 874, 877 (1963). Here defendant did not meet its burden. If it had wanted automatic radiator valves on all 15 floors, it should have said so explicitly. Even the Government witness conceded that there was no way of telling from the floor plans that automatic valves were intended for the 8th through the 15th floors.

Since we find that defendant's plans and specifications were not so clear as to make its interpretation binding on plaintiff, we must next proceed to the second issue, the formulation of which is based on the well-defined principle that 'when the Government draws specifications which are fairly susceptible of a certain construction and the contractor actually and reasonably so construes them, justice and equity require that construction be adopted.' Peter Kiewit Sons' Co., et al. v. United States, 109 Ct. Cl. 390, 418 (1947) cited with approval in WPC Enterprises, Inc. (supra). Thus we need only look to see whether plaintiff's interpretation of the contract requirements was reasonable.

Reference Case 52

J. A. Ross & Company v. United States
115 F. Supp. 187, 192, Ct. Cl.; 1953

The language of this opinion speaks eloquently to the relationship between change orders and delay damages:

It [the contractor] was granted an extension of time of 15 days and an increase of price of approximately $15,000 for the additional work required, but it has not been compensated for its excess cost incident to the delay. This it is entitled to recover. It is entitled to recover this, notwithstanding the fact that it accepted the extension of time and the $15,000 for the cost of the additional work without reserving the right to sue for the excess costs incident to the delay. The delay was a breach of contract. The amount paid [in the change order] was not in satisfaction of damages for the breach of the contract, nor was the extension of time given.

Plaintiff was also unreasonably delayed 29 days in connection with the installation of the 6-inch water main. . . .

Plaintiff was paid $4,000 for the installation of this new main, but it has not been compensated for its increased cost resulting from the unreasonable delay. . . .

In this case Plaintiff accepted the $4,000 'without prejudice or [sic] any claim for increased costs resulting from delays in performance'; but, independent of this reservation, we think Plaintiff is entitled to recover, because this was a breach of contract.

Reference Case 53
Sheehan v. Pittsburgh
213 Pa. 133; 1905

A contract for street work provided:

All loss of damage arising out of the nature of the work to be done under this contract or from any unforeseen obstructions or difficulties, which may be encountered in the prosecution of the same, or from the action of the elements, or from any encumbrance on the line of work, shall be sustained by the parties of the second part [the subcontractor].

No charge shall be made by the contractor for any hindrance or delay from any cause during the progress of the work, but it may justify his asking an extension of time.

The court refused to apply either the no damage clause or the time extension clause to delays resulting from the city's failure to procure rights of way. The court concluded:

Not withstanding the breadth of the language of the agreement that all loss or damages from unforeseen obstructions and difficulties and from delay were to be borne by the contractors, it is clear that the delay from the City's failure to obtain complete right of way was not in the class of difficulties and delays which were in the mind of the parties, for the agreement itself was based on the assumption by both parties that the complete right of way had been secured so that work could be begun at any point and proceed without interruption.

. . . For the same reason the provision for extension of time only on written assent by the Director of Public Works is not applicable.

Reference Case 54
Terry Contracting v. State
295 N.Y.S. 2d 897; 23 N.Y. 2d 167

Terry Contracting entered into a contract with the state by which it undertook the construction of the superstructure of a precast, prestressed continuous concrete girder bridge consisting of three spans across the Oneida River in Onondaga County, New York.

In one of its causes of action, Terry sought to recover the increased cost of fabricating the bridge's cantilever girders in a vertical position, the one approved by the state, rather than the less expensive horizontal position that Terry desired to use. Terry contended that the state committed a breach of contract by refusing to approve the contractor's proposal to use horizontal fabrication, and therefore that Terry was entitled to recover increased costs involved in using the recommended vertical method. Terry relied principally on a single paragraph in the specifications which left the method of forming the girders to the contractor's discretion. The court of claims, however, from an examination of the specifications as a whole, found that the contract and specifications contemplated vertical casting.

Basic Facts

Following are the basic facts of the situation as described by the counsel for Terry Contracting (and extracted from the appellate brief):

> The second cause of action is for the sum of $1,225,117.80 for increased cost of fabrication of girders arising out of disapproval by the State of the method chosen by the claimant for such fabrication. . . . The work included the fabrication of 24 concrete cantilever girders, each of which was approximately 145 feet long, 14 feet high and 4 feet wide, and weighed approximately 250 tons each.
>
> The contract contained the following provision for the forming of the girders:
>
> > 7. FORMS: The method of forming shall be left to the discretion of the Contractor. The Contractor shall, however, submit plans for the forms he intends to use to the Engineer for his approval prior to undertaking the making of forms. On the design of the forms special precautions shall be taken to prevent the introduction of stresses in a vertical direction due to the shrinkage of the

concrete. This is particularly important if the Contractor elects to use rigid steel forms.

The method of forming the girders necessarily determined the position in which they were to be cast. Claimant submitted its bid on the basis of casting the girders in horizontal position, i.e., building the forms so that the concrete would be poured into the forms resting on the 14 foot side, then rotating the girders so that the 14 foot side would be in a vertical position.

The State, acting by Blanchard, its Deputy Chief Engineer in charge of bridges, would not approve horizontal method of casting except on the withholding of progress payments during the performance of the work.

The progress payments during the fabrication of the girders in a vertical position amounted to $1,281,813, spread over a period of two years and two months. Compliance with the condition imposed by the State for horizontal casting would have suspended such payment for such amount and such period.

The Basic Difference in Approach

The argument by counsel backed up by voluminous testimony demonstrated the difference in cost of each approach. Examination of the arguments in the testimony shows little real difference of opinion. It is clear that casting the 14-foot high by 145-foot long girders in a horizontal position would have been much less expensive. Further, it would have permitted easier placement of prestressing tendons and reinforcing steel, and better control of the concrete placement. The analogy would be the comparison between placement of a 14-foot wide highway slab versus a 14-foot high retaining wall.

The state engineers did not insist that the horizontal scheme would not work; they were just not as certain about its reliability because of the additional handling required in rotating the girder from the horizontal to its final vertical position.

Apparently it was rather clear from the documents that the State had contemplated a vertical installation. The contractor argued that he had bid on the basis of the less expensive approach, and because of that obtained the low bid and was assigned the contract.

In estimating the additional cost or damages, counsel for Terry developed a total cost of $2,301,880 on the basis of unit prices compared to the sum of $1,281,813 included in the low bid (and paid by the state). On this basis, the suit for damages for the vertical casting requirement was held to be $1,020,078. With the addition of interest, the suit for damages for that specific method of fabrication was $1,225,118.

Case for the Contractor

Counsel for the contractor argued first on the facts, and secondly on four points of law that it was the prerogative of the contractor to select the method of fabrication. On the basis of facts as developed by testimony, counsel presented the following argument (as extracted from the appellate brief):

> The controversy relates to the right of claimant to exercise its ingenuity in so forming girders as to save large sums in their fabrication; a saving of which the State obtained the benefit since claimant based its bid on the economical method contemplated by it.
>
> The girders were ultimately to be placed in the bridge structure so that the 14-foot or long side would be in a vertical position. However, if the forming for concrete pours were so constructed so that the 14-foot side of the forming stood vertically it would be far more costly than if such side were in a horizontal position, and then, after the pour solidified, the girder be tilted so that the long side then stood in a vertical position.
>
> The State conceded that claimant's proposed method was economically feasible and practical. Nevertheless, during contract performance, the State's engineers insisted on the vertical method of pour being employed, under penalty of non-payment of progress payments provided for until completion and placement of the girders were accomplished.
>
> The question then is, did the contract preclude plaintiff from the right to employ its own devised, economically feasible, and practical method and compel it to use the complicated, costly method which the State insisted upon?
>
> The contract expressly provided "The method of forming shall be left to the discretion of the contract."
>
> The plans showed and were designed in detail toward the vertical method of forming, but expressly stated that this was a "suggested" method.
>
> It is claimant's position that since it was given the option of determining the method of forming, and since the detailed method shown on the plans was expressly stated to be only "suggested", that it had a right to assume it would be permitted to employ such more economical method of attaining the required result, as it might devise, and that it might safely bid accordingly. The determinations in the Courts below have the effect of making the "suggested" method the required method, thereby depriving claimant of the exercise of its option which the contract allowed it.

Though the State's engineers conceded neither plans nor specifications required by the vertical method of forming nor precluded the employment of the horizontal method, we believe the Courts below were misled by the testimony of these same engineers that they devised the plans to show the vertical method of fabrication.

Plaintiff does not dispute that the plans indicated a method of forming and fabrication based on the assumption that the "suggested" method therein contained would be employed. However, since claimant was informed this was merely a "suggestion", it contends it was not precluded from employing its own practical and far less costly method.

Counsel then proceeded to quote at length from the testimony of the State engineers to verify the argument.

Findings

The court of claims dismissed the cause of action involving the method of construction on the ground that the claimant failed to prove any breach of contract by the state. The appellate division affirmed the dismissal. The court of appeals found that the records sustained the finding that the contract called for vertical casting of the bridge's cantilever girders, and the state's refusal to approve horizontal casting method did not constitute a breach of contract.

Reference Case 55

Town of Poughkeepsie v. Hopper Plumbing & Heating Corp.
260 N.Y.S. 2d 901

In November 1964, the Union Free School District awarded a plumbing contract to Hopper Plumbing & Heating Corp. for the Hagantown Elementary School at a contract price of $102,250. Previously in July 1964, the Central School District had awarded a plumbing contract to Hopper for the Sheafe Road School at a contract price of $57,545.

The town of Poughkeepsie entered an action to enjoin the defendants (Hopper and the two school districts) to prevent performance by Hopper of the plumbing work in the schools until Hopper submitted its plans for a plumbing permit from the town. At this time, Hopper had done a substantial part of the contract on the Sheafe School and was starting work on the Hagantown School.

The Poughkeepsie Plumbing Code and Ordinance requires that all new plumbing work be inspected to insure compliance with requirements of the code and to assure that the installation and construction of the system is in accordance with approved plans. Also, any person may not work as a plumber in the township unless he has passed an examination by the Board of Plumbing Examiners and received from them a certificate of competency and a license. In taking the action, the Town of Poughkeepsie first stated that Hopper had not filed plans, had filed no application for license, but admitted that the contracts had been entered into under the provisions of the General Municipal Law.

The court reviewed the general process that the plans for these schools had undergone. First, they were prepared by architects licensed to practice in New York State. They were approved by each respective school board and pursuant to Section 408 of the Education Law, the plans and specifications were submitted to the Commissioner of Education, New York State, for approval. The appropriate department under the commissioner reviewed the plans and specifications comparing them with a set of State Standards that appear in a school building code compiled by the commissioner for the construction of schools. Both sets of plans had been approved by the state.

The court also reviewed the general procedure that the school boards and architects followed in monitoring the quality

of the work. However, this chain of safeguards, although com-
mendatory, was not on the main stream of the questions of law
as described by the court:

*Upon these facts, the issues are well defined: is the plumbing
contractor who performs this work within the Town of
Poughkeepsie in accordance with the general requirements of
the State Education Law and the General Municipal Law and
the plans and specifications for the erection of new public
schools under contract with respective school boards subject to
the regulations of the plaintiff's Plumbing Code?*

*Two defenses are raised: first, that Hopper is exempt from the
provision of the Code because it is working on public school
contract, and second, that it is unconstitutional. This case may
be disposed of by reason of Hopper's exemption from the provisions of the Code, question as to the constitutionality of the
Code is not reached.*

The court considered a number of citations by the parties
including one which seemed to indicate that local regulations
would prevail: *City of Kingston v. Bank* (45 Misc. 2d 176, 256
N.Y.S. 2d 276). This decision enjoined an unlicensed plumber
from performing a contract for the Kingston Board of Education
in violation of the city plumbing ordinance. In the referenced
case, plans and specifications were submitted by the architect
engaged by the board of education to the city plumbing inspector and these specifications required that inspections were to be
made by the city plumbing inspector as well as the architect. In
keeping with these specific requirements, the plumber applied
for a certificate of competency, was examined and failed. This
introduced the question of voluntary submission to the control
and regulation of the municipal plumbing code, as distinguished from the case.

The court cited the education law providing for approval of
plans and specifications by the commissioner of education, and
stated that the provisions of this law clearly show that the legislature had preempted the area of plans and specifications and
vested it exclusively in the commissioner of education.

The court noted that the town argued beyond this point (that
is in the actual field of construction after design) that there was
no preemption of authority. They claimed that the legislature
acted only in the design sphere, and that to insure the health
and safety of the pupils, the police power of the town must be
exercised to enforce its planning code and ordinance. The court
did not agree.

Reference Case 56

Trans-World Airlines Inc. v. Travelers Indemnity Co.

262 F. 2d 321, Mo.; 1959

A construction contract included liquidated damages of several hundred dollars combined to represent damages to the owner of the property as well as to the airline leasing the property at the airport. The project was completed late, and the airline decided to sue for its actual damages which they computed to be approximately $3.5 million.

The court found in favor of the contractor (Surety). In explaining its ruling, the court held:

> where a contract and bond provides for the penalties to be paid in the event of a failure to comply with the terms of a contract, are clearly binding upon all the parties, and that special or unliquidated damages may not be collected in addition to liquidated damages which are clearly provided for and spelled out in the contract . . . the general rule enforced by the courts of the State of Missouri and elsewhere is to the effect that where the parties especially provide or stipulate for liquidated damages, such liquidated damages take the place of any actual damages suffered and that any recovery for breach is limited to the amount so agreed upon. The rule is stated in 15 Am. Jur. 264, Damages, p. 697, as follows:
>
>> The effect of a clause for stipulated damages in a contract is to substitute the amount agreed upon as liquidated damages for the actual damages resulting from breach of the contract, and thereby prevent a controversy between the parties as to the amount of damages. If a provision is construed to be one for liquidated damages in case of a breach, and the recovery must be for that amount. No other or greater damages can be awarded, even though the actual loss may be greater or less.

Reference Case 57
Turner Construction Company v. State of New York
253 App. Div. 784 3d Cir.; 1 N.Y.S. 2d 158

In this case, the appellate division ruled in favor of Turner Construction. The ruling was made on the basis that the state had directed a method of performance not required by the contract, and different from the method chosen by the contractor. The court held:

> The Court of Claims has found that the State's inspectors were wholly unreasonable in requiring the contractor to cut a large number of brick in the body of the brick work on the exterior walls of nine buildings. The Court below was fully justified in this finding. The requirement of the State's inspectors was not authorized by the contract or specifications and was arbitrary. It made it necessary for the contractor to set up special cutting benches around the walls of these buildings and to have bricklayers cut a large number of these brick, when substantially the same result and the result wholly within the contract could have been accomplished by following the method suggested by the contractor of using six-inch stretchers which could be obtained commercially.

Reference Case 58

United States v. Citizens and Southern National Bank of Atlanta, Ga.
367 Fed. 2d 473; 1966

A subcontractor sought reimbursement against its general contractor to recover damages for an alleged breach of contract on the ground that the general contractor failed to coordinate progress of the subcontractor's plastering work with that of other subcontractors. The court reversed an award in favor of the subcontractor on the ground that a substantial amount of the extra costs proved by the subcontractor and claimed to be caused by the general contractor could be attributed to factors for which the general contractor was not responsible. The appeals court, therefore, concluded that the entire claim on the subcontractor had to be rejected. Citing *Lichter* v. *Mellon-Stuart* (Reference Case 36), the appeals court held: "On the whole record it appears that a not insubstantial part of the extra costs for which plaintiffs [subcontractor] sought reimbursement could be attributed to factors for which Lee [general contractor] was not responsible. As the evidence does not provide any reasonable basis for allocating the additional costs among these contributing factors we conclude that the entire claim should have been rejected."

Reference Case 59

United States v. Rice

317 U.S. 61; 63 S. Ct. 120; 1943

In 1932, paragraphs 3 and 4 of the standard form construction contract used by the U.S. Government read as follows:

3. Changes. *The contracting officer may at any time, by a written order, and without notice to the sureties, make changes in the drawings, and(or) specifications of this contract and within the general scope thereof. If such changes cause an increase or decrease in the amount due under this contract, or in the time required for its performance, an equitable adjustment shall be made and the contract shall be modified in writing accordingly.*

4. Changed Conditions. *Should the contractor encounter, or the Government discover, during the progress of the work, subsurface and(or) latent conditions at the site materially different from those shown on the drawings or indicated in the specifications, the attention of the contracting officer shall be called immediately to such conditions before they are disturbed. The contracting officer shall thereupon promptly investigate the conditions, and if he finds that they materially differ from those shown on the drawings or indicated in the specifications, he shall at once, with the written approval of the head of the department or his representative, make such changes in the drawings and(or) specifications as he may find necessary, and any increase or decrease of cost and(or) difference in time resulting from such changes shall be adjusted as provided in Article 3 of this contract.*

The Supreme Court was asked to decide whether damages for delay could be recovered under either paragraph. A unanimous court held that damages for delay could not be recovered under these paragraphs: "It seems wholly reasonable that 'an increase or decrease in the amount due' should be met with an alteration of price, and that an 'increase or decrease . . . in the time required' should be met with alteration of the time allowed; for 'increase or decrease of cost' plainly applies to the changes in cost due to structural changes required by the altered specification and not to consequential damages which might flow from delay taken care of in the 'difference in time' provision".

Rice could have been interpreted in one of two ways. On the one hand, one could say that although delay damages may not be included in a change order issued under paragraphs 3 and 4 of the contract, they could be collected in a subsequent independent action by the contractor for breach of contract. On the other hand, *Rice* could have been read to hold that a contractor's only remedy for delay incident to a change order is an extension of time, and damages can under no circumstances be recovered. The subsequent history of what has become known as the Rice Doctrine shows that courts have opted for the first of these alternatives, consistently entertaining actions for delay damages based on breach of contract.

Reference Case 60
Vernon Lumber v. Harseen Construction Co.
60 Fed. Supp. 555; 1945

During World War II, Vernon Lumber contracted to furnish a large quantity of lumber to Harseen Construction Company. Vernon, in turn, arranged for the purchase of the lumber from a mill in North Carolina. The contract between Vernon and Harseen did not specify the lumber source. The War Production Board, under its wartime powers, assigned higher priorities to the output of the North Carolina mill and reassigned the lumber elsewhere. Vernon Lumber sought to be relieved from performance of the contract by indicating that conditions beyond its control had made performance of the contract impossible. The court, however, found against Vernon Lumber stating:

> If conditions beyond the control of the plaintiff [the lumber supply company] have made it impossible for plaintiff to procure the required lumber, performance of the contract has been frustrated, and plaintiff would not be liable for its default. If Rules and Regulations of the War Production Board made it impossible for plaintiff to procure the lumber, the Rules and Regulations would be a bona fide excuse. But the reply does not allege impossibility, and in failing to do so is insufficient as a defense. . . .
>
> The term "impossible" does not mean an absolute impossibility. If it did, impossibility of performance could be negatived merely by showing that the required lumber was available at some backwoods source not known to anyone but the inhabitants of the surrounding area. "Impossible" must be given reasonable and practical construction . . . but it is not satisfied by the allegation employed herein that plaintiff sought to procure the lumber "from its usual and regular channels as well as elsewhere." . . . Under the contract as it is presently written, plaintiff is under obligation to furnish the lumber if it can be obtained. To be excused from this obligation, plaintiff must allege "impossibility" of obtaining that lumber. Only then would the defense have merit.

Reference Case 61
Wallis et al. v. Inhabitants of Wenham
90 N.E. 396, Mass.; 1910

This was a contract in which time was of the essence. The contractor was to coordinate his work with other contractors and the owner, and liquidated damages were set at ten dollars per day for delay. The contract included an authorization for extensions of time for delay "in the prosecution or completion of the work by the neglect, delay or default of any other contractor or by any damage which might happen" by fire, strike, or weather. The contractor did not finish on time, but claimed that he was delayed by actions of the owner, and therefore institution of liquidated damages was precluded. The Massachusetts Supreme Court agreed, noting:

that under such an agreement as this, owner cannot hold the contractors liable in the amount of the stipulated damages for any delays which have been due to his own fault. Russell v. Dibandeira, 13 C. B. N.S. 149; Kenny v. Monahan, 169 N.W. 591, affirming 53 App. Div 421; Home Bank v. Drumgoole, 109 N.Y. 63; Marsh v. Kauff, 74 Ill. 189; Palmer v. Stockwell, 9 Gray 237; Amoskeag Manuf. Co. v. United States 17 Wall. 592. But in many of the decisions in which contractors have been completely exempted from such liquidated damages for a failure to finish the whole work within the stipulated time it has been either assumed or found as a fact that the whole of the delay was due to the fault of the owner or of persons for whose conduct the owner was responsible. Ludlum v. Vail, 166 N.Y. 611, affirming 53 App. Div. 628; Perry v. Levenson, 82 App. Div. 94; Boden v. Maher, 105 Wis. 539, Weber v. Collins, 139 Mo. 501; Altoona Electric Co. v. Kittaning Street Rwy., 126 F. 559; District of Columbia v. Camden Iron Works, 15 App. Cas. D.C. 198; Dunavan v. Caldwell & Northern R.R., 122 N.C. 999. So in Cornell v. Standard Oil Co., 91 App. Div. 345, the contractor finished the work as soon as the owner allowed him to do it. This was the principle applied in Champlain Constr. Co. v. O'Brien, 177 F. 271, in which the owner was found to be principally at fault for the delay which had occurred, but it was impossible to apportion the responsibility between him and the contractor. The builder is not relieved from his contract, but the owner cannot recover for delays which have been caused by himself or by those for whose conduct he was responsible. The parties are taken to have understood that the contractor's time limit was extended by the amount of such delays.

Reference Case 62

Wertheimer Construction Corp. v. United States

406 F. 1071

In this case, Wertheimer Construction Corporation was penalized for delay in the completion of its contract, and brought action for remission of damages. The job involved construction of 183 dwelling units for the National Capital Housing Authority in Washington, D. C.

The work to be accomplished was divided into two stages, each to be "progressively completed, suitable and ready for occupancy" within a prescribed number of consecutive calendar days. Plaintiff was liable for liquidated damages for each calendar day of delay until work was either completed or accepted. The period of delay would not include unforeseeable causes beyond its control or its fault or negligence, including "unusually severe weather". There was delay by a paving contractor that was recognized by the Housing Authority. However, this recognition did not extend to both stages as described by the trial commissioner:

The contracting officer granted plaintiff 130 days extension of contract time for completion of group 1 buildings due to delay caused by a paving contractor, but granted no extension of contract time for completion of group 2 buildings. The testimony of both plaintiff's and defendant's witnesses establishes, however, that the delay of the work on group 1 buildings interfered with the planned sequence of the operations with a resultant delaying effect on the work on group 2 buildings. Plaintiff claims that it should have been granted 70 days extension of contract time for completion of group 2 buildings, but, as set forth in finding 5(f), 15 days extension of time is found to be warranted.

The contractor claimed that it should not have been penalized for certain of the delay time because the real cause was bad weather, and a suitable request for extension of contract time had been made to the contracting officer. After comparing weather conditions in the region in similar months during a preceding eight year period, the contracting officer granted a 22 day extension for each group. The contractor felt that the period of delay should have been substantially longer. However, the contractor's evidence was found to be vague and intangible, and the trial commissioner found against the contractor on this premise.

The contractor indicated that vandalism was an unforeseen problem. In this regard the commisssioner's report noted:

> In denying plaintiff's request for an extension of contract time because of delays due to vandalism, the contracting officer emphasized that it was not defendant's responsibility under the contract to protect the project from theft or damage while it was in the hands of the contractor, and that there was no requirement in the contract for an extension because of delay due to vandalism. In reaching this conclusion, it is clear that the contracting officer was in error because of the contract provisions which exonerated plaintiff from liquidated damages because of any delays in the completion of the work "due to unforeseeable causes beyond its control and without its fault or negligence," do not depend upon fault or responsibility of defendant. Moreover, when one couples this language with the contract language which provided that the contractor should not be relieved from payment of liquidated damages because of delay caused by failure of the contractor to adopt reasonable and continuous protective methods, the conclusion is inescapable that if the delay was because of the above unforeseeable causes and was not caused by failure of the contractor to adopt the protective methods, then the contractor was entitled to be relieved from payment of liquidated damages. The contract is, of course, to be interpreted so as to harmonize all provisions whenever it is possible to do so. In preparing its bid, plaintiff anticipated that there would be some vandalism, and during the construction period, plaintiff had two or three watchmen on duty at all times. In addition, plaintiff alerted the Police Department "to keep watch as much as they could." Nevertheless, the evidence is clear and uncontradicted that there was extensive vandalism on the project, including approximately $4,000 to $5,000 in damage to window glass, and that plaintiff was delayed by the vandalism. As set forth in finding 7(d), plaintiff adopted reasonable and continuous protective methods, but was delayed by vandalism which was unforeseeable, beyond its control and without fault or negligence, to the extent of five days on both group 1 and group 2 buildings. . . .
>
> . . . The contracting officer denied plaintiff's request for an extension of the contract time because of delay which plaintiff asserted was due to errors in the drawings. As set forth in finding 8(b), the weight of the evidence establishes that there were no serious errors in the drawings, and that the corrections in the drawings were handled expeditiously and that the errors in the drawings did not cause plaintiff any significant delay in the over-all progress of the work.

An adjacent road that passed close to both groups of buildings required a retaining wall and grade alteration which caused a delay. After review of the facts, the contracting officer allowed a 12 calendar day delay on two buildings in group 1, and a 106 calendar day delay on site and landscaping of group 2 (but not on the houses themselves).

The contractor further contended that it was unreasonably delayed because the government failed to provide inspectors to inspect the work after the buildings had been substantially completed. The trial commissioner's report quoted the contracting officer's statement on this allegation as follows:

The Authority refused on this project, just as it has on all other projects, to accept any buildings for use and occupancy until they were brought to a satisfactory stage of completion and quality of workmanship to comply with the contract. Numerous punch lists were made on these buildings, and checked and rechecked by the project personnel representing the Architect and the Authority until satisfactory completion of contract work and punch list items. The Authority was constantly pushing the Contractor and his personnel to satisfactorily complete the buildings so that they could be taken over. A review of the memoranda of acceptance for occupancy will reveal that buildings were finally taken over subject to completion of miscellaneous work on exterior of buildings and site work and landscaping, and in some cases completion of interior work. If the Contractor's personnel had been diligent in the satisfactory completion of contract required work and punch list items, the amount of punch listing would have been greatly reduced and the buildings could and would have been taken over sooner than they were. However, they failed to properly check and supervise the mechanics' work, and therefore, any delay is the Contractor's responsibility.

Based on the foregoing facts it is my determination as Contracting Officer for the Authority that the Contractor experienced no delay on the part of the Authority in accepting buildings for use and occupancy that was not caused by his personnel and . . . no time extension is granted.

As to the tenth cause of delay asserted by the Contractor in his letter of February 9, 1962 . . . relating to alleged delay by the Authority in accepting buildings for use and occupancy, and for which an extension of 30 days was requested, I find the facts, as they apply to Group 2, to be as follows:

For the reasons set forth in detail . . . above, the Contractor is entitled to no extension for alleged delays in acceptance of buildings for use and occupancy. . . .

After these quotations, the trial commissioner's report summed up the acceptance situation as follows:

At the trial the evidence established that the buildings were "substantially" completed prior to acceptance by defendant. Plaintiff, apparently relying upon the above-quoted Section 34 of the General Conditions, claims that it should have been allowed an extension of the contract time "as a result of the failure of the defendant to inspect and accept the dwelling units when substantially completed." A fair reading of Section 24 of the General Conditions and of the above-quoted paragraph 2 of Section 3 of the Special Conditions, however, compels the conclusion that when the work was substantially completed plaintiff was obliged to notify defendant of that fact, but that defendant was not then obliged to accept the buildings. The language of the Special Conditions is obviously permissive and embraces the exercise of discretion by the defendant as to whether a building was reasonably safe, fit and convenient for the use and accommodation for which it was intended. Moreover the buildings were, as previously indicated, to be "completed, suitable and ready for occupancy." As set forth in finding 10(i), the record does not support plaintiff's contention that defendant's inspectors were tardy in making inspections or that the inspections were unnecessary or improper, or that defendant failed to accept the buildings promptly after they were completed and ready for occupancy.

The contractor had an additional claim for time extensions for the execution of change orders. The Housing Authority testified that they had developed a time extension for contract group 1 of thirty-four calendar days and for group 2 of forty-nine calendar days. These extensions were calculated by dividing the contract dollar amount by the contract days, and applying proportional extensions for change order work. However, it was further testified that after these figures had been reached, the contracting officer had conferred with representatives of the Public Housing Authority, which had to approve the extensions, and they disagreed with this formula approach. In this regard, the court opinion commented:

As set forth in finding 11(c), although at the trial plaintiff attacked the above-mentioned formula and on each of several change orders adduced evidence to the effect that a certain number of days were required for a subcontractor to complete the work under the change order, it failed to show how the change order affected either group of buildings or the project as a whole so as to justify additional extension of the contract time. Plaintiff, accordingly, failed to establish that it was entitled to additional time extensions because of change orders. . . .

. . . In its petition, plaintiff alleges that defendant breached the contract by failing and refusing to accept the work when it was substantially completed, and that as a result, plaintiff incurred additional costs; but in view of the conclusion heretofore reached that the record does not support plaintiff's contention that defendant failed to accept the buildings promptly after they were completed and ready for occupancy, this claim for additional costs is not sustained.

The trial commissioner found that after considering all the findings of fact on the excusable delay, the contractor was entitled to recover the sum of $4,450 that had been withheld as liquidated damages.

Reference Cases

Topical Cross-Reference

	Plans & Specifications	Contract	Exculpatory Clauses	Quantum Meruit	Ambiguity	Privity	Building Codes	No Delay Clause	Owner	Architect/Engineer	Unforeseen Conditions
1. Aetna Insurance Co. v. Hellmuth, Obata & Kassabaum, Inc., 392 F. 2d 472		X				X				X	
2. Arc Electrical Construction Co. Inc. v. George A. Fuller Co. Inc. 24 N.Y. 99, 247 N.E. 2d 111, 299 N.Y.S. 2d 129; 1969										X	
3. Benjamin v. Toledo Plate & Window Glass Company, 8 Oh. L. Abs. 264; 1929											
4. Bentley v. State, 41 N.W. 338, Wisc.; 1899									X	X	
5. Bethlehem Steel Corp. v. City of Chicago, U.S. Court of Appeals, 7th Cir.; 1965; 350 F. 2d 649		X									
6. Bloomfield Reorganized School District R-6 v. E.M. Stites, 336 S.W. 2d 95, Mo.; 1960		X									
7. Blount Brothers Corp. v. Reliance Insurance Co., 370 F. 2d 733	X										
8. Blount Brothers Construction Co. v. United States, 346 F. 2d 962	X					X					
9. Brandt Corp. v. City of New York, 14 N.Y. 2d 217; 199 N.E. 2d 493; 1964		X									
10. Burke v. Ireland, 166 N.Y. 305; 59 N.E. 914; 1901							X		X	X	
11. Carroll Electric Co. v. Irwin and Leighton, 80 Pa. Super. 438; 1923		X									
12. Cauldwell-Wingate Company v. State of New York, 276 N.Y. 365; 12 N.E. 443; 1938		X	X						X		
13. Citizen's National Bank of Meridian v. L. L. Glasscock Inc., 243 S. 2d 67		X		X					X		
14. City of Lawton v. Sherman Machine & Iron Works, 182 Okla. 254, 77 P. 2d 567									X	X	
15. City of Littleton v. Employers Fire Insurance Company, 653 P. 2d 810		X								X	
16. Clark v. Ferro Corp., 273 F. Supp. 230	X				X						
17. Collins v. Baldwin, 495 P. 2d 74											
18. W. G. Cornell Co., Washington, D.C. v. United States, 376 F. 2d 299						X					
19. County of Tarrant v. Butcher & Sweeney Construction Co., 443 S.W. 2d 302		X							X	X	
20. Depot Construction Corp. v. State of New York, 41 Misc. 2d 764; 246 N.Y.S. 2d 527		X		X							
21. Joseph F. Egan, Inc. v. City of New York, 17 N.Y. 29 90; 18 A.D. 2d 357	X	X							X		
22. Fanderlik-Locke Co. v. United States F/U/O Morgan, 285 F. 2d 939, 10th Cir.; 1960		X						X			

Schedule	Contractor Method	Delay Factors	Impossibility	Subcontractor Delay	Contract Breach	Substantial Performance	Liquidated Damages	Setting Damages	Waiver	Time Extension	Remarks
	X										Bonding company claims supervising architect responsible for poor work
				X	X						Architect refuses proper progress payment; substantial completion
		X				X					Substantial completion
											Collapse; owner responsible
X											Milestone schedule
											Contractor fights liquidated damages
							X	X			Subcontractor claims paint specifications are impossible
		X	X	X	X		X	X			Ambiguity in specifications; found for contractor
									X		Final payment as waiver
											Building collapsed; found for owner
X				X							Time is of the essence can be one-way clause
X		X						X			Delay in phased construction due to unforeseen conditions
											Unforeseen conditions; found for owner
											Engineer's field decisions are factors in fraud
		X	X								Tanks collapse due to lack of design details by engineer
X						X					Performance specifications; parol evidence
					X	X		X			Substantial completion
X											Substitution or "equal to"
						X		X			Substantial completion; power of architect/engineer to change specifications
											Change in scope
								X	X		Waiver; duress
				X				X			Privity

Reference Cases

Topical Cross-Reference

(Continued)

	Plans & Specifications	Contract	Exculpatory Clauses	Quantum Meruit	Ambiguity	Privity	Building Codes	No Delay Clause	Owner	Architect/Engineer	Unforeseen Conditi...
23. Fanning & Doorley Construction Co. v. Geigy Chemical Corp., 305 F. Supp. 650	X										
24. Forest Electric Corp. v. State, 275 N.Y.S. 2d 917									X		
25. Foundation Co. v. State of New York, 233 N.Y. 177		X		X							
26. Gasparini Excavating Co. v. Pennsylvania Turnpike Commission, 409 Pa. 465; 1936		X						X	X		
27. General Building Contractors v. County of Oneida, 282 N.Y.S. 2d 385		X	X						X		
28. Hammermill Paper Co. v. Rust Engineering Co., 243 A. 2d 389									X		X
29. Harper Drake & Assoc. Inc. v. Jewett & Sherman Co., 182 N.W. 2d 554		X			X					X	
30. Herbert v. Aitken, 5 N.Y.S 839; 25 N.E. 954; 1890										X	
31. Hersey Gravel Co. v. State, Supreme Court of Michigan, 305 Mich. 333; 9 N.W. 2d 567; 1943		X	X								X
32. Hollerbach v. United States, 233 U.S. 165; 1914	X	X	X								
33. Johnson, Inc. v. Basic Construction Co., 429 F. 2d 764, D.C. Cir.; 1970		X					X	X			
34. Johnson v. Fenestra, Incorporated (Erection Division), 305 F. 2d 179, 181, 3rd Cir.; 1962											
35. Peter Kiewit Sons' Co. v. Iowa Southern Utilities Co., 355 F. Supp. 376; 1973									X		
36. Lichter v. Mellon-Stuart Company, 305 F. 2d 216 3rd Cir.; 1962											
37. Luria Engineering Co. v. Aetna Casualty and Surety Co., 206 Pa. Super. 333; 1965											X
38. Luria Brothers & Co. v. United States, 369 F. 2d 701	X										X
39. MacKnight Flintic Stone Co. v. The Mayor, 160 N.Y. 72; 54 N.E. 661	X										
40. Meads & Co. v. City of New York, 191 App. Div. 365, N.Y. 1920; 181 N.Y.S. 704										X	
41. Meyers v. Housing Authority of Stanislaus County, 60 Cal. Reptr. 856	X				X						
42. Moore v. Whitty, 299 Pa. 58; 1930											X

Schedule	Contractor Method	Delay Factors	Impossibility	Subcontractor Delay	Contract Breach	Substantial Performance	Liquidated Damages	Setting Damages	Waiver	Time Extension	Remarks
		X	X								Impossible performance in specifications; found for contractor
		X		X				X			Owner as coordinator; found for contractor
					X						Change in scope obviates contract unit prices
											Owner failed to plan
											Owner as coordinator; exculpatory clauses
	X							X			Owner's right to monitor construction
										X	Documentation base; damages
											Architect as supervisor
		X									Exculpatory clauses; borings wrong
											Dam foundation; borings wrong; exculpatory clauses
				X	X						Subcontractor right to abandon
		X		X							Subcontractor delayed by general contractor's failure to deliver material
X											Schedule milestones
	X			X				X			Subcontractor delayed by prime contractor; had to work piecemeal
		X		X							Subcontractor wanted release due to strike delay
	X									X	Poor plans; slow owner response
			X			X					Performance as defense (classic)
	X										Contractor selection of method of work
											Ambiguity v. scope
		X		X							Subcontractor wanted release due to union and strike

Reference Cases

Topical Cross-Reference

(Continued)

	Plans & Specifications	Contract	Exculpatory Clauses	Quantum Meruit	Ambiguity	Privity	Building Codes	No Delay Clause	Owner	Architect/Engineer
43. Mullinax Engineering Co. v. Platte Valley Construction Co., F. 2d 553, 10th Cir.; 1969										
44. Nathan Construction Co. v. Fenestra Inc., 409 F. 2d 134						X				
45. New England Foundation Co. v. Commonwealth, 327 Mass. 587, 100 N.E. 2d 6; 1951	X				X					
46. Race Company v. Oxford Hall Contracting Corp., 268 N.Y.S. 2d 175			X							
47. Roanoke Hospital Assoc. v. Doyle & Russell, Inc. and Federal Insurance Company, Cir. Ct., Roanoke, Va.; Review by Supreme Court of Virginia, Record #740212; 1975			X							
48. Reetz v. Stackler, 24 Misc 2d 291, 201 N.Y.S. 2d 54; 1960			X				X			
49. C. W. Regan Inc. v. Parsons, Brinckerhoff, Quade, & Douglas, 411 F. 2d 1379	X	X					X			X
50. Kirk Reid Co. v. Fine, 139 S.E. 2d 829	X									X
51. L. Rosenman Corporation v. United States, U.S. Ct. Cl., #211-65	X				X					
52. J. A. Ross & Company v. United States, 115 F. Supp. 187, 192, Ct. Cl.; 1953										
53. Sheehan v. Pittsburgh, 213 Pa. 133; 1905							X	X		
54. Terry Contracting v. State, 295 N.Y.S. 2d 897; 23 N.Y. 2d 167	X									
55. Town of Poughkeepsie v. Hopper Plumbing & Heating Corp., 260 N.Y.S. 2d 901	X						X			
56. Trans-World Airlines Inc. v. Travelers Indemnity Co., 262 F. 2d 321, Mo.; 1959										
57. Turner Construction Company v. State of New York, 253 App. Div. 784 3rd Cir.; 1 N.Y.S. 2d 158									X	X
58. United States v. Citizens and Southern National Bank of Atlanta, Ga., 367 Fed. 2d 473; 1966										
59. United States v. Rice, 317 U.S. 61; 63 S. Ct. 120; 1943										
60. Vernon Lumber v. Harseen Construction Co., 60 Fed. Supp. 555; 1945										
61. Wallis et al. v. Inhabitants of Wenham, 90 N.E. 396, Mass.; 1910									X	
62. Wertheimer Construction Corp. v. United States, 406 F. 1071									X	

Schedule	Contractor Method	Delay Factors	Impossibility	Subcontractor Delay	Contract Breach	Substantial Performance	Liquidated Damages	Setting Damages	Waiver	Time Extension	Remarks
											Site not ready for paving; substantial completion
		X		X							
						X		X			Substantial completion; curtainwall
						X					Performance specifications for pile driving
									X		Literal interpretation as waiver
								X	X		Types of damages
									X		Effect of supplementary signing as waiver
											Flood; architect/engineer responsibilities to supervise temporary work
						X		X			Substantial performance; limit of damages
											Ambiguity v. scope
X					X			X			Damages for delay from changes
										X	Precedent damage by owner
	X										Contractor method in unusual technique
											Code jurisdiction
							X	X			Liquidated damages limit recovery for actual damages
	X										Inspectors cause increase in scope
X				X	X			X			Subcontractor fails to separate costs of delay and loses
		X			X			X		X	New doctrine in no delay clauses
		X	X								Definition of impossible
		X					X				Delay by owner
						X				X	Substantial completion

Part IV·Case Study

The John Hancock Tower:
A Case Study in Delay

By Rita Tatum, *formerly Associate Editor*
Building Design & Construction

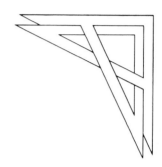

Glass curtainwalls have caused problems for a number of buildings, including Chicago's Civic Center, New York's Chase Manhattan Bank, towers in Dallas and Milwaukee, and even a building on the campus of Massachusetts Institute of Technology. One of the most publicized is the sixty-story, rhomboid-shaped John Hancock Tower in Boston.

When professionals in the design and construction industry say, "it can't happen here," they had best study the excellent credentials of the Hancock team: as the Hancock building illustrates that no firm—no matter how large or experienced—is totally immune.

John Hancock Mutual Life Insurance Company is far from a first-time owner. New York City architect, I. M. Pei & Partners has been designing outstanding high-rise buildings across the country for years. With more than 100 years' experience in the field, Gilbane Building Company of Providence, R.I., has tackled much more complex buildings with success. H. H. Robertson Company of Pittsburgh, subcontractor for the curtainwall, and Libbey-Owens/Ford Company of Toledo, Ohio, the manufacturer, have worked with glass for years.

With such well-respected names attached to its new headquarters building, it would have appeared that Hancock had little to worry about when it broke ground August 21, 1968. There had been some local resentment at the idea of a skyscraper dominating Boston's Back Bay, but that centered on the innovative design and projected appearance of the tower. No one involved in the groundbreaking that summer day expected that the building would be plagued with curtainwall problems that would help delay Hancock's occupancy until mid-1976, nearly eight long years later.

With the clarity of hindsight, some critics now claim the curtainwall problem could have been predicted. They insist more extensive wind tunnel tests and a closer study of insulated glass problems in other high-rise buildings could have prevented the glass breakage, or at least caught the flaw sooner. The fact remains that the problem was not foreseen by some of the best designers and constructors in the country.

As a result, Hancock is now suing all parties involved in the project for an undisclosed amount encompassing not only the cost of replacing the glass units, 10,344 in all, but also for lost rentals and lost use of the building. Countersuits and cross-suits have been filed by several of the principal parties.

The final dollar amount for the delay claims is not known; first, the Middlesex Superior Court in Cambridge must weed through the nineteen-count suit filed September 15, 1975, to decide who the potentially liable parties are. Because of the complexity of the case and the litigation process, the final results may take years.

The suit brought by Hancock accuses Gilbane of breach of contract, negligent construction, and breach of warranty. Robertson is faced with breach of warranty, negligent design and construction and breach of contract. LOF, the glass manufaturer, is confronted with four counts of warranty violations covering expressed, implied, by sample, and mechantability. LOF is further called to task for negligent selection, design, and manufacture of the glass units, as well as negligent supervision of installation.

Pei, architect for the building, must defend itself against breach of contract in both design and construction as well as two counts of negligence in design and supervision. Also named in the suit were the Aetna Casualty and Surety Company of Hartford, Connecticut, which furnished the performance bond for Gilbane and the Federal Insurance Company of New York, which furnished Robertson's performance bond.

The suit claims Hancock signed a written contract with Pei on November 17, 1967, under which Pei assumed responsibility for the design of the building including all architectural, site planning, and engineering services as well as supervision of all construction. "The curtainwall consisted of a pressure-equalized system of metal work, glass and glazing . . . , containing approximately 10,000 insulating glass units, each unit consisting of two panes of glass approximately 5 feet by 11 feet, hermetically sealed and separated by one half inch of dehydrated air space . . . ," claims the suit.

On January 27, 1971, Gilbane also signed a written contract to select and furnish all materials, labor, equipment, and services for the construction of the building in accordance with the drawings, specifications, and conditions provided by Pei.

Robertson's contract to install the glass was signed by Gilbane on November 26, 1969, more than a year before Gilbane actually contracted with Hancock to build the building. There has been some speculation that Gilbane may have had some form of oral agreement with Hancock, prior to their general contractor status, for provision of construction management services.

According to the suit, LOF also had contracted to supply Robertson with the glass units on January 11, 1971, more than two weeks before the Gilbane contract. The suit claims "significant numbers of glass units" began failing in November 1972. By September 1973, Pei directed all glass units in the curtainwall be replaced. But replacement did not start until late May 1974, with work being completed in May 1975.

The suit claims " . . . John Hancock has sustained substantial damages, including but not limited to the cost of labor and materials for removing and repairing the glass units in the curtainwall, additional design, engineering and construction costs, increased operating expenses and other costs for the Tower, the deprevation of the use of the Tower, diminution in value of the Tower, and lost income on rentals for the Tower."

According to Hancock officials, the building originally was scheduled to open in February 1973, or four and a half years after the first shovel of earth. However, this date seems to have been adjusted for delays due not only to several construction strikes in the area, but also some early foundation problems. Hancock denies any delays due to slow completion of working drawings or any other design or construction time spender.

Nevertheless, even the initial date seems to encompass some unnamed delays. Chicago's 110-story Sears Tower, for instance, broke ground in August 1970. That building, the nation's tallest, began opening its doors to Sears personnel in September 1973, just three years later. Nor can the time difference between the two buildings be totally credited to Boston's poor soil conditions or brutal winters. Chicago's clay soils have challenged many tower projects, and that city's winters are certainly a match for Boston's.

Besides the glass replacement, Hancock also agreed to add more L-bracing in the building's core, which explains the time difference between the final glass repair in May 1975 and the occupancy date of mid-1976. In a press release issued March 1975, Hancock said Pei had advised the company "that in order to insure satisfactory performance of the building over the long term under extreme and rare wind conditions which could possibly occur over the next 100 years, stiffening members should be added in certain locations within the central core of the building." After the reports of two consultants, Pei recommended the L-shaped members be installed between beams and columns in the building's core area. The additional bracing installed was to prevent cracking of partitions in the core area under extreme winds, a common occurrence in tall buildings. But the architect denied any suggestion that the bracing was in any way related to the building's glass problems.

From the beginning, the Hancock building seemed born under a bad star. Early into construction, the building experienced foundation problems when shoring slipped and street settling occurred. Dropping in some places as much as a foot, the foundation settling contributed to damages suffered by utility companies and a couple of nearby buildings, including historic Trinity Church. Various litigation resulted, including *New England Telephone & Telegraph* v. *John Hancock* for damages to wires and cables; *Boston Edison Company* v. *I. M. Pei* for damages it claimed occurred to steam, electrical, and other conduits, steam services, cables, manholes, and other property of the utility; *Boston Gas Company* v. *Concord Construction Company* for damage to gas lines; *City of Boston* v. *Gilbane* for damages to the city's water conduit, sewer pipes, streets, sidewalks, and edgestones due to property settling; the *Young Women's Christian Association* v. *Hancock* for damages; and the *Episcopal Church* v. *Hancock* seeking $4 million for damages to the 99-year-old Trinity Church that forced repair of cracks in its foundations, walls, and ceilings.

All but the YWCA and Episcopal suits were settled out of court. Speculation had it that a nearby Sheraton hotel, which also suffered damage, was subsequently bought by Hancock.

However, Hancock's present suit does not mention either the foundation costs or the extra bracing. These delays may surface later. Even excluding delays before the February 1973 date, Hancock could not occupy the building for three and a half years.

Most designers and contractors realize that any delay costs them money. Not only does delay involve direct staff costs and overhead, but, with key personnel tied up on a delayed project, new assignments may be lost in the process. What many forget, however, is the tremendous cost to the owner in lost rental income and lost use of the building. That cost on the Hancock building runs into many millions of dollars.

The building features more than two million square feet. Hancock planned to occupy two-thirds of the space, leasing the final third to other firms.

According to the Codman Company, which does detailed yearly surveys of square footage rentals in the Boston area, most of the city's office space is leased under the New York definition of rentable space. Unlike the national definition, which includes corridors, stairwells, restroom facilities, and spaces for maintenance, the New York rental policy also includes a percentage of floors devoted to mechanical and electrical equipment.

Hancock planned to let 670,000 square feet to other firms. Assuming that all of that space was occupied in February 1973, Hancock has lost millions of dollars. According to Codman, average rentals in new office buildings that year varied from $8.75 to $10.25 a square foot. "But Hancock offered a great buy for the Boston market," said R. Duff Ramsey of Codman. "Our sources indicate that the average rental contract there was around $8.50 a square foot."

Remembering that in 1973, new office space in the Boston area was at a premium because there was not enough to go around, Hancock theoretically lost $5.7 million in income each year for three and a half years. Multiplied out that comes to a total of nearly $20 million lost. Although the assumption for that loss is based on total occupancy from day one, it does not reflect lost reinvestment interest.

The value of the additional space to Hancock personnel should be also considered. During the repair and readjustment period, many Hancock people occupied approximately 1.3 million square feet elsewhere, at a direct rental cost to Hancock. Using a low value figure of $5.00 a square foot and multiplying 1.3 million square feet times three and a half years, totals $23 million lost. Once again, a number of variables were ignored to simplify the figuring. There was no consideration given, for instance, to Hancock personnel's efficiency under one roof rather than scattered about in other space. Also, there was no discussion of better organization of work because of the added space, because these factors are very intangible.

Therefore, in addition to the $30 million Hancock claims it spent over the original construction estimate of $95 million, the losses include an additional $43 million in lost rentals and lost usage. This also does not take into account the change in rental status from 1973 to 1976 in the Boston area. While 1973 was an owner's market for office space, that situation changed in late 1975, according to Codman, because of the addition of five million rentable square feet in new buildings, so that Boston became less of a seller's market that it had been. Nor does the $43 million consider any inflation.

While Hancock did not claim all delays were caused by curtainwall problems in its initial suit, at least two and a half years can directly be connected to window breakage.

Hancock first became aware that the glass was not performing as well as it should in November 1972. However, reassured by all parties involved in the design and construction of the project that some glass breakage was normal, the insurance company claims it was not aware of all the ramifications.

By January 1973, however, the whole nation knew of Hancock Tower's problems. Hurricane winds on January 20 helped break some sixty-five glass panels and damage another one thousand.

A team of experts from Massachusetts Institute of Technology, headed by consulting engineer Robert J. Hansen, investigated the cause. Before this time, glass breakage was attributed to objects blown from open floors against glass on lower floors.

After months of testing, Hansen came up with a solution: replace all 10,344 glass units with one-half inch thick tempered glass. But, he cautioned, the tempered glass would have to undergo the same detailed testing the original panes did.

Tests run by Hansen's team on the insulated windows measured the deflection and breaking point of the glass, wind velocities around the building, and deflection of the mullions. The group also reexamined the Purdue University wind tunnel tests conducted before the building was constructed. At Purdue, tests were run in ten-degree intervals around the building's circumference.

So in addition to running the tests in smaller intervals, Hansen extended the testing to include six of the proposed monolithic panes inserted in the building's problem areas.

Boston's building code requires glass pressure tolerances of eighty pounds per square foot. However, one source indicated the original double-pane windows had variances of ± twenty pounds per square foot—with some testing as low as sixty psf while others tolerated up to one hundred psf.

Hansen conducted a number of tests in the building. On the thirty-fifth floor, his team developed a detailed testing station stocked with air pressure gauges, wind velocity devices, and wind deflection sensor monitors, using twelve miles of wire and cable into a central switching box to route signals to various recorders.

During the testing, Hansen meticulously watched three critical areas where glass breakage had occurred with the double panes: the WNW and SSE corners of the ninth floor and the WNW corner of the eleventh floor.

The researchers also watched oscilloscopes that monitored signals from fifty sensors located throughout the building. Although generally the oscilloscopes watched all signals, operators could zero in on any one instrument proving critical at the moment.

When winds in the Boston area reached velocities of forty miles per hour, scientists used a Sanborn machine that plotted readings from eight different instruments at the same time.

Because of the massive volume of data coming in, researchers used a scanner to monitor the series of instruments of ten milliseconds each. Readings were recorded on one channel of a four-track recorder. One of the remaining channels was used as a timing device, with the other two constantly monitoring deflections of specially instrumented windows.

The tapes, along with all the other information gathered by the MIT group, went back to the school's campus where a computer sorted the information and readied it for analysis.

One phenomenon the researchers observed was the wide variance of wind speeds from one part of the building to the next. For instance, while wind, measured at one hundred feet above the building, was twenty-five miles per hour, some problem corners were simultaneously registering wind speeds as high as sixty or seventy miles per hour.

Sensors on the problem areas indicated wind coming from the same direction as the rooftop reading, leading some to believe the phenomenon probably was part of a downdraft or turbulence from that downdraft, combined with currents created by surrounding buildings. However, Hansen's team found that the phenomenon did not fit a uniform rule-of-thumb.

Nevertheless, Hansen was able to predict that the tempered glass would solve the problem. The process required all panes to be replaced and new adaptors installed in the window frames, and also caused an increase in capacity of the building's heating system, which had been originally designed to take advantage of the insulated glass.

In May 1974, work began on replacing all of the building's original windows with the stronger, tempered safety glass. Specially designed octopus machines were used in the reglazing. Composed of a vacuum pump mounted on wheels with four large suction cups attached to the lever-like rotating arm, the machine was used both for the removal of the old glass and the installation of the new.

On the top three floors and four mechanical floors, the glass was installed from the exterior using a roof hoist and one of the octopus machines. The rest of the glass units were installed from the inside.

For the interior installation, seven machines, each operated by three men, were used for glass removal and installation. One machine removed the panes while another behind it installed the new glass units. Safety netting to catch any potential glass breakage was used throughout the reglazing and moved downward as the glass installation progressed.

New gaskets and aluminum extrusions also were installed. The extrusions took up the gap between the existing panes, which were as much as one and one-fourth inch thick, and the newer, one-half inch thick tempered panes.

The Hansen report and the results of his tests—the most advanced window reaction tests probably ever conducted— probably will make up Hancock's case. The details will probably surface years from now when the court battles are over.

It is safe to predict that there will be no winner in the melange of suits—just a redistribution of losses. Further, new losses in time, reputation, and legal costs can be guaranteed. The suit is bound to damage the parties professionally, even if in the end they are found to be not responsible. Publicity has a way of playing up the suit angle and playing down the results from the suit years later.

The Hancock lesson should be clear: no project or team is immune to problems, problems cause delay, and delays in monumental projects tend to have devestating impact on the project and its participants.

Bibliography

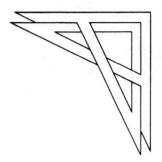

Cohen, Henry A. *Public Construction Contracts and the Law.* New York: McGraw-Hill, 1961.

Dunham, Clarence and Young, Robert. *Contracts, Specifications and Law for Engineers.* New York: McGraw-Hill, 1971.

Greenberg, Max. "Are Construction Contracts Fair?" *Civil Engineering,* May 1975, pp. 56–59.

Jabine, William. *Case Histories in Construction Law.* Boston: Cahners Books, 1973.

Sweet, Justin. *Legal Aspects of Architecture, Engineering, and the Construction Process.* St. Paul, Minn.: West Publishing Co., 1970.

Walker, Nathan, and Rohdenburg, Theodor. *Legal Pitfalls in Architecture, Engineering, and Building Construction.* New York: McGraw-Hill, 1968.

Case Index

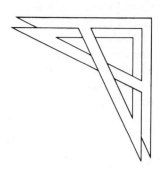

Index

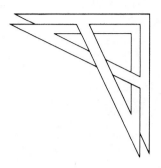